New Music Composition

New Music Composition

DAVID COPE

SCHIRMER BOOKS
A Division of Macmillan Publishing Co., Inc.
NEW YORK

Collier Macmillan Publishers
LONDON

90-1004

Copyright © 1977 by SCHIRMER BOOKS
A Division of Macmillan Publishing Co., Inc.

SCHIRMER BOOKS
A Division of Macmillan Publishing Co., Inc.
866 Third Avenue, New York, N.Y. 10022

Collier Macmillan Canada, Ltd.

Library of Congress Catalog Card Number: 76–21376

Printed in the United States of America

printing number
1 2 3 4 5 6 7 8 9 10

Library of Congress Cataloging in Publication Data

Cope, David.
  New music composition.

  Includes index.
  1. Composition (Music) 2. Music--Theory--20th
century. I. Title.
MT40.C73   781.6'1   76-21376
ISBN 0-02-870630-7

To my wife

Contents

Introduction

If there is one characteristic of any viable art form that remains constantly active, it is *change*. While to the placid or unobservant listener Western music may seem to be conveniently consistent and reliable, that is certainly the one thing it is not. Traceable harmonic vocabularies began with the perfect open intervals of the fourth and fifth and proceeded (though often at snail's pace) through triadic structures, seventh and ninth chords until, running out of available equal tempered notes, cluster chords of all possible pitches were formed. Melodic tradition likewise ebbed from stepwise scalular chants through triadic outline and nonharmonic counterpoint to finally achieving a panchromatic (twelve tone) basis during the first part of this century. Rhythm, timbre, and texture followed similar simple to complex paths, but less quickly, saving a great deal of their exploration for twentieth century creators.

This *change* is as inevitable a part of music as it is of life. Those who would deny it, or who exemplify the perfection of musical craft as that of the seventeenth to nineteenth centuries (as many do), are indeed wrong. Though many a great masterpiece was produced during these years, it is undeniable that brilliance of craft and musicianship are evident in thousands of works before and after this "sacred" so called "common practice period."

New Music Composition has been written with three basic concepts in mind: (1) There is no *right* way to compose music, no *right* style, just different ones. Each individual must decide a mode of expression for himself, and though a social climate may call for a single language, it is by no means necessarily right. (2) There is no progress in art. While it may at first seem plausible that a late romantic symphony is far superior to the more simple fluctuations in a tenth century single line chant, careful consideration proves that *possibly* the latter is more sophisticated. Certainly, a comparison of "progress in the arts" to, for instance, "progress in the sciences" is inapplicable. (3) Whatever one's definition of music (it matters very little in the final analysis), there are elements in it which make craft and consistency fundamental to its quality. While arguments may rage concerning the direction to take when teaching music (present–past or past–present), this book predicates itself on the reader's thorough knowledge and craft in the musics of the past. There is absolutely no substitute for a confident repertoire of accessible former musical styles *before* beginning a study of the present.

New Music Composition is designed to cover the basic areas of composition of the twentieth century while placing a strong emphasis as well on the newer musics of the past forty years. The need for this is appreciable when it is realized that most theory classes now deal so completely with traditional techniques (inclusive of the major traditional techniques of this century) that a book dealing with such for a *composition* course makes it valuable more as a reference tool or at best a manual for review. It is truly the *new music* and an organized approach to the teaching of it that is the focus of this book.

Many fine reference books exist which cover one, two, or possibly three of the subjects included here (cf. Appendix II); however, this text strives to cover as many areas of contemporary composition as possible in a single volume, in as objective a manner as possible. This procedure avoids the long reference lists often substituted for texts in composition classes. *New Music Composition* is based on the aesthetic assumption that freedom of expression is truly achieved by knowledge of as many procedures as possible and that exclusiveness of any one system leads the student away from freedom and knowledge and towards a confused relationship between his own embryonic style and those of his peers. The author does not compose musics which reflect any single one or, for that matter, any conglomerate of most of the techniques presented in this volume, nor does he expect the student after completion of the text to do so; this is a matter solely for personal taste and style. By studying and evaluating carefully the ideas presented herein in their entirety, it is hoped that the reader will be *self-led* to individuality.

The format of *New Music Composition* is designed around twenty-seven chapters, concise and direct in nature, with explanation and assignments designed to coincide with two semesters of composition (thirty weeks) or three quarters (thirty weeks), with time left for review or extra study in one or more areas (one week for review in the quarter system and one and one-half weeks in the semester system). There is an easy application to a two- or three-year format (i.e., one chapter every two or three weeks instead of one a week). Thus the book provides both teacher and student with a neat directional study and work design intended to cover basic new musics applicable to one, two, or even three years of study, depending upon depth of coverage desired.

The beginning chapters try to carry over from traditional backgrounds and bridge the gap gently from learned bias to exploration of new ideas. The order of the chapters themselves is not always historical (i.e., many of the concepts presented occurred simultaneously or were well known before others discussed earlier). Often chapters which are closely related are separated (e.g., Chapter 2, on twelve-tone techniques, and Chapter 18, on total organization) for purposes of review and extension. Such organization avoids as well the possibility of getting into 'ruts' of one craft or another. Equally important in the organizing of chapters is the concept of reinforcement. The book provides a great deal of reinforcement in terms of the chapter organization, content, assignments, and works for study.

Each chapter includes definition, procedures, techniques and/or instrumentation, examples, assignments, and a brief list of works (by no means comprehensive) for further study via both scores and recordings. The examples are all by the author and were composed not as representations of his own style but as the best way to demonstrate the point under discussion. The listening is intended to deal with the materials of the chapter for use in the classroom and during private study. Often the works were chosen not as an abrupt introduction to new techniques but rather as a presentation of them by way of the reader's already extant style familiarity. Duplication of works on occasion helps the reader to relate numerous techniques to a one work concept, possibly reevaluate a work previously heard in a different light, and continue to establish the reinforcement technique so important to the book. The lists are brief simply due to the practical aspect of potential listening time; further works can be found in many of the reference books in Appendix II.

The three appendices reflect a distinct necessary addition to the book. Appendix I serves to aid the composer in the practical aspects of writing music (an often-neglected aspect of composition instruction). Appendix II gives suggestions, chapter by chapter, of related books (or sometimes materials) which would serve as excellent further study on any given chapter topic. Appendix III is an alphabetized glossary of terms which the author hopes will be used from the outset. No two individuals arrive at the beginning of this book with the same vocabulary; thus it is hoped that this last appendix will help provide a common language for the composer.

Though a wide variety of applications can be found, the author's current usage is based on seminar study (one meeting per week) of the book, with a chapter for every two weeks, allowing the student not only the opportunity to complete at least one assignment but to have it *performed*—at least in a classroom situation. The two-week usage also affords opportunities for performance of many of the examples in each chapter as well as discussion of the text, and allows for performance and study of as many of the "works for further study" as time permits. The student also meets with the teacher once a week on a private basis for consultation on a larger project which may or may not interact with the assignments from the seminar. In this way, each student obtains practical and usable techniques from a variety of new styles *and* completes larger works demanding of form and content.

It is with these concepts in mind that the author hopes to aid the reader in discovering the techniques, processes, instruments, and procedures of new music composition.

DAVID COPE

New Music Composition

1

Harmonic Progression and Chromaticism

Elasticity of viewpoint for the composer and student of composition is most important, and the choice of the subject of harmonic progression and the chromatic variation of such for the first chapter of this book is not to shy away from other approaches towards structure in music (e.g., counterpoint, melodic considerations, etc.). Indeed, these will be taken up in detail later in the book. Rather, due to the approach of most general theory studies, it seemed most logical to begin at this point.

There are a number of acoustical properties of sound which, when viewed abstractly (i.e., without the interference of listener subjectivity), are most important when defining harmonic progression. The overtone series supplies enough information to provide evidence of significant cause-and-effect relationships for basic terminology and analysis.

Example 1
Overtone series based on D fundamental.

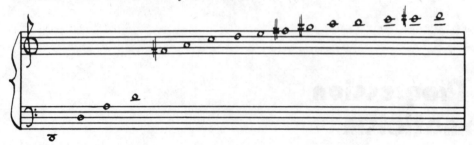

First it should be noted that since this series exists in one form or another in all sounds except the sine wave, it has a subsequent "built-in" natural familiarity. Though these tones are for the most part so soft as to be inaudible in themselves, they contribute (along with the envelope; cf. Chapter 14) to the timbre characteristics of pitches and combinations of pitches. One need only press silently five or six low keys on the piano keyboard (without depressing the damper pedal) and then strike a higher key somewhat loudly (a note within the overtone structure of one depressed below) to activate aurally a member of the series.

Example 2
Struck pitch (B in treble clef) activating overtone series members without pedal (damper: piano) depressed.

When the struck note is released it will continue to be heard even though its strings inside are stopped by a felt damper. What has happened is sympathetic vibration; that is, the played note has initiated vibrations in the overtone series of one or more of the "open" strings ("open" because the depression of these lower keys has lifted the dampers from their strings).

Observing the overtone series in an abstract way (making each note present, dynamically equal and, for now at least, "in tune" [cf. Chapter 8 on microtones]), one finds generous information as to:

1. *texture* (thin at the bottom, thick at the top; a general technique of traditional voicing and orchestration);
2. *consonance and dissonance* (perfect intervals such as fifths and octaves appear first from the bottom of the series, while strong dissonances like the minor second and major seventh appear much higher);
3. *interval strengths* (stronger root-producing intervals occur first from the bottom of the series, and the weaker ones higher; these strengths are useful in both vertical harmonies and horizontal root movement strength);
4. *roots* (in example 1 all roots are D, below the fourth D from the bottom note, and thus the strongest note of any interval or group of intervals can be derived);
5. *progression strengths* (horizontal application of the series in terms of root and interval strength).

In music, it must be understood that none of this portends correctness but rather a given effect equaling the desired result (called "working" in most composition languages). Therefore, the information more concretely considered below is not given as laws or rules, but as concepts, always to be juggled by the creator to make a piece "work." Here, then, are more sophisticated distillations of the above; materials which the composer can knowledgeably use to generate successful harmonic progressions derived from this same bit of overtone information.

Texture is an integral aspect of harmonic progression. When texture tends toward duplication of overtone construction, one finds sonorous and balanced chord formations. When the series is inverted (small intervals on the bottom, large on top), a completely different chord is heard, even though the notes (transposed by octaves) may be the same. The result is thick and clustered low sonorities with an almost severed upper portion nearly divorced from harmonic implications. Obviously if clarity is needed, the former application would be appropriate. On the other hand, if clusters and ringing separation are required, the latter would be preferable. Since both cluster techniques and texture are discussed in separate chapters, it will suffice to mention here that overtone series observations, and the limitless varieties and subtleties between the two extremes mentioned, are a critical factor in the development of chords and harmonic progression.

Consonance and dissonance (the tension factor within or between any given notes or chords) are subject to a great many variations.

Subjectivity and especially context are evident villains in forming a perfect definition here. A major seventh chord for example, can have many different meanings dependent on the environment in which it is placed:

Example 3
Consonance and dissonance as subject to musical context (measure 1. relatively neutral; 2. relatively dissonant; 3. relatively consonant).

In the abstract, however, it is important to note the basic comparison of intervals in terms of consonance and dissonance in order to be aware of their potential contextual usages. Example 4 shows the five basic groups of intervals:

Example 4
Five basic groups of intervals: 1. open/perfect; 2. ambiguous/ contextual; 3. consonant; 4. relatively dissonant; 5. harshly dissonant.

Perfect consonances are called such due to the fact that they create "beats" when out of tune, beats which get faster as the separation becomes larger. The perfect fourth is sometimes considered a dissonant interval (e.g., traditional two-voice counterpoint) requiring resolution; however, again one must point to style (e.g., twelfth-century organum considered it quite consonant) and context. The augmented fourth (diminished fifth), which splits the octave in half, does not fit any category but its own and tends to be completely dependent on style and context for description.

Spacing is a critical aspect of consonance-dissonance relationships. A major seventh five times separated by octaves tends to lose its harshness and indeed be overshadowed by the then *more* dissonant major second inverting their relationship in terms of dissonance. In this and all other interval discussions a displacement of more than one octave tends to weaken dissonance.

Example 5
Spacing as an aspect of consonance–dissonance relationships.

Interval strengths tend to follow the order proceeding upward in the series: octave, fifth, fourth, third, sixth, second, and seventh. Again, octave separation weakens the interval somewhat, though in extreme cases the intervals nearest to perfect consonances tend to feel resolved (see example 5 where the "weak" interval of the seventh loses many of its characteristics and gains the strength of the octave).

Roots are defined usually by the bottom note of all odd-numbered intervals (thirds, fifths, and sevenths) and the top note of all even-numbered intervals (seconds, fourths, and sixths). To obtain the roots of intervals beyond the octave, these intervals should be reduced to within the octave for analysis and then replaced in the original position (e.g., the root of a ninth is not the bottom note as its odd numbering would indicate, but rather its top note as its reduction to an interval within the octave, a second, would be). When more than one of the strongest intervals in a given chord is present, usually it is the bottom or lowest one which is the stronger (unless spacing, for example, made the bottom interval so weak as to regress its strength).

This information, combined with the interval strengths presented before, leads the reader to a quite accurate analysis (and thus composition) of any type of chord. In a C-major triad, for example, the strongest interval present is the *fifth,* its *lower* note the root: C.

Example 6
Root position C major triad: root C.

The triad in first inversion presents the strongest interval as the *fourth* and therefore its *upper* note the root: C.

Example 7
First inversion C major triad: root C.

The second inversion, like the first, has again the *fourth* as the strongest interval with its *upper* note the root: C.

Example 8
Second inversion C major triad: root C.

While acoustics do play havoc with complex chords such as the ones shown in example 9, the intervals do function in much the same manner for root identification.

Example 9
Roots (black notes) of various chords.

Progression strengths are defined by a combination of interval strengths (in terms of both vertical and horizontal relationships) and dissonance. The term *direction* is often interchangeable herein. Using D (dissonant), N (neutral), and C (consonant), one can begin to define a progression no matter what its content or complexity and likewise compose progressions from these concepts.

Example 10 shows a weak-root consonant chord structure moving gradually towards a strong-root dissonant chord structure with root movement growing from weak intervals to strong.

Example 10
Directional progression.

Example 11 is a consistent environment of harsh dissonant chords compiled of growing interval and root strength as well as increasing horizontal root strengths.

Example 11
Dissonant progression of growing strength.

Example 12 is longer and includes a wide variety of textures as well as contrasts. Note here that often root movement and/or interval strengths are overshadowed by sudden increases of dissonant intervals.

Example 12
Progression of increased variety and contrasts.

Root position is a very important consideration in progression strength. In the extremes, roots never occurring in the bass voice will weaken a possibly otherwise strong progression. On the other hand, roots always appearing in the bass voices may strengthen a progression (unless it is weak to begin with, in which case its weak characteristics would be strengthened). One should be constantly aware of root placement in the chord and recognize the various subtle variations of the extremes. Though no set rules exist here, the mind and ear should follow root position in the chord for possible negating relationships in regard to progression strength.

In analyzing or composing such progressions as examples 10, 11, and 12, it is not necessary to start from any one source, proceeding in order to completion; however, these examples were conceived from texture overview to progression strengths as outlined at the beginning of this chapter. Should another approach be found more satisfactory it should be noted that (1) a *method* should be established (a smooth order of recognizable observations) and (2) all of the five main characteristics be at least considered during composition.

The list of harmonic progressions does indeed become endless, but with the criteria for interpretative analysis and composition thus established, *direction, motion,* and *balance* are at least abstractly measurable and one can proceed through any diverse music and maintain a credible stability of analytical procedure and understanding.

Example 13
Examples of directed and non-directed (diverse) progressions.

Chromaticism, herein defined as any note outside the framework of the previous context of materials, can be used for variety in any style. Outside the traditional "leading-tone" connotation (secondary dominants, diminished sevenths, etc.) chromaticism, when loosed within harmonic progression, provides further direction and motion. Example 14A is a pandiatonic (all the notes within a key without chromatic alteration) chorale with a nearly random selection of dissonance, root strengths, and progression. The same selection is shown in example 14B, but with the slow and careful addition of chromaticism not only supplying variety but a *direction* and *motion* the chorale did not have in its first statement.

Example 14
a. Random pandiatonic chords; b. chorale of directed use of chromaticism for variety, direction and motion.

Chromaticism too, like dissonance, works in a variety of ways. When context is continuously diatonic, chromatic notes add the increasing tension and direction shown in example 14B. Conversely, however, when context is highly chromatic to begin with, tension and direction must be achieved by other means (e.g., ordered dissonance, progression strength, etc.) *or* a change towards less chromaticism (diatonic).

Example 15
Chromatic passage becoming less and less so.

With this latter example it is important to note that it is vital to know the techniques of subtracting tension as well as adding it. Direction is a twofold manifestation: towards something, away from something. Both must be clearly controllable.

Returning to the initiation of this chapter, it is important to realize that the overtone series is useful even when applied in melodic and contrapuntal ways:

Example 16
a. Melody based on overtone series; b. two voice counterpoint based on overtone series.

Note in example 16 the slowly evolving chromaticism that the series provides. This is not to suggest that some natural rule is implied but that again, as was stated earlier, recognizability of aural phenomena, even in the abstract, is a valuable tool for the composer whether he wishes to apply it, negate it, or usefully employ the myriad sophistications between the two extremes.

It is best to point out now that however detailed a chapter's approach may become, the *overview,* the structural *form* of musical ideas, is what makes the craft of the specifics significant. As so many have pointed out, any note, any chord may follow or be followed by any other, and it is the *temporal* nature of music which evolves style and the framework around which any line, any progression, any counterpoint may grow and develop.

A macroconceptual approach, the beginning of a composition from an overview, is often as effective as a microconceptual one. While compositions may grow from a single note, motive, or harmonic structure, it is frequently important to begin with a double bar. Sketching a work (even in graphic terms as a start) in its complete form before even a note or chord has been written, telescoping it always outward and retaining the ever important overview, helps allow the composer to not always begin at the beginning when detail comes to the fore, but rather anywhere intuition suggests.

Example 17
Brief example of overview with one possible realization.

ASSIGNMENTS

1. Compose a slow sustained passage for piano in which *dissonance, root strength, harmonic progression,* and *chromaticism* move independently, finally coming together in a strong consonant and diatonic ending.

2. Begin a harsh striking passage for instrument (any available) and piano and slowly invert the overtone flow in such a way that the solo instrument (high) separates itself from the continuing piano dissonances into a long lyric and consonant line.

3. Slowly introduce chromaticism to a diatonic single line, giving direction while strengthening the melodic intervals as much as possible. At the highest point of chromaticism slowly reverse the procedure until the line has returned full cycle.

4. Compose a passage for three available single-line instruments in which the dissonance, root strengths, and chromaticism are consistently variable, while applying a continuously strengthening progression of intervals between roots.

5. Write a short piece for piano which is consonant and strong in all areas, beginning with a basic overtone texture, and slowly invert this texture without altering any of the aforementioned consonances and strengths.

6. Compose a short quartet in which no chord root is allowed to be in the bass voice (all other options are at the discretion of the composer).

7. Analyze the example below for root strength, dissonance, chromaticism, progression strength, and texture, and compose as completely different an example as possible yet with the same exact characteristics as analyzed:

Example 18

8. Compose a short three-voice work (for three available instruments) which moves slowly towards the sixteenth overtone. Use consonant, strong roots and strong progressions at the outset which slowly get weaker as the work evolves.

9. Add notes to the following example which would invert every shown aspect of its character (as discussed in the chapter):

Example 19

10. Overview (in graphic terms) a short work for piano which should not have an increase of tension or direction (i.e., whatever begins the work should be retained as consistently as possible throughout).

WORKS FOR ANALYSIS

Consult the most recent Schwann Catalog for current in-print recordings of these works. Publishers are usually obtained through libraries, music stores, or distributors of music. This list is not meant to be comprehensive, only suggestive of further study.

Barber, Samuel: *Adagio for Strings* (continuous use of dissonance, texture, and root strength for direction and tension).

Bartók, Béla: *Concerto for Orchestra* (excellent command of all facets of harmonic progression and chromaticism).

Berg, Alban: *Concerto for Violin and Orchestra* (from the open consonances at the outset to the second-movement Bach quotation, a very good study in texture and extremes of dissonance developed over long periods of time).

Chavez, Cárlos: *Sinfonia Antigona* (extreme texture development and divergence of dissonant and consonant structures).

Copland, Aaron: *Piano Variations* (consistency of dissonance and progression strengths throughout).

Dahl, Ingolf: *Concerto for Saxophone* (balanced use of overtone-influenced texture and strong root progressions through dissonant passages).

Henze, Hans Werner: *Concerto for Violin and Orchestra* (consistent chromaticism with fluctuating root strengths paralleling harmonic progression).

Honegger, Arthur: *Pastorale d'Eté* (Simplistic texture but not so obvious progression techniques with often nonmatching root progressions with consonance-dissonance relationships).

Hindemith, Paul: *Mathis der Maler* (ending is a strong reference to all the strengths mentioned in the chapter).

Ives, Charles: *Central Park in the Dark* (slow but highly contrasting overlays of complex textures and progressions).

Ligeti, György: *Requiem* (very consistent textures not following the overtone series complex).

Messiaen, Olivier: *Turangalila Symphonie* (consistently contrasting overlaps of the various progressions and chromaticism throughout).

Prokofiev, Serge: *Symphony No. 5* (third movement especially is a strong textural and chromatic opening to the overtone series).

Stravinsky, Igor: *3 Pieces for String Quartet (1914)* (constant dissonance with consistently weak progressions and hidden roots).

Villa-Lobos, Heitor: *Bachianas Brasileiras No. 1* (ebbing and flowing tensions built around vertical structures strong in roots and extremely strong progressions).

2

Twelve-tone Processes

Chromaticism, extended to its fullest degree in equal temperament, leads to the concept of the use of all twelve tones before any one is repeated. Initially it would seem that this pantonal (inclusive of all tonal centers, each pitch as its own center) or atonal (exclusive of any tonal centers) process must be carefully maintained throughout a given composition for it to have any consistent validity; however, as one can easily see from the concluding discussion in Chapter 1, constant chromaticism is as directionless as constant diatonicism. Twelve-tone procedures have provided many composers with a medium of consistency without direct aural association with traditional harmonies and their inherent leadings and allowed for explorations into other areas of musical craft: timbre, rhythm, melodic development, etc. Regardless of the strictness implied, or the numerous varieties of subtle composer nuances in the use of twelve-tone processes, it has remained an important concept for all composers to grasp and extremely useful even for those who do not apply it directly in their works.

Construction of a *row* is usually the first step in the process, and probably the most important; for as easy a pitch storehouse as the row may seem, the musicality of the resultant work may very well rest on this basic set of notes. Example 20 shows a row whose intervallic setup is such that tonality is avoided in nearly every choice (note the lack of strong intervals—fifths, fourths, and even thirds—present between notes or even between sets of three or, in some cases, four notes of the row):

Example 20
Very atonal (pantonal) row.

In contrast to this is a row which maintains a strong consistent chromatic vocabulary but seeks traditional tonal concepts (e.g., triads, strong progression, etc.):

Example 21
Very triadic and nearly tonal row.

The augmented fourth (diminished fifth) in a row, even with a note in between, is a very unpredictable variable: in rows attempting atonality, an augmented fourth may strongly hint of the "leading tone to fourth degree of the scale" tones of a dominant-seventh chord, suggesting tonality; on the other hand, in a very tonal approach to the row (as in example 21), the augmented fourth may be the weakest and necessarily the most atonal aspect (C-sharp major triad to the F-sharp major triad: notes 7–9 to notes 10–12).

Obviously there exists between these two extremes a nearly limitless number of rows with varying degrees of built-in tonal suggestions. Aside from its tonal aspects, example 21 exemplifies a procedure of twelve-tone process known herein as *subsets*. In example 21, each of the four successive note groups (trichords) is a triadic formation. When it is known that the row will be used vertically as well as horizontally, it is important to anticipate possible combinations in terms of harmony. Rows have been constructed around hexachords (six-note groupings), quatrachords (four-note groupings), as well as trichords and variable unbalanced collections (two and ten, for example). Example 22 shows each of the other major types of row subset construction with the significant relationships between each of the subsets extrapolated for demonstration.

Example 22
Hexachord and quatrachord rows and analysis.

The fascination with manipulative rows can become obsessive but it is most important to note the significant and very useful ramifications of such. Melodically the row can become balanced and include sequences, inversions, etc., all potentially musical material. Harmonically, such available resources make for consistent harmonic language and available variation. Row construction in the most musical way possible, along with constructive subsets, is an important facet of twelve-tone processes.

Along with transposition of the row (designated herein as *O*—*original*—with 1–11 for the transpositions), *inversion* (mirror, or opposite direction of exact interval, known herein as *I*), *retrograde* (use of the row in reverse, herein known as *R*), and *inversion retrograde* (mirror and reverse, herein known as *IR*), are the usual variations. To make such materials readily available in complete form, a *row box* is usually constructed. Example 23 is just such a box constructed from the row shown.

Across the top of the box is the original row itself. Down the left-hand side is the exact inversion of the row (mirror; that is, each interval of the original is in turn inverted: a major third up in the original equals a major third down in the inversion). It is important to make sure that each interval is exact and that no mistake has been made (e.g., a major third up being made a minor third down). To make a final check of the inversion at this point in the construction of the box would be to make certain that the left-hand column down contains all twelve pitches (most easily done by beginning with the note C and finding all chromatic notes up to and including B). Once this is done, one must fill in horizontally all the remaining notes of the total 144 squares. This is done by finding the interval from the row above by comparison with the left-hand column and progressing by that same interval completely across the box, thus filling in eleven notes across to complete.

When finished, the row box will contain all four versions of the

Example 23
Row and resultant row box.

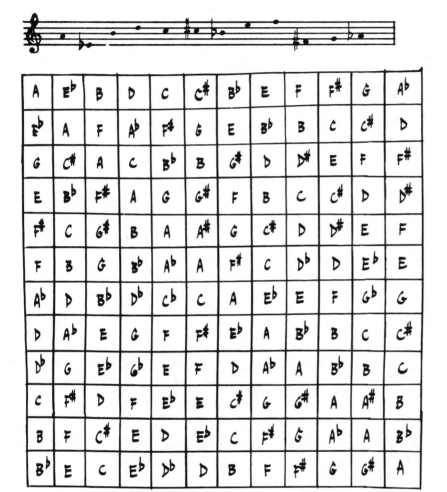

A	Eb	B	D	C	C#	Bb	E	F	F#	G	Ab
Eb	A	F	Ab	F#	G	E	Bb	B	C	C#	D
G	C#	A	C	Bb	B	G#	D	D#	E	F	F#
E	Bb	F#	A	G	G#	F	B	C	C#	D	D#
F#	C	G#	B	A	A#	G	C#	D	D#	E	F
F	B	G	Bb	Ab	A	F#	C	Db	D	Eb	E
Ab	D	Bb	Db	Cb	C	A	Eb	E	F	Gb	G
D	Ab	E	G	F	F#	Eb	A	Bb	B	C	C#
Db	G	Eb	Gb	E	F	D	Ab	A	Bb	B	C
C	F#	D	F	Eb	E	C#	G	G#	A	A#	B
B	F	C#	E	D	Eb	C	F#	G	Ab	A	Bb
Bb	E	C	Eb	Db	D	B	F	F#	G	G#	A

row from all twelve available notes (forty-eight versions). The original and all of its transpositions are read from left to right. All transpositions of the inversion are read from the top to the bottom. The retrograde from all available notes is read from the right to the left and the inverted retrograde and all its transpositions from the bottom to the top. While it may seem time-consuming at first, the row box is a great aid in the heat of composition, avoiding the otherwise necessary figuring and refiguring of the various formats until the best is found. With the box, all versions are immediately accessible and quickly used or discarded.

Once a row is composed, checked for possible errors (e.g., the presence of less than twelve tones, or unwanted interval strengths) and a row box completed, the materials are ready for composition. This may be, as was mentioned in Chapter 1, either from a previously conceived overview (macroconceptual) or from a motive (in this case, subset) within the row itself. Before presenting the wide variety of nonexclusive row alterations for musical purposes, the two major abstract approaches to row composition without deviation will be examined.

Category 1 includes compositions in which only one version of the row is used at a time to produce both the harmonic and melodic materials. Example 24 shows a row and a short excerpt with all the details of note numberings present. Here the first, fourth, and ninth notes of the row are used melodically while the remainder are present harmonically. This is changed as the excerpt continues.

Example 24
Row and excerpt using row with partial analysis.

Only the original form of the row has been used here and it can be readily seen that even the original with no transposition (since it contains all twelve notes) can produce almost an endless variety of possibilities. Transposition can add variety and sequence; inversion, though probably not immediately recognizable, can provide another nearly limitless supply of related materials consistent but ever variable. Retrogrades are more difficult to recognize unless obvious care has been taken about subset organization, and inversion retrograde is usually the least used, though it does present extraordinary potential for variation. Recognizability here does not refer to either "counting-the-notes" or even noting the form (O, I, R, IR) of the row used, but merely a *gestalt* recognition of aural consistency.

Category 2 compositions employ more than one version of the row simultaneously. Great care must be taken in this framework, as the row itself will no longer provide the consistent chromatic language it did in category 1. The potential for sudden octaves, open fifths, or triads in an otherwise dissonant environment is quite high over an extended period of time. This can be carefully watched, and indeed, to some composers, this form of composition offers the strictest of platforms from which to compose (somewhat like the strict fugal practices of the eighteenth century). Obviously the more simultaneous versions of the row used, the more opportunities for inconsistent harmonic and melodic materials to exist. Example 25 first shows the row, then a random application of three versions simultaneously. A rigorous application of the harmonic progression analytical techniques found in Chapter 1 will yield a totally haphazard nondirectional result.

Example 25
Row with random excerpt.

Example 26, on the other hand, shows the same row and versions of such with composer control and comprehension of the vital aspects of progression. Analysis here will yield a quite drastic difference from example 25, even though the same notes essentially were used: a strong directional progression.

Example 26
Controlled excerpt from row of example 25.

Obviously example 26 has produced a much more consistent and musical result born of compositional care and the use of rhythmic variation to avoid the "accidents" of the row's simultaneity. It can be argued that any music takes this care; however, in category 1 the avoidance of the "accidents" was not one of the musical essentials of the twelve-tone procedure.

Both category 1 and category 2 present special problems and solutions, but it should be evident that twelve-tone processes are as musical as the composer makes them, and in no way need they serve as so-called crutches. Category 1 seems easily accomplished at first, but almost immediately appears not flexible enough for "built-in" row subsets to be melodically recognizable (since melodic notes must be picked often nonconsecutively from the row). Category 2 seems almost to defeat the intent of twelve-tone processes in that it definitely allows a note to repeat itself before the other eleven have sounded. Yet it does offer great variety if handled with care (especially the care offered in Chapter 1) and as well the opportunity to practice the craft of composing within a very strict, almost constantly contrapuntal form from the outset.

Example 27 shows both categories in separate excerpts, with each bent on musicality and, especially, the vertical and horizontal exposition of the various row subsets (same row in each excerpt). Note the difference in sound as well as the comprehension of the row itself. Whether or not "counting" one's way analytically through a composition is a useful procedure is beside the point here (though doing it at least once is quite valuable). One must have a *reason* for using the row and not just plant it, expecting another consistent flow of sound to automatically *work* musically or do anything but add another piece to the incredibly long list of works somehow obtaining validity with only such consistency or reasoning.

Example 27
Categories 1 and 2 in excerpts from given row.

Example 28
Row with excerpt using repetitions.

The varieties of row manipulation are as vast as the works utilizing it. Note and chord repetitions are very frequent and the resultant "out-of-order" row treatment can lead to manifold new techniques. Example 28 shows a row and an excerpt using such techniques, with repetitions of vertical sonorities occurring. Note as well here that the last note of the row (in the melody) has become the first note of the next version (this is quite a common overlap) and that the harmonic material from the original statement of the row is repeated again under the second version. All this leads to a very free use of twelve-tone procedures, bending the row whenever the composer feels it does not suit his needs. Lost notes, or "skeletonized" rows, especially after many repetitions, can be quite successful; adding notes can also be successful (thirteen- and fourteen-note rows) if the reason is musical.

Example 29
Row and two different variations.

These experiments can lead to complete breakdown of procedure at times, offering the potential of row usage whenever it is suitable and abandoning it when it is not.

In the direction of more control of row deviations, subsets offer perfect ground. Example 30 shows a hexachord row in which the second hexachord is exactly the same as the first, transposed up a diminished fifth. This offers the composer the possibility of overlapping rows in groups of six notes. As well, this same row in trichords has the second and fourth subsets as mirror inversions of the first and third. This type of extremely motivic and controlled row evolution can lead to intricate category 1 and category 2 combinations with interchanging subsets (four for two; three for one), overlapping as many notes as desired (e.g., considering E–G–F-sharp as the end of an interchanged subset row, with F beginning a new row, then allowing three new pitches to be added, creating in essence a fifteen-note row), skeletonizing (i.e., since there is only one three-note motive here, breaking the row apart and using the notes between the trichords to evolve new rows and consequent subsets: F-sharp–F–D, notes three, four, and five), etc.

Example 30
Hexachord and trichord row with mirror inversion subsets.

Complicated hexachord relationships can be more easily formed from the augmented fourth concept: if all the notes of the first hexachord remain within and inclusive of the interval of an augmented fourth, any version (retrograde, inversion, retrograde inversion, or transposition of the original) can be composed in the second hexachord. Obviously this is not a rule, as many nonaugmented fourth concept hexachordal relationships can be formed. It is, however, a good starting point for the uninitiated.

Creation of rows with such immense interval consistency as discussed above can provide the composer with vast opportunities for exploring the potential of note relationships. Simultaneously, one must not forget the purpose of such undertakings and let the machinations of note names dominate over musical direction and motion. One can become so preoccupied with accounting for notes and their reason for being that the initial intent can be lost.

ASSIGNMENTS

(In each of the assignments given below it is suggested that a row box be completed both for the practice of such and the always present possibility that an assignment started well may blossom into a movement or eventually a complete work.)

1. Construct an atonal row and compose from it a short piece for piano using category 1. Purposefully collect melodic notes which provide strong consonant harmonies.

2. Compose a work for solo instrument strictly adhering to an atonal row, using only the original with no transpositions. Make as interesting as possible using octave displacement, rhythmic variations, etc.

3. Compose a row very triadic in nature and utilize as much of this character as possible in a short excerpt for any instrument and piano. Use only category 1 and emphasize the triadic formations as much as possible in the piano accompaniment.

4. Using a row which is in some form related internally by hexachords and quatrachords, compose a short work for voice without words using overlaps and skeletonizing as much as is musically possible.

5. Analyze example 31 for row present, then compose a completely different excerpt based on the same row.

Example 31

6. In a two-voice invention for piano and using category 2, create a consistent vertical vocabulary using the original and inversion of the row.

7. Compose a work for soprano, alto, and bass voices using a very triadic row with each voice a category 2 different version (I, R, IR) of the row. Carefully determine a weak-to-strong harmonic vocabulary based on the information from Chapter 1.

8. Using a rather free-form row (neither triadic nor atonal), compose a work for two available instruments (not piano) including at least one version of all forms of the row (category 1).

9. Construct a highly controlled row in which the second subset is the inversion of the first (hexachords) and compose a short work for piano using all forms of the row except inversion. Begin the piece in category 1 but evolve quickly into category 2.

10. Begin a work for voice and piano built on a row of your own choosing. Slowly deviate from the row first by simple techniques of note or chord repetition, and then by skeletonizing to the point that the piece is no longer twelve-tone at all. Modulate thus in such a manner that the change is not an overly noticeable one.

11. Construct a row and its complete box. Find in it a completely different row by making angular (nonskipped) lines starting anywhere in the box. Start an excerpt for any instrument(s) with the original row and slowly (as unnoticeably as possible) modulate to the completely new row using category 1 only.

WORKS FOR ANALYSIS

Consult the most recent Schwann Catalog for current in-print recordings of these works. Publishers are usually found through libraries, music stores, or distributors of music. This list is not meant to be comprehensive, only suggestive of further study.

Babbitt, Milton: *String Quartet No. 3* (very strong use of motivic subsets, overlap and subset rearrangement).

Berg, Alban: *Lulu* (Berg's free use of the row as well as triadic references to romantic harmonic vocabulary are quite obvious in this and other of his works after 1925)

Boulez, Pierre: *Le Marteau sans Maître* (good use of row for consistency and credible recognizability of motivic structures).

Dallapiccola, Luigi: *Parole di San Paolo* (somewhat strict use of row techniques with very musical results).

Křenek, Ernst: *Pentagram for Winds* (strong use of serial techniques but with constant twists of variations of the row to new consistencies).

Martino, Donald: *Concerto for Wind Quintet* (somewhat strict use of the row yet obtaining a very original but consistent result).

Petrassi, Goffredo: *Concerto No. 5 for Orchestra* (flexible use of very free rows).

Riegger, Wallingford: *Symphony No. 4* (inviting lyricism throughout with the twelve-tone techniques almost completely hidden).

Rochberg, George: *Symphony No. 2* (strict use of strong row techniques throughout; very thorough use of all versions).

Schoenberg, Arnold: *Concerto for Piano and Orchestra* (good use of row techniques and procedures with freedom used for musical reasons; works such as *Five Pieces for Orchestra* and *Gurrelieder* and others before 1920 give good insight into the not yet twelve-tone process but high level of chromaticism present in the works of this original mind).

Schuller, Gunther: *Symphony* (dramatic use of the row in a very controlled manner).

Weber, Ben: *Concerto for Piano and Orchestra* (straightforward use of row with little deviations).

Webern, Anton: *Concerto for Nine Instruments* (as with most of Webern's small output, this work is concise and direct and explores only the most musical of the row's aspects; row construction is highly evolved as well).

Webern, Anton: *Variations for Piano Solo* (excellent example of category 2 consistency).

Wolpe, Stefan: *Chamber Piece No. 1* (twelve-tone composed music in the most traditional of processes).

Wuorinen, Charles: *Concerto for Piano* (very involved subsets and evolution of new variants from original rows).

3

Melodic Direction

Creating good melodic lines is an integral part of music composition and one which cannot be overlooked, no matter what style or process is in use. Example 32 is an eight-bar melodic phrase which in miniature exposes a number of very basic melodic concepts:

Example 32
Eight bar melodic line.

Disregarding for the moment information from Chapter 1 regarding overtone influence and interval strength (they will be discussed later in the chapter), this line—as most lines do—tends to *flow*. Lines tend to resist constant angularity by reacting to skips with at least temporary stepwise motion often in the opposite direction. *Flow* is the least approachable definition of melodic line since so many have it while resisting every vocabulary for distinct rules, laws, or even suggestions. In general, however—like diatonicism and chromaticism—stepwise motion provides a base of flow around which skips provide the very necessary variation.

Climax is a most important consideration in composing melodic lines (example 32 tends to climax on the C-sharp). Melodies seem to have points at which one or more of the following occur: highest note, loudest note, harshest or smoothest note in articulation, fastest (shortest) or longest note. In general, climax is the most extreme of one or more of the musical components of a melodic line. Melodies tend to have points of rest called *cadence* (physical from both the instrumental point of performance as well as from the listener's viewpoint). Cadences occur at phrase (or breath) endings at which one or more of the following are present: lowest note, longest or one of the longer notes, strongest interval approach, and/or most concrete note in terms of horizontal interval and root strength.

Melodic *direction* moves towards climax from the outset, towards cadence from the climax and towards continuing line from the cadence. *Balance* is usually obtained by striking the climax at the pivot point (no matter where it occurs in the phrase) around which equal shares (not at all necessarily equal lengths) of growth and resolution towards cadence occur.

All of the elements (flow, climax, cadence, direction, and balance) are present to some degree in example 32. They present a mobile around which the melodic line may vary and grow. At the same time it should be pointed out that these five linear ideals do not necessarily contribute to a successful line if none are wanted or needed. Example 33 shows a divergent melodic phrase which does not flow (except in consistency of idea), does not really cadence (it merely stops, as all things must), has very little direction or climax (since the angular line possesses a number of climaxes and thus a shattered direction), and little balance. At the same time it has as much *character* as example 32.

Example 33
Divergent melodic phrase.

The point to be made here is that general characteristics are important only in that they be known, and not that they should necessarily be incorporated into a line unless their result is desired.

Knowing in advance what type of subtle combination of the basic ingredients of line is desired is most critical and can best be learned through the analysis of a number of lines, all different in purpose and style. Example 34 shows five separate and distinct lines, each of which possesses some or most of the qualities described so far. Each is briefly analyzed in terms of what is shown and not with reference to context (that will be discussed later). The first line is twelve-tone and each successive melody becomes less and less chromatic and complex, with the last being overtone-derived.

Example 34
Five distinct and separate melodic lines.

Each of these single lines, regardless of style, has to some extent the elements of climax, cadence, flow, balance, and direction. While each of these elements may be intuited, it is when one or both of the following is applied that knowledge of the above attributes is critical: (1) long extended lines of many phrases, and/or (2) lines with harmonic accompaniments or contrapuntal texture.

Extended melodic lines of many phrases (often such phrases may be marked by only slight breath cadences, suggesting one very long single line) are extremely difficult to compose, as suddenly the five elements under discussion must become telescoped to cover the complete line. Climax of the entirety must be observed from the outset so that intentional inner phrase climaxes do not detract from the direction toward the largest climax of the group. In extremely long lines it is most difficult to hold back the tendency to bring direction to an end earlier than desired. Minimal beginnings serve best, with a "saving" of materials for climactic use. Consistent flow can become easily boring, as can constant angularity; beginning with one or the other and slowly modulating to the climax is often effective. Balance is unwieldy in such macromelodic terms, and often only cadence can provide realizable assurance of successful balance around climax. Obviously the strongest melodic cadence should be present in the final notes of the line, and imbalance will become apparent if such a cadence tends to stop rather than end. Internal cadences, whether grouped in twos or threes as traditionally done, or gathering strength progressively through the melody, should not be quite so concrete as the last (much as internal climax should not overshadow the critical one). Example 35 is a twenty-five–measure line which follows the suggestions given above. It is a very lyrical melody with only hints of internal cadences, phrase balances, etc., yet conceived with a defined direction and climax in mind:

Example 35
Twenty-five-measure lyric line.

Phrases (and thus cadences) are marked with parenthetical breath marks ('), interval climaxes with asterisks (*), and direction with arrows. Note the singular evolution of flow from stepwise motion to larger and larger skips (however, not entirely allowing angularity to take over). Note that the full climax is the highest note, the loudest note, and is preceded by one of the largest skips of the line to help "pronounce" its existence. Balance must be left to the listener's and composer's ears. Again, each of these elements can and should be avoided at times when individual style and craft demand. A brief example of such divergence is shown in the excerpt in example 36, wherein the climax of an ostensibly long lyric line is the softest note of the phrase, touched with delicacy, marking even more emphatically the distinguished and fullest climax present:

Example 36
Line with indirect climax.

Introduction of harmonic accompaniment or contrapuntal texture to line should be done with the greatest of care. Though strong lines can carry weak or contrary harmonies through a given passage, even the best of melodies can be heavily damaged by an antagonistic participant.

Harmonic progression, especially when the considerations of Chapter 1 are applied, can add further momentum to lines of any length. Detractions usually occur when harmonic vocabulary or progression becomes more interesting than the musical linearity desired. At the same time this is not to say that harmonic progression should be dull and lifeless, only "serving" melodic direction; indeed, it can not only contribute but most certainly take over at times (especially at points of cadence and climax) to give the basic thrust of musical direction. With the concept in mind that harmonic cadence is achieved usually by the strongest of progressions leading to the strongest and most relatively consonant of chords (resolution or suggestion of resolution in cadences of forthcoming phrase cadences), it can be observed that "staggered" melodic and phrase cadences tend to weaken both, yet aid the composer who wishes to overlap for purposes of hiding internal breaths for long lyrical lines (see the potential present for harmonic accompaniment of example 36).

Example 37 shows two brief examples of melody with accompaniment. The first is category 1 twelve-tone composition with melodic notes extracted from the row at times when such helps provide harmonic consistency (note the effect here of melody "serving" harmony). The second is a category 2 twelve-tone excerpt with the row as melody and all its motivic subsets very much apparent (note the contrapuntal harmony of simultaneous versions of the row, producing an almost random collection of notes sounding often as if belonging to a separate work).

Example 37
Melodies with harmony: a. category 1–12-tone; b. category 2–12-tone.

Neither of these excerpts is "wrong." They exemplify simply two of the extremes in vertical with horizontal approaches: (1) that melody should somehow be derived from or because of harmonic vocabulary, or (2) that melody should necessarily be contradictory of harmonic or contrapuntal textures (N.B. They will interact regardless of composer attempts that they should not). Moreover, counterpoint (evident to some extent in even the most highly vertical of musics) helps to bridge the gap of melodies strung over harmonic poles in recitative style.

Example 38 is a melodic line in an environment which aids its direction, flow, climax, cadence, and balance, yet achieving a definitive character of its own, often breathing new life into sequences or repetitions:

Example 38
Melody with analyzed harmonic accompaniment.

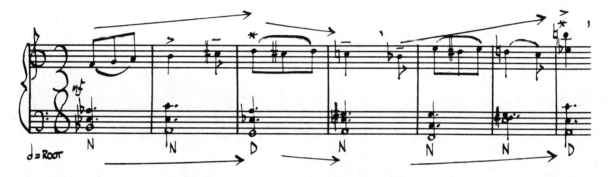

Note the Chapter 1 analysis of harmonic progression, along with this chapter's own melodic correlation. The coincidence of strengths at certain times, while avoiding it at others, is done consciously with the complete overview of the example in mind in conjunction with composer intent.

It is important at this point to note two very significant attributes of music which, while being alluded to often in this book, will not get the attention that, say, timbre does: dynamics and articulation. Each of these elements plays an extremely important role in the compositional processes of melodic and harmonic concepts. Strict definition, however, is most difficult indeed. As has been pointed out already, many climaxes land on the softest, not the loudest, note of a line. As well, contradictory harmonic articulations such as harsh attacks can easily make an already lyric line appear more so. Hopefully without appearing to sidestep the issue, one might state that dynamics and articulation are contextual variables which indeed rely almost entirely on a particular environment for definition. If indeed any generalization can be applied to their contribution, it is that they both can constructively contribute to line evolution or contradict it as powerfully as can harmony, counterpoint, or silence.

Rests can also contribute to potency of melodic direction or fall into cadence. Example 39 shows two brief uses of rest in the context of a single phrase. Note that the first use is just before the climax and is just the hiatus to effectively set it apart from the remainder of the material. The power of silence at this point (it will indeed be discussed in greater detail under Rhythm) is such that even a weak climax could be enhanced by the pause. The second interruption with silence is shown just before the final cadential note. This, though working in a very different way from with climax, helps to announce the finality of the last note and aids its agogic cadential properties with breath and preparation.

Example 39
Use of silence in context of single phrase.

Study and practice in the composition of melodic lines and lines with harmonic or contrapuntal textures is extremely crucial in the craft of composition as a whole. No book, no source of materials can possibly replace this practice or give a fraction of the potential sources of musical invention possible. Constant analysis of melodic lines, especially in early composition processes, is necessary in order to observe when cohesion is present and when it is not, and why. Certainly, everything is possible and can work in the proper context. It is the intention here only to give the reader the tools for understanding how to achieve a desired result.

Lines may begin from a single motive (generally, three to six notes) and blossom outward into full melodies. Such procedure can be very effective if it does not become a case of explaining each note in terms of motive (or the inversion, retrograde, or inversion retrograde). Though many prefer the overview approach described earlier, the motivic concept is nonetheless a valid and useful one. Tools for varying the motive to obtain material for generation of line include: adding notes (filling in skips), augmenting and/or diminishing intervals within the motive, skeletonizing (omitting a note or notes), elongating (adding notes to the beginning or end of the motive), repetition (repeating a note in the motive), transposition, inversion, mirror, retrograde, inversion retrograde, and augmenting durations or otherwise altering the rhythmic frame of the motive. The list of variances can be a very long and creative one. Example 40 shows a number of versions of a given motive and the construction of two phrases: (1) a "construction" in which most of the notes (including overlapping) can be accounted for as motivically generated, and (2) a motive-derived line in which flow, direction, climax, balance, and cadence remain the basic elements. Again it is emphasized that nowhere need the composer account for notes in terms of anything except his own instinct.

Example 40
Motive with six variations with two phrases built in different ways from such.

Line need not depend on one voice for existence. It is possible in a large ensemble to have line exist as entrances of instruments on different notes rather than a straightforward run of notes in a single instrument. Such lines portend material presented in the next chapter, but it is important to note that, while melodies of this type are often difficult to hear, they constitute as significant an approach to linear composition as do the other lines presented in the chapter. "Entrance lines" such as these preclude harmony in such a way that it is often difficult to distinguish the two: one follows the entrances for line, but each addition of a note adds equally to vertical sonorities, and the subtraction of already sounding instruments also presents linear potential. As well, such attention to the ends of notes being as individually articulated as the beginnings of notes (particularly when not releasing together) is a particularly valuable source of new melodic vocabulary to be considered in more depth later in this book.

ASSIGNMENTS

1. Compose two lines for the same instrument, the first of which exemplifies flow, climax, direction, balance, and cadence in the basic sense as described in this chapter. The second line should diverge from the norm of the first as much as possible yet still retain line definition. Harmonize each line twice with piano accompaniment; one is to complement the line, and the other to be as opposite as possible.

2. Write ten lines for an available instrument, with the first being an example of strong flow, climax, direction, balance, and cadence as described herein. Each of the following lines in turn should be subtly losing one or more of the strong elements, with the last of the ten being almost the opposite of the first. Change only a limited number of notes from first to last example, retaining as many as possible.

3. Compose a category 1 twelve-tone excerpt (harmony and melody) according to Chapter 2, making the *line* as lyrical as possible.

4. Analyze the line and harmonic direction in example 41 and compose a similar-length short piece for piano. It should be different but based on the same attributes of example 41.

Example 41

5. Write ten lines for unaccompanied voice, each of which exemplifies one aspect of chapter content. Analyze each according to its purpose. Avoid as much as possible the other aspects of the chapter regarding line.

6. Compose a long (forty to sixty measures) line, marking all of the cadences and climaxes as done in the chapter (example 35). The line should be as lyrical as possible. Be sure to include dynamics and articulation.

7. Create a twelve-tone line for any available instrument and contrast it with as divergent an accompaniment as possible, while making the excerpt work.

8. Using example 41, include four complete rests of a quarter-note length, and make each contribute to rather than detract from the material present.

9. Write a short work for piano. Analyze it completely for attributes of line, harmony, and their compatibility. Alter notes as needed.

10. Construct a pattern of symbols (those used in Chapters 1 and 3) to describe a set of three phrases. On a separate sheet compose an excerpt in any style to comply with your requests of line and harmony.

11. In a category 2 twelve-tone process, compose a short two-part invention for two different instruments, in which, by virtue of observed vertical strengths (not voice crossing), the lines exchange importance at least three times.

12. Sketch a motive. Derive a non–twelve-tone melodic line of over thirty bars in length from this motive. Avoid boredom or conspicuous use of the motive, but let it stand as an obvious source of the line. Note climaxes and cadences.

WORKS FOR ANALYSIS

Consult the most recent Schwann catalog for current in-print recordings of these works. Publishers are usually obtained through libraries, music stores, or distributors of music. This list is not meant to be comprehensive, only suggestive of further study.

Bartók, Béla: *Music for Strings, Percussion, and Celesta* (line in all guises: alone, with harmony, in contrapuntal texture; divergence but direction throughout).

Britten, Benjamin: *Peter Grimes (4 Sea Interludes)* (active interchange from melodic to harmonic direction and importance).

Carter, Elliott: *Sonata for Cello* (line getting stronger because of its contrasting harmonic accompaniment).

Crumb, George: *Ancient Voices of Children* (strong emphasis on solo line with articulate emphasis on growth from smooth flow to leaping angularity).

Hindemith, Paul: *Music for Brass and Strings* (strong melodic line with cohesive strength continually in the harmonic vocabulary).

Kay, Ulysses: *Markings* (divergent melodic and harmonic cadences but with resultant overlap, smooth transitions).

Ligeti, György: *Lontano* (line present but only by instrument entrance; at first sounding as if without melody, further inspection nets strong melodic and motivic presence between, not within, instruments).

Mahler, Gustav: *Symphony No. 9* (exemplifies Mahler as a master of long lines building to stepladdered climaxes; overlapping harmonic and melodic cadences as well as constant balance between stepwise flow and angularity).

Rachmaninoff, Sergei: *Symphony No. 2* (very long lines of characteristic balance, flow, and climax).

Respighi, Ottorino: *Pines of Rome* (familiar lines with overlapping harmonic ostinati and resultant staggered cadences between line and harmony).

Ruggles, Carl: *Sun Treader* (complex struggle of many lines interweaving for dominance; cadence and balance almost completely sublimated towards linear drive).

Schuman, William: *Symphony No. 6* (very long lines beset constantly with contrasting harmonic and percussive conflicts; line benefits from the combination).

Scriabin, Alexander: *Symphony No. 5* (lines derived from harmonic sonorities and subsequent motives).

Stravinsky, Igor: *Dumbarton Oaks Concerto* (neoclassical lines in a bastard harmonic environment).

4
Pointillism and Klangfarbenmelodien

Pointillism in music is line with a majority of notes separated by octave displacements, rests, and/or different articulations and dynamics. Derivation of pointillistic process is a natural extension of melodic practice, carrying vital elements of line to their extreme. Flow (now weakened by drastic leaps and spaces), direction (splintered by lack of recognizable singularity of pitch motion), and climax (often difficult to find due to the multitude of high notes and leaps) are the most affected by pointillism. Cadence (helped by agogic "landing" of notes in terms of duration) and balance are the least affected. Example 42 shows a line and four pointillistic versions of that line. The first version is octave displacement. Note the weakening of interval strength and immediate lessening of flow. The subsequent two versions apply first rests and different articulations, each without octave displacement. Note that these middle two versions are not as drastic in variation as the first, nor as interruptive of flow and direction. The final version is a combination of rests, displacement, articulation, and dynamic contrast, and demonstrates one potential of pointillism. Note that none of the first three versions is that different from the original, always maintaining some number of consistencies with it. The fourth version, however, is strikingly different and marks a total conceptual difference in the study of melodic line and its comprehension.

Example 42
Line and four pointillistic versions.

At this point one might ask, "Why this departure?" First, the individual elements of pointillism are in no way new to music. Throughout history one can find examples of octave displacements, rests in themes, and articulation variations within line. It is, however, the combination of these simultaneously which gives a uniqueness—an extreme which parallels the relationship of chromaticism to twelve-tone writing. Most important in pointillism is the care which each note receives. The connective tissue of long lyric lines often allowed composers a certain luxury: many notes existed only to prepare or unravel a climax, direction, or flow, and some notes (such as those found in quick scalewise runs) could be left out, misperformed, or slurred over without great loss to the line or work itself. With pointillism, however, each note is vital in and of itself, while at the same time contributing to the melodic line. Example 43 shows two lines, one being very lyrical in nature, the other contrasting by pointillistic procedures in the extreme. Both serve individual purposes. While to the so-called natural instincts of the human ear the first may be considered the *only* line present, the second melody presents drama, intensity, and immediacy, with each note a unique and functioning contributor to the whole.

Example 43
Contrasting lyric and pointillistic melodic lines.

Programmed aesthetics may have some listeners mark pointillism as "pointlessly" unraveled melodic contour; it nonetheless draws the ear outward for the quality and distinctness of each note in the line.

Combination with twelve-tone procedures is due not only to historical proximity but to the cohesion constant chromaticism gives in the space, time, articulation, and dynamic extremes which pointillism provides. As well, extreme pointillism applied to diatonic and otherwise traditionally lyric lines seems forced and needless. Indeed, the elements which contribute so successfully to such lines more often than not need little tampering. Example 44 shows a twelve-tone pointillistic excerpt. Note that even though leaps occur from the outset, they continue to expand to give at least some direction towards climax and a subtle flow. Likewise a slight increase in note duration towards the end of the example helps give strength to the cadence and as well helps provide direction.

Example 44
Twelve-tone pointillistic excerpt.

In a further extreme of octave displacement, one finds almost a two-part counterpoint present in a single line (a sort of "hocket" technique), with the higher and lower notes forming groups of linear direction and individual flow:

Example 45
Two part counterpoint in a single line.

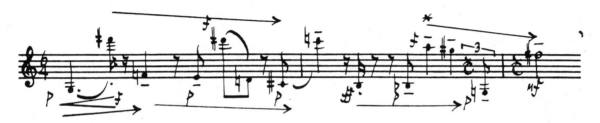

Note carefully the arrows for direction and the asterisks (*) for climax used for analysis of melodic line.

From these examples one can confront a somewhat major compositional problem: aside from two-part spatial counterpoints as above, how can pointillistic line in the extreme, with its leaping and rests, be used in harmonic texture without being easily lost in its environment? One obvious way is to make certain that the pointillistic line is of different timbre than that of its harmonic texture:

Example 46
Timbre control of pointillistic line in homophonic framework.

A second solution is to have the harmony as pointillistic as the line:

Example 47
Pointillistic harmony and line.

Texture varies here, but this can add yet another uniqueness to the totality of the composition's vertical and horizontal structure. Category 2 twelve-tone process can help contribute the necessary pitch complement for such variety as in example 47. The simultaneity of more than one row can slow down the use of all 12 notes (often otherwise spent within the framework of a measure or less) as well as offer a further extreme to the nuances of pointillism: highly variable harmonic structures. Example 48 shows just such category 2 variety with the presence of a wide cross-section of harmonic language; a variety which often seemed out of place in lesser extremes now serves as yet another available possibility for the composer of pointillistic texture.

Example 48
Pointillism in a cross section of harmonic vocabulary.

Klangfarbenmelodien offers yet another solution to the pointillistic frame of reference (harmonic or contrapuntal background). It adds the concept of potential timbre change to each note of the line, thus extending still further the unique qualities of the individual note (or "event" when speaking of two or more notes connected either vertically or horizontally). Example 49 shows one aspect of *klangfarbenmelodien* (literally translated, *sound-color-melody*) for violin, horn (in C), and flute, and explores these timbre aspects of pointillism:

Example 49
Klangfarbenmelodien.

Phrases are quite possible in *klangfarbenmelodien* passages, usually structured from long notes or longer periods of silence. Extreme pointillism does lead, however, to a norm of constant variation in and of itself, quickly becoming less and less dramatic. The potential, therefore, of consistently pointillistic works with *klangfarbenmelodien,* is traditionally not in long forms but rather in short pieces, precise in form and drama. Longer works are usually constructed from a number of short movements contrasted by tempo or texture variations. Example 50 shows the opening bars of three movements of a work in *klangfarbenmelodien* style, and some possible contrasts for form.

Klangfarbenmelodien can be used successfully within a context of a variety of other textures, and is useful for contrast and idea, but it need not be an absolute which, once begun, must be adhered to. Example 51 shows a brief passage for violin which begins in a quite lyrical and connected manner. It modulates to a short burst of pointillism and returns once again to the former texture, showing one possible contribution of pointillistic techniques to otherwise continuous textures: variation.

Example 50
Opening of three klangfarbenmelodien *movements and some possible contrasts.*

Example 51
Klangfarbenmelodien *modulating from a lyric line.*

In ensembles of potentially wide timbre variances, *klangfarbenmelodien* can as well serve a useful function of variation without becoming a staple for the entire work.

Klangfarbenmelodien in the extreme does present a new word to the vocabulary of this text and one which will be used extensively in later chapters: *parameter.* Briefly defined, parameter is a measurable limit and, while obviously useful in terms of instrumental performance restrictions (i.e., highest note, loudest sound, etc.), it is also a highly valuable reference term when tackling balance, direction, and climax. *Klangfarbenmelodien* can, if reaching the available parameters at the beginning of the work, make further climaxes into anticlimaxes, direction only a diversion, and balance almost impossible except for very large forms. It is often very wise to be constantly aware of the parameters of any given situation so that *klangfarbenmelodien* is not merely a device but an effective tool for truly musical composition.

ASSIGNMENTS

1. Compose a short work for an available single-line instrument in which a lyric and relatively diatonic line slowly modulates through octave displacement, etc. (see example 42) while becoming more and more chromatic, ending with a derived row in as extreme a *klangfarbenmelodien* style as is possible.

2. Write a short trio for diverse instruments in *klangfarbenmelodien* style in which no two instruments ever sound simultaneously.

3. Analyze example 52 in terms of harmonic and melodic direction (Chapters 1 and 3) and attempt to achieve the same goals in a highly pointillistic framework.

Example 52

4. Compose a short piece for piano and available instrument in which the piano is harmonic and continuous in texture and the other instrument is highly pointillistic inclusive of *klangfarbenmelodien.*

5. Compose a category 1 twelve-tone work for piano in which the extremes of octave displacement become actively contrapuntal.

6. In a brief piece for three voices without text (but using notated vowel sounds for varying timbre), evoke strong *klangfarbenmelodien* inclusive of extremely diverse rhythms.

7. With the rhythmic structure shown in example 53, compose a work for piano in category 2 twelve-tone process with vertical texture varying from one to six voices.

Example 53

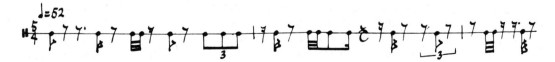

8. Begin with three measures of each of five movements for piano, applying *klangfarbenmelodien* completely in each, yet having each movement contrast with each of the others. Use a single category 1 row.

9. In a work for solo voice (syllables for text), compose the opening three measures, the measure of climax, and the final three measures conclusion. All should be *klangfarbenmelodien,* but the melodic vocabulary in terms of notes is free.

10. Compose a trio for piano and two available instruments. Analyze the completed brief piece in terms of the melodic and harmonic techniques described in Chapters 1 and 3. The piece should be category 2 twelve-tone process and inclusive of as many techniques of *klangfarbenmelodien* as possible.

WORKS FOR ANALYSIS

Consult the most recent Schwann Catalog for current in-print recordings of these works. Publishers are usually obtained through libraries, music stores, or distributors of music. This list is not meant to be comprehensive, only suggestive of further study.

Berio, Luciano: *Circles* (good use of occasional *klangfarbenmelodien* and pointillism, contrasting "events," and longer lyrical line).
Boulez, Pierre: *Sonata No. 2 for Piano* (advanced pointillism throughout with control over climax, direction, and drama).
Cope, David: *Triplum* (category 1 twelve-tone process with heavy use of *klangfarbenmelodien* at times, while at others modulating into homophonic sections).
Copland, Aaron: *Piano Variations* (highly dissonant pointillism almost throughout with excellent development of dynamics and articulation).
Crumb, George: *Eleven Echoes of Autumn* (often heavy use of *klangfarbenmelodien* with an abundance of rests and dynamic growth).
Davidovsky, Mario: *Synchronisms No. 6 for Piano and Electronic Sounds* (contains contrasting uses of pointillism on the keyboard and *klangfarbenmelodien* on tape with lyrical lines and vertical sonorities on the piano).
Erickson, Robert: *Chamber Concerto* (good use of modulating *klangfarbenmelodien* within harmonic textures with lyric lines).
Henze, Hans Werner: *Der Junge Lord* (good use of vocal pointillism within orchestral textures).
Ligeti, György: *Aventures* (heavy use of dramatic pointillism).
Nono, Luigi: *Espressione* (occasional pointillistic and *klangfarbenmelodien* techniques as contrasts to more homophonic ones).
Ruggles, Carl: *Evocations for Piano* (harsh pointillism in contrapuntal style almost without letup throughout).

Stravinsky, Igor: *Elegy for J.F.K.* (pointillism used sparingly for contrast in a free atonal texture).

Stockhausen, Karlheinz: *Nr. 5 Zeitmasse for Five Woodwinds* (constant application of *klangfarbenmelodien* techniques throughout).

Webern, Anton: *Cantata Op. 29* (like most of Webern's works, this is a striking use of *klangfarbenmelodien;* note the brevity of this and most of his output and the constant use of extreme pointillistic techniques).

Webern, Anton: *Symphony for Chamber Orchestra, Op. 21* (exemplifies again the extremes of both brevity and *klangfarbenmelodien;* note especially the importance of each note within the directed confines of each line).

5

Polytonality

It is important never to forget the potential continuing evolution of techniques past. Such is the case with tonality in polytonality (also inclusive of *polymodality*). Defined simply as the simultaneity of two or more keys or tonal centers, polytonality is a divergent and plastic process which can allow for a wide variety of musics.

The first major consideration in polytonality is the choice of key relationships. For the purposes of this text two categories exist: consonant and dissonant. A consonant relationship is one in which the keys chosen have five or more notes in common between them. A dissonant relationship occurs when less than five notes are in common. These common notes do not include the octave (i.e., each tonality or modality consists of seven pitches). An example of this would be to contrast the relationships of C major to F major and C major to F minor. In the first instance the relationship is consonant, as six of the seven tones are in common; in the latter case the relationship is dissonant (when considering the natural minor), as only the notes F, G, and C are in common.

In consonant relationships it is important to observe carefully the note differences present. It would not be polytonality at all if, for example, C major and F major were the chosen keys and B and B-flat were avoided. It is indeed the *differences* between the keys which validates polytonality. In dissonant relationships, care must be maintained to thoroughly establish the keys present, as often the high degree of chromaticism present can approach atonality rather than polytonality.

There are a number of ways to establish two or more centers clearly:

1. Separate the key areas so that each is heard distinctly:

Example 54
Polytonality with separated key centers.

2. Establish the tonal centers of each key so no doubt can exist as to their separate identities. Maintaining strong progressions and lack of chromaticism within each key helps in this area. As well, it is important to define clearly what mode of minor—or indeed what mode—is chosen, and to strive constantly to emphasize contrasting notes between keys once established. Example 55 shows C major and E-flat major in polytonal texture.

Example 55
Close but strong polytonal structure.

Note the immediate cross-relationships developed between keys as well as their tonal centers strengthened by repetition and strong progressions (this in spite of the fact that they are not spatially separated as in example 54).

3. Avoid quick or numerous modulations from one key center to another. This weakens relationships and confuses the conflict of centers. Modulations work best when the tonal center stays the same but the mode around it changes (e.g., D major to D minor; D major to D Phrygian). Staggered modulations also help maintain polytonal textures. Example 56 shows a modulation from C major to C minor in one key while the other key remains constant:

Example 56
Polytonal modulation.

4. Chromatic alterations other than modulation (secondary dominants, etc.) can occur but should be minimalized if polytonal contrast is to be maintained. Since altered chords represent a way to achieve chromatic variety in a single tonality, they need not be quite so necessary in polytonality. If altered chords are used, repetition can be useful in establishing them as members of the key they represent, hopefully avoiding a breakdown of cross-relationships between keys. Example 57 shows the use of an altered chord in two situations. In the first it is used in such a way that momentarily the augmented sixth chord in C major sounds like a dominant seventh in C-sharp major (the other key). The second excerpt chooses an altered chord which does not exist naturally with the other key (dominant of the dominant in C major, equally the Neapolitan sixth altered chord in C-sharp major). The polytonality of the second example is far more consistent.

Example 57
Two uses of altered chords in polytonal texture.

Each of the above four points should be observed in order to concentrate the opposition of keys so that when used together they produce a clean set of two distinct keys sounding simultaneously:

Example 58
Distinct polytonality.

Further separation can be achieved by timbre (e.g., strings on the bottom sonority, with woodwinds on top), articulation (e.g., staccato on the bottom, legato on top), dynamics (e.g., soft lower key center, bright and loud upper), and material (e.g., ostinato on bottom, clear melodic counterpoint on top). Each of these furthers the unique differences between centers and thus provides successful raw material for composing polytonal textures.

The use of dissonant polytonal relationships further articulates the wide diversity this source material provides. Example 59 shows an extreme separation in terms of all the above collected suggestions. Wide spacing between the key centers, different timbres for each, completely different material, articulations, and dynamics, as well as strong establishment of keys, all contribute to the clean polytonal aspects of this excerpt:

Example 59
Contrapuntal polytonality.

At this point, however, one must digress and suggest the possibility that the composer may wish a more subtle intertwining of the two or more keys in use. While great care must be taken to constantly evaluate the successful establishment of key centers, nearly all the above suggestions can be abandoned with a very different yet still polytonal result:

Example 60
Intertwined polytonality.

Note in this example the lack of range separation of the two keys (D-flat major and F major) and the consistency of dynamics, articulation, material, and timbre. Polytonality is maintained, however, by sustained cross-relationships of different key notes and strong tonic-dominant progressions in each key. Here the effect is a continuous flow of similar material deeply involved in chromatic development *without* either of the two former alternatives: traditional altered chords or atonality. It is with this approach that many composers have achieved highly chromatic and evolutionary passages without either submitting to the governance of row domination or resorting to observed traditional formats. Noteworthy here is that instead of abandoning a technique (in this case, tonality) and creating another, extension of a given process has revealed yet further materials and expansion.

Harmonic analysis in terms of Chapter 1 is easily applied to example 60; however, as with earlier examples in this chapter, it should be cautioned that single root definition, etc., tends to be very misleading. Example 61 shows a brief polytonal excerpt with two separate analyses. The first analysis proceeds as if nothing but the vertical structures themselves are important; the second shows the presence of two roots, two directions, etc., recognizing the polytonality present. Suffice it to say that analysis in both manners is correct in certain circumstances. When polytonality is separated in the extreme (as in example 59), the second mode of analysis is the most logical choice. When polytonality is used to create chromaticism in a nontraditional way and with atonal influences (the polytonality becoming blurred), the first mode of analysis should be acceptable.

Example 61
Polytonal excerpt with two different root analyses (open note).

The use of three or more tonal centers becomes difficult indeed and separation of at least one tonality is suggested. As well, a lightening of texture in at least one of the keys is most helpful if anything but chromatic chaos is to be achieved. Example 62 shows three distinct keys (D minor, F minor, and B Dorian) in combination:

Example 62
Three keys in polytonal texture.

Note the separation of the upper Dorian and its complete uniqueness of material. Though the lower two keys are closely spaced, the D minor is nearly a pedal point while the F minor is a single-line melody, clearly a separate entity. Each of the three maintains identity yet contributes to the overall polytonal texture.

If the three keys are not separated and strengthened (not only in tonal center but unique in materials, timbres, or textures), the result is more chaotic than the same with two keys and, unless the tonalities are clearly consonant in relationship, near atonality is reached as well as a muddying of overall texture. Example 63 shows two brief excerpts of consistent three-key–centered polytonality. The first is dissonant with little but a vain attempt at strong tonal centers to hear distinctly the keys in operation. The second excerpt is less muddled in that the spatial separation, clear vertical sonorities, and constant cross-relationships help maintain a semblance of three-key operation.

Example 63
Three-key-centered polytonality: a. mixed; b. spatial separation.

Polytonality can be highly effective in contrapuntal situations in which each voice is in one key. Example 64 shows a clean, clear-cut three-voice counterpoint with each voice maintaining completely separate musical characteristics while contributing to the flow of the entireity.

Example 64
Three-voice polytonal counterpoint.

Obviously, single lines defining keys in contrapuntal textures is the best route for clarity in the use of four or more keys. It must be cautioned here that the borderline of psychoacoustics is fast approached (i.e., the reasonable assurance that the keys can be recognized by the listener). It is quite possible and reasonable, however, to use polytonality *not* for clear listener recognition of keys but rather the *gestalt* of multiplicity. Indeed, even chaos can be a composer-desired effect. Example 65 is the result of seven different keys (six contrapuntal ideas and a seventh of chords splashing through the resultant texture). Some of the lines exchange materials and all modulate freely. The result is not the distinct polytonality discussed earlier but the general *effect* of such.

Example 65
Polytonality with seven different keys.

Atonality, though approached, can be dismissed by the total lack of the notes E-natural and G in the example. Finally, it is important to note the significance of polytonal procedures. As with other ideas mentioned in previous chapters, they need not be maintained throughout a work for validity, but can simply provide needed variety. The nuances and subtleties are just touched upon herein, and the composer can create a significant reservoir of materials between the extremes suggested.

ASSIGNMENTS

1. Compose a short consonant polytonal work for piano with each key thick in texture yet widely separated. Make clarity of key centers a dominant feature of the work.

2. In a short work for piano, use dissonant related keys in polytonality, with both keys in the same register overlapping constantly. Make clarity of key centers a dominant feature of the work.

3. Compose a polytonal work for voice and piano with the separate instruments having the separate keys (dissonant in relationship), with each modulating and concretely establishing new tonal centers, but still polytonal.

4. In a short work for two pianos, have each piano maintain a separate key in consonant relationship with each other; however, using at least one altered chord and avoiding sudden bursts of correlation between keys. Make clarity of key centers a dominant feature of the work but do not separate them by range.

5. Analyze example 66 in two ways: (1) single analysis; (2) double analysis for clarity of polytonality present. Choose the best approach and compose a brief excerpt using the analysis as a guideline.

Example 66

6. Compose a work for three voices (with syllables only) in which each is a separate mode. Make clarity of key centers (three) a dominant feature of the piece. Use both consonant and dissonant polytonal relationships but do not modulate or include altered chord suggestions (chromaticism within line).

7. Compose a piece for piano in which the two or more key centers are not clear (but analyzable on paper), but rather add nontraditional chromaticism to the texture.

8. Using four available instruments (not piano), write a short work exploring the contrapuntal aspects of polytonality. Use four keys but make each voice clearly different in material, articulations, timbre, and approach to strengthening tonal center.

9. Using only borrowed material in different keys (recognizable hymn tunes, popular songs, etc.), combine first two and then three in a short work for any available instruments (inclusive of piano), preferably as many as possible. Key relationships can be either consonant or dissonant, whichever works best.

10. Compose a work for two pianos in which one is contrapuntal and harsh and the other highly vertical and thick-textured. Use dissonant key relationships and highly chromatic (both altered-chord and modulations) vocabularies in both instruments; strive for clarity of the altering key centers.

WORKS FOR ANALYSIS

Consult the most recent Schwann Catalog for current in-print recordings of these works. Publishers are usually obtained through libraries, music stores, or distributors of music. This list is not meant to be comprehensive, only suggestive of further study.

Bartók, Béla: *String Quartet No. 5* (use of occasional polytonality and especially polymodality as variation technique).

Becker, John: *Symphony No. 3* (constant use of polychords as well as some extended polytonality).

Berio, Luciano: *Sinfonia* (polytonality as a result of quoted material present in the third movement).

Colgrass, Michael: *As Quiet As* (Ivesian use of quoting and polytonal references throughout a soft texture of lush sonorities).

Cowell, Henry: *Sinfonietta* (occasional use of polytonality for variation and addition of chromaticism).

Diamond, David: *Symphony No. 4* (constant polytonality created from intertwining and self-generating motives in different keys).

Foss, Lukas: *Baroque Variations* (liberal use of polytonality based on Baroque quotations and their overlays).

Griffes, Charles Tomlinson: *Poem for Flute and Orchestra* (occasional use of polytonal texture as an extension of extremely thick tertian chords).

Harris, Roy: *Symphony No. 3* (good use of polytonality with often distinct spatial separation and dissonant relationships).

Honegger, Arthur: *Symphony No. 2 for String Orchestra* (thick-textured polytonality with especially difficult aural realization due to intertwining of common timbres).

Ives, Charles: *Central Park in the Dark* (good use here of polytonality, which is present to some degree in almost all his works).

Ives, Charles: *Three Places in New England* (excellent treatment in the second movement of growing dissonant relations in polytonal frameworks).

Milhaud, Darius: *Symphonies (5) for Small Orchestra* (each of these works is a study in close-knit polytonality with very often indistinct tonal centers).

Schuman, William: *Credendum* (good changes of key within a polytonal setting going from major to minor on the same note).

Shostakovich, Dmitri: *Symphony No. 1* (polytonality used throughout often for humorous effects; usually consonant relationships).

Stravinsky, Igor: *Petrouchka* (excellent use of dissonant—augmented fourth—relationships in polytonality; space and particularly timbre are used to help further establish the already strong key centers).

6

Interval Exploration

Aside from atonality and polytonality, yet quite possible within
each, the exploration of intervals other than thirds or triads and their
inversions is an important addition to the vocabulary of extending
potential sound materials. Such musics are not bent upon avoiding
tertian harmonies (chords constructed in thirds) but rather to create
yet further structures for harmonic and melodic invention. Before
beginning discussion of individual interval possibilities, a number
of concepts must be articulated.

It is, for example, very important to realize that most successful
works are not born completely of a single interval. Even the
simplest of triadic chorales contain most possible intervals, with
nonharmonic content often providing the remainder. Example 67
shows a very simple four-part chorale. Yet within it exists every
vertical interval (condensed within the octave) possible (e.g., minor
second as passing tone E–F resolving to D–F, etc.). While this may
be immediately obvious, it does bear observation, as a great many
first compositions based on intervals other than the third suddenly
become immaculate from the variation which interval multiplicity
provides. Therefore, regardless of the interval basis of examples
discussed later in the chapter, core intervals should predominate but
not exist in a state of overkill.

59

Example 67
Four part chorale with interval demonstration.

Interval exploration may be vertical or horizontal or both. Again, however, an overabundance of a single interval either way can produce boredom. Vertical concepts include "stacking" (or the "in turn" placement of like intervals one upon the other either simultaneously or in rhythmic addition), octave displacement (the perfect fourth becoming a perfect eleventh, etc.), and inversions (exactly the same approach as in triadic harmony). This latter concept is most important as it not only provides change of root position and resultant variation, but as well often creates new intervals. Example 68 shows stacked fourths and the resulting inversion possibilities. With the first inversion alone the new intervals of the sixth, fifth, and second are added to the fourths (as well as the sevenths and thirds present in the chord already, reduced within the octave). Thus, with just one inversion, all intervals in one form or another come into existence.

Example 68
Stacked fourth chords and inversion possibilities.

In general, every aspect of triadic harmony can be applied to harmonies constructed on other intervals. Once established, for example, an environment becomes stable and new notes, whether consonant or dissonant, can be "nonharmonic." Example 69 shows an extreme of this in an excerpt based on seconds. The dissonance becomes a constant in which the third-beat minor seventh chord becomes nonharmonic. Though this may very well invert many a traditional conception of terms, such terms may be applied nonetheless. Chromaticism need not be random or arrived at by planing, but can easily develop from many of the altered-chord concepts of traditional harmonies. Example 70 shows examples of traditional chromatic concepts applied to textures composed of other than tertian harmonies. The first is a secondary fourth chord of the dominant and its resolution (all in quartal harmony) within its key. The second example is a modulation from C-tonality seconds harmony to FGA-tonality seconds harmony by use of a traditional pivot chord technique (note that modulation can also exist from one type of chord to another, e.g., seconds harmony to quartal harmony; but this is not highly successful if applied too often or without fully establishing not only the key but also the constancy of interval environment). The third example is a Neapolitan-fourth chord and its resolution. It is important to note that deriving chromaticism from traditional sources is only one possible technique. Example 71 shows chromaticism derived from a combination of other processes. The excerpt is in seconds harmony and the alteration from major to minor and back provides the opening source of chromaticism. The second measure explores the potential of planing (i.e., the parallel motion of all voices upward or downward by other than diatonic routes). The third measure evolves chromaticism from the contrapuntal leanings of the now melodic lines.

Example 69
'Second chord' chorale with seventh chord as non-harmonic.

Example 70
Example of chromaticism applied to non-tertian harmonies with traditional approaches (secondary dominant; modulation; Neapolitan sixth).

Example 71
Interval exploration chromaticism derived by other means.

Analysis is no more difficult with these materials than with triadic ones (and often it is easier) if the techniques of Chapter 1 are applied diligently. Vertical sonorities of *any* type can have variety through as many structured nonharmonic and chromatic concepts as traditional and nontraditional sources (note the examples of twelve-tone applications and others near the end of the chapter). Moreover, as obvious as it may seem to some, there is no interval or vertical structure which is *right.* History has proven successfully that while indeed a vast amount of musics based on tertian harmonies were composed during the so-called common-practice period, this represents but a bare fraction of the musics of the Western world and even less of the musics of the world as a whole.

Use of intervals other than the third in *melodic* lines is so commonplace that only two suggestions need be given. The first is to avoid overconsistency; that is, to avoid a continual exploration of one interval, which usually leads not only to boredom but also to the experimental aspects of the compositional process becoming too obvious. Secondly, it is important to note that tertian melodies, when *leaping,* often do so around their harmonic structures. If a smooth flow of melodic line is desired, a "like" leaping technique may be applied to all but harmonies built in seconds. Example 72 shows just such variation and leaping in process:

Example 72
Fourth chord melodic leaping technique.

Note the quartal leaping occasionally giving just enough hint of the harmonic vocabulary in use without dissolving the line with fourths.

For organizational purposes the study of interval exploration here will progress from fifths to fourths to seconds and sevenths (thirds and sixths being the primary substance of well-explored tertian harmonies). Composing with perfect fifths as the staple of a work (both vertically and horizontally) is, as has been shown, a great deal more difficult than may initially appear. Example 73 shows a texture of five notes with four perfect fifths. Observe that with the creation of each interval beyond the single two-note fifth, new intervals are created. With the three bottom notes there are two fifths and a ninth (becoming a second when condensed). With four notes there are three fifths, two ninths, and a thirteenth (a sixth when condensed to within the octave). With five notes a seventeenth is added (a third when condensed). The root here is the lower note of the lowest fifth.

Example 73
Five-note texture; four perfect fifths and resultant new intervals present.

The inversion of this chord and the resultant interval ramifications are shown in example 74:

Example 74
The inversions of a five-note fifth chord.

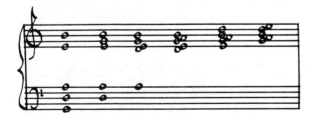

Most important in this and other nontriadic interval environments is to avoid resolving dissonances traditionally or the structure reverts to triadic units. Example 75 demonstrates two sets of chordal movements. Note that in the first excerpt the progression has all traditional dissonances resolving in such a way that tertian harmony is obtained. In actuality, no fifth chord has occurred. The resolution solidly suggests that the first chord was really a triad with nonharmonic tones present (or a ninth chord with only one nonharmonic tone).

Example 75
Two motions of a fifth chord: a. as resolution in tertian harmony; b. as fifth chord interval exploration.

The second excerpt has the first chord move to another chord based on fifths even though its inversion (root, however, remaining on the bottom acoustically as the lowest note of the lowest fifth) slightly weakens the fifth-chord feeling. Example 76 is a complete phrase with fifths as the basic unit of structure. Note the varying texture, inversions for variety, and chromaticism present in the harmony. The lyrical melodic line on top once outlines leaps of fifths but otherwise maintains stability and generation of climax, etc. based on the examples of Chapter 3.

Example 76
Complete phrase with fifths as the basic unit of structure.

Works in fourths (often called quartal harmony) function much as do those in fifths, with the difference that fourths—traditionally—

often seek resolution to thirds (common-practice technique primarily). It is therefore common to see such works have more of a prevalence of fourths in order to establish them as compositional norms and lose the feeling of expected resolution. Fifths are more frequent in tertian harmony and provide not quite so many problems.

Example 77 shows a short contrapuntal phrase constructed from fourths. Note the heavy usage of vertical fourths here to establish their dominance. As well, note the total lack of third resolution typical of triadic compositions.

Example 77
Short contrapuntal phrase built around the interval of a fourth.

Little that is new need be added with the study of seconds and sevenths, except that they are harsher in dissonance and—even more so than fourths—tend to feel a programmed need to resolve based on triadic tradition. Often, therefore, compositions tend to employ enormous amounts of unresolved seconds before admitting other (nonharmonic) intervals, into their company. Example 78 shows a chord built in seconds and one in sevenths, the resultant inversions, and a short excerpt using both simultaneously (a subject to be covered later):

Example 78
Chords in seconds and sevenths with example using both simultaneously.

Note another feature here: immediate chromaticism which further allows the interval ingredients themselves to become a foundation of the environment and avoid triadic responses.

The augmented fourth (diminished fifth) is a difficult specimen in that it divides the octave equally and thus cannot exist by stacking. It can, however, exist—as can the others—by separate groups not necessarily connected by continuous interlocking of the same interval. In example 79 the chord of four notes is really two augmented fourths a major second apart. The subsequent excerpt is quite complex, as the interval itself implies constant chromaticism, weak root structure, and a continual lack of strong harmonic direction when used exclusively.

Example 79
Augmented fourth chord and short excerpt using interval exploration of augmented fourths.

Works can be (and actually already have been, in preceding examples, but not in concentrated form) composed using more than one interval as the basis for exploration. Such is obviously the case in so-called tertian harmony, which indeed requires fifths to share almost equally in the environment of thirds. Since multiple stackings of one-interval chords produce another or often many other intervals, it is natural to use this as a starting point for two intervallic vocabularies. Example 80 shows a fifth chord consisting of three notes, providing the composer with another interval (the ninth or, condensed, the second). The inversions shown mark the second here as a prevalent interval; indeed, a natural one to use.

Example 80
Three-note fifth chord and new interval potentials.

Extensions of multiple interval explorations to beyond two can become very complicated, and often such works lose their conceptual point. Interval exploration can exist in other processes. Example 81 is a twelve-tone excerpt with the seventh (and octave displacements) as the basis for its primary vertical and horizontal interval materials:

Example 81
Twelve-tone excerpt with seventh interval exploration.

Klangfarbenmelodien can also serve as a vehicle for potential interval exploration:

Example 82
Klangfarbenmelodien *with interval exploration.*

Note here the added consistency that the predominance of the seventh offers the otherwise drastically disconnected line. In both twelve-tone and *klangfarbenmelodien* processes, applications of interval exploration can provide a further source of direction and continuity.

Polytonality offers a most interesting palette for utilizing interval exploration, as the tonal aspects of polytonality often give a mistaken impression that harmonic sources are triadic (or must be so). The tonal centers can be helped by choosing separate intervals for each center while the opposite effect can be obtained by choosing the same interval for both.

As repetitious as it may have become, it is again important to articulate the concept that processes—in this case interval exploration—need not exist throughout an entire composition. Though the assignments which follow may call for such processes, interval exploration can be used as a solid technique for variation within a work whose texture may be quite different.

ASSIGNMENTS

1. Compose a work for piano which uses a five-note texture of intervals of a fourth and all the inversions possible. Develop chromatic variation through a single traditional modulation to a key two sharps or flats or more removed from the original.

2. Compose a short piece for three available instruments based on the interval of the fifth. Employ all inversions of an implied six-note stack of fifths and obtain chromatic variation through the use of traditional altered chords of your choosing.

3. In a brief piece for an available instrument and piano, explore the interval of the second (major and minor) and subsequent octave displacements (ninths, etc.). Establish the second harmony so strongly that a minor triad (which should appear in the composition) becomes very obviously nonharmonic.

4. In a work for two pianos, develop fifth-chord harmonies over which a lyrical melodic line explores the interval yet does not become overly angular. Achieve chromaticism by planing.

Example 83

5. Analyze example 83 for both the interval explored and the harmonic-melodic strengths. Compose a short piece attempting to achieve the same strengths but using a different interval as source material.

6. Compose a work for piano in which quartal harmony and secundal harmony help distinguish consonant polytonality in the same relative range.

7. Using an interval of your choice, stack it to determine what other interval might suggest "natural" simultaneous exploration. Compose a short work exploring both as equally as possible. Attain chromaticism by altering the major or minor quality of one or both of the intervals. The piece may be for an ensemble of instruments available.

8. Compose a category 2 twelve-tone work in which the interval of the fourth is predominant. Utilize a projected five-note stacking and all the inversions possible. Compose the work for three or more voices on syllables.

9. Using non–twelve-tone *klangfarbenmelodien,* explore the interval of the second with emphasis on the *major* second. Provide chromaticism by "collecting" stacked major seconds in the occasional vertical structures. The work should be for piano and at least two other available instruments.

10. Write an extended work for a solo instrument not utilizing any harmonic textures. Use fourths and fifths as the intervals explored but do not make the line *klangfarbenmelodien* (i.e., avoid constant leaps). Achieve chromaticism by implied traditional altered chords and modulations. Analyze the results in terms of Chapter 3 techniques.

WORKS FOR ANALYSIS

Consult the most recent Schwann Catalog for current in-print recordings of these works. Publishers are usually obtained through libraries, music stores, or distributors of music. This list is not meant to be comprehensive, only suggestive of further study.

Bartók, Béla: *String Quartet No. 3* (extensive use of seconds throughout; a large number of his other works, inclusive of a number of the *Mikrokosmos,* employ interval exploration).

Berg, Alban: *Wozzeck* (fourth chords used in spots and in a very highly chromatic climate).

Copland, Aaron: *Symphony No. 3* (strong use of open fifths and exploration of the interval in stacking).

Hindemith, Paul: *Nobilissima Visione* (relatively constant use of fourths as intervals for exploration).

Husa, Karel: *Apotheosis of this Earth* (much use of seconds and sevenths throughout to obtain both vertical and horizontal materials).

Prokofiev, Serge: *Piano Sonata No. 7* (constant use of interval exploration but with a variety of different intervals both simultaneously and at different times).

Ruggles, Carl: *Men and Mountains* (exploration of seconds throughout).

Sessions, Roger: *Symphony No. 2* (much exploration of fourths with a great deal of chromatic variation and often modulating to triadic harmonies).

Walton, William: *Concerto for Viola and Orchestra* (frequent use of fourths for variety from an otherwise tertian harmonic vocabulary).

Webern, Anton: *Piano Variations Op. 27* (primarily atonal but with interval exploration of fourths in various places throughout).

7

Cluster Techniques

Interval exploration of multiple seconds creates dense clouds of sound called *soundmass* or *clusters.* These groups of seconds have a separate distinction from compilations of other intervals in that they create knots of sound with as few as three intervals. Successive addition of notes (seconds) establishes a block of sound materials acting and reacting in very different ways from chords discussed up to this point.

Clusters form a most important new contribution to vertical structure in that individual pitches cease to be valid in themselves and are only important as they contribute to the whole mass. The larger the clusters the less importance each note has.

In example 84 the vertical cluster covers more than an octave. Note the notation of a large natural and sharp sign, signifying that both natural and sharp versions of the notes shown exist, thus creating a completely chromatic mass inclusive of *all* notes from D to E (for more on this notation see Chapter 22).

Example 84
Three chromatic clusters, two of which have missing notes.

Two other completely written-out versions of this same cluster are to its right. One note (different in each case) has been removed from each to help make the point that individuality of pitch ceases to be of real significance in cluster writing. It is, first of all, difficult even to locate the missing notes visually. Though there is a slight difference aurally, it is not a significant one and would probably not be heard if the listener were not alerted to it. It is as if clusters represented the exact opposite of *klangfarbenmelodien* in that they tend to lessen the importance of individual pitch and strengthen only their contributive aspects.

Four exceptions to this concept should be pointed out. First, the outer notes are by far the most important and, in most cases, deletion of these notes can easily be detected. Therefore, careful consideration of the notes on either extreme should be maintained at all times. Secondly, if a cluster should be diatonic (or consistently of a scale other than chromatic) and only one note be *outside* that framework, its disappearance would surely be noticed (conversely, introduction by accident of a note outside the cluster reference would be conspicuous). Third, timbre plays an important role. Though one often assumes that clusters will be produced on a piano or other instruments with timbre continuity (e.g., string orchestra), they can be produced by a selection of instruments of uniquely different timbres. When the latter occurs, a subtracted note may become quite noticeable, depending on the sharpness and clarity of the timbre of the missing note (or, again, the accidental adding of a note). Finally, in large clusters which involve some skips, some of the pitches again contribute to harmonic significance, and displacement can be harmful to the texture and pitch vocabulary present. With these exceptions in mind, however, the cluster's ability to diminish note importance is a most significant concept and one which can be a very valid and useful one. Especially notable is its relevance to indeterminacy (i.e., if in *chromatic* clusters only the outer notes are significant as pitches, the internal structure becomes somewhat indeterminate in makeup, and a note added or subtracted will be of minor consequence).

Vertical analysis of clusters becomes very difficult here. Obviously the roots in example 84 can be found without great time consumption. However, their significance must be severely questioned. The acoustical properties of soundmass are such that all intervals become imploded, leaving little but a visual analysis without much meaning. In most cases the lowest note (root or not, though it is usually the lower note of the lowest fifth and therefore the root anyway) is taken as the note used for progression outline, if indeed progression of successive different clusters takes place at all.

The *use* of clusters will somewhat explain this latter point. Example 85 shows a possible application of soundmass. The excerpt demonstrates the *percussive* potential of thick chromatic clusters (produced here by left forearm slaps on the lower portion of the piano keyboard). The clusters here are very short and, while not harmonizing the violin line, do indeed contrast and bring out further its lyric qualities. The brevity of each cluster and the lack of great movement one to another does not lead the ear to progression in the usual sense (if progression is heard at all). Indeed, clusters used in this manner need very large interval separation to occur before motion is even perceived (progression notwithstanding). Note here the notational device (again refer to Chapter 22) of merely indicating the outer notes with the inner notes implied only by the vertical lines. The large natural and sharp again indicate a complete chromatic cluster (in this case white and black keys on the keyboard). The notational shorthand is quickly understood, and performance (even in sightreading) is quite simple. As well, note again that if the performer were to miss one note in the large block of sound, the listener would miss virtually nothing.

Example 85
Application of soundmass.

Example 86 shows yet another cluster potential quite different from that shown in example 85. Here the keyboard palm clusters splash softly about, with the damper pedal down so that each mass

contributes to a growing and ringing cloud of sound. The short
spurts actually add continuity to the same violin line as example 85
(same notes, that is, except that *klangfarbenmelodien* has been
applied). The clusters here, though not producing any strong root
progression or contributing to climax development except in rhythmic stretto, do pervade the music with a continuous climate of
consistent vertical language. Note here yet another notation for
clusters (cf. Chapter 22).

Example 86
Another notation and use of cluster chords.

In example 87 the clusters have been written out due to the small
"holes" and lack of exact chromatic or diatonic build. Observe the
implications of many internal notes regaining a portion of their
importance and independence. Moreover, the cluster appears more
to be cluster*s* than one single vertical unit. Again, the piano
performs a short progression of these polyclusters with violin on top
and harmonics blending the mood of the entire passage. The
soundmass here is verging on possible root(s) definition and consideration for progression.

Simultaneous clusters separated by some distance (polyclusters)
can be extremely effective and useful compositional material. They
can be similar in nature and thus homophonic (e.g., keyboard
white-key palm clusters) or they can be quite opposite, distinguish-
ing each as a separate entity and thus viable for contrapuntal idioms
(e.g., one cluster being major seconds and the other minor seconds).

Example 87
Notated clusters where missing notes become important.

Spacing obviously becomes an important consideration in cluster formation. Example 88 shows the same type of cluster as performed in example 85, yet the sounds are now displaced over a wide range of the (in this case) two keyboards. Some notes are knotted in second clusters but the overall structure follows a somewhat strict overtone influence, the bottom being spread and the top predominantly clustered.

Example 88
Cluster with overtone influence in composition.

The appellation *cluster* here is a loose one, as the sonic environment has very important internal notes and a very predominant and analyzable root (useful for progression as well). Yet all twelve notes are present, with many occurring more than once. To help in observing the increased importance of individual notes and root notes, one need merely drop out a few (or even one) to see and hear a marked difference. Even if the notes were just octave displaced to retain the twelve-note panchromatic sound, the change would be noticeable. The example (88) would be even more potent (in terms of individual note importance) if performed by a string orchestra instead of the two pianos, as the decay characteristic of the piano is relatively fast, while the sustaining instruments could bring out the inner lines. As was mentioned before, the performance on sustaining instruments of distinctly differing timbres would make the note importance even more observable and restore that importance to its former status while still under the umbrella of the generalized term *cluster.* Too often clusters are thought of as being peculiar to the piano (probably because of the ease of performance and notation), when indeed ensemble and orchestral potentials are very high.

With spacing noted for its power to diversify and create a vast world of cluster potentials, nuances, and subtleties, several other concepts should be noted in terms of the purer-form (or closely-spaced) cluster. Types of clusters used are quite varied indeed and, while individual notes may lose strength, intervals between them do not, especially when content is consistent. Example 89 is a set of three clusters with the notation of example 84:

Example 89
Diatonic, chromatic and whole tone clusters.

The first is a diatonic cluster (in this case, for ease of performance, the white keys of a piano keyboard) and is a very *consonant* one in comparison with the second, a totally chromatic mass. The third is made up exclusively of major seconds (as the second was constructed of minor seconds) and, like the first, is very consonant. It has, however, only six notes (being in reality of whole-tone origin); while obtaining a chromaticism the first cluster does not have, it is far more open in sound and, with the augmented fourths constantly persisting, presents an unusual sound indeed. It is quite consonant, but literally lacks any strong root whatsoever, making a consistent progression of such clusters quite distinctly directionless and without marked definition.

There is, of course, a numerous supply of clusters based on various Western and Eastern scales as well as the composer-constructed varieties possible for constant exploration.

Clusters are extremely useful for a variety of circumstances in works where clusters do not predominate. Climaxes, for example, can be effectively pronounced with cluster accompaniments. Example 90 presupposes that the clarinet has performed for some time prior to the excerpt illustrated, with a nonclustered piano texture background. The brief hiatus in the piano adds drama to the sudden burst of thunderous double forearm clusters in the piano with damper pedal down for slow ringoff.

Example 90
Dramatic use of single cluster.

Cluster ostinati can be quite effective even without melodic overlay. Note in example 91 that the accents and rhythms are the important elements, with pitch a very passive contributor. Even in non-ostinato passages, clusters can be very effective if musical life and direction can be maintained through rhythm and/or accents.

Example 91
Percussive clusters with accents as predominating compositional force.

Again, this example need not exist in a framework of constant cluster applications.

Example 92 shows an intervallic overview of two potential movements. The first shows a slow accumulation of vertical intervals until the cluster (climax) is reached, and then a slow retrograde back to the opening sonority, providing an archlike form.

Example 92

Two movement overviews showing two variable cluster uses.

The second overview shown is a movement in which the cluster plays only a very small part, adding drama to a dancelike section and acting more as a percussion instrument than a "constructed" interval predominance (interval of a second).

As has been seen, the cluster or soundmass takes on many guises, analyses, and uses. Above all, however—and most spectacular at this point in compositional study—one must return to the one constantly reiterated substantial impact: many individual notes are no longer important in themselves and can often be missed or even left out with no significant impairment to the chord structure, passage, or work. Once this concept is established, understood, and utilized successfully in composition, a great portion of the chapters which follow will not seem completely removed from tradition. Indeed, as remote as many of the remaining techniques may seem from one's musical heritage, no *revolution* has taken place; it is all a step by step *evolution* as inevitable as that in any viable and living phenomenon.

ASSIGNMENTS

1. Compose a work for piano with clusters as the sole compositional material, obtaining direction and climax from dynamics, rhythm, pitch levels, accents, etc. Note that though two clusters may be used simultaneously, all must be in seconds (major and minor).

2. Write a passage of clusters for piano (different types for each hand) and create a type of canon with imitation and spacing an integral part of the passage.

3. Create a scale unlike those familiar to you and, with it as a basis, compose a passage for an available instrument and piano with clusters created from this synthesized scale pattern. Make both instruments homogeneous with one another.

4. Begin a work for four or more available instruments (not piano) which originates in an obviously nonclustered texture and slowly modulates to a predominantly clustered environment.

5. Using closely knit consonant clusters, slowly introduce dissonant notes to create tension until a full panchromatic cluster is created. Create this in piano as accompaniment to a vocal line with text of your own choosing. The vocal line, however, should be highly lyrical and connected.

6. Choose one of the overviews in example 92 and realize it in a work for piano and three other available instruments.

7. Analyze example 93 in terms of type of cluster (consonant/dissonant), type of material (scale) used for construction, and root importance (if any). Create as opposite a cluster as possible and use just once in a short work for instrument and piano. The remainder of the material should be polytonal.

Example 93

8. Compose a work based on a very widely spaced cluster in which very few seconds as such occur, but in which all twelve notes appear. Write for as many instruments (inclusive of piano) and voices as possible, with emphasis on creating fluctuating clouds of sound with internal pitches important both due to spacing and timbre difference. Constantly overlap pitch beginnings and endings and octave displacements.

9. Accompany the line in example 94 with clusters twice. The first time try to contrast the line and give it more individuality. The second time try to obtain a consistency with the line, adding to its qualities.

Example 94

10. Compose a work for piano beginning with three-note closely spaced clusters, and slowly expand to full octave clusters. As well, modulate the type of cluster (consonant to dissonant) used. Make the outer notes as melodic as possible, with contrary motion a prime consideration.

WORKS FOR ANALYSIS

Consult the most recent Schwann Catalog for current in-print recordings of these works. Publishers are usually obtained through libraries, music stores, or distributors of music. This list is not meant to be comprehensive, only suggestive of further study.

Becker, John: *Symphony No. 3* (very percussive use of cluster chords in complete orchestra framework and texture).

Constant, Marius: *24 Preludes for Orchestra* (occasional use of clusters in the orchestra, well-balanced by other sonorities).

Cowell, Henry: *The Hero Sun* (a predominance of keyboard clusters throughout this work).

Crumb, George: *Black Angels* (a great number of cluster knots for string quartet, with almost every texture conceivable used as well).

Ives, Charles: *Majority* (very large consonant and dissonant clusters prevail in this work notable as well for its date of composition—1921—and its idiom: voice and piano).

Kagel, Mauricio: *Improvisation Ajoutée* (full of huge organ clusters, often with stacking approach and release).

Ligeti, György: *Requiem* (widely spaced clusters for choir and orchestra knotted at points; good study for spacing of clusters and analysis).

Penderecki, Krzysztof: *Threnody for the Victims of Hiroshima* (large cluster bands throughout the strings inclusive of glissando; notation unique for its time; see Chapter 22).

Riegger, Wallingford: *Music for Brass Choir* (closely knit cluster bands with very subtle dynamic approach; very dissonant).

Ruggles, Carl: *Angels* (clusters obtained through constant intertwining of manifold contrapuntal lines in close proximity; always in motion).

Stravinsky, Igor: *Le Sacre du Printemps* (good use of accents and rhythmic ideas with soundmass; notable especially is the "Danses des Adolescentes").

Varèse, Edgard: *Equatorial* (effective use of large-spaced clusters throughout with ever-changing consonance/dissonance relationships).

Xenakis, Iannis: *Akrata* (clustered masses of effects and glissandi for very interesting orchestral soundmass).

8

Microtones

While a thorough study of acoustics is impossible in a text of this size, it should be valuable to note briefly the major tuning systems in order to better understand the implications of and needs for microtones.

The overtone series (see Chapter 1) supplies a number of specific intervals which, when played a few cycles (vibrations per second) off target, produce *beats:* these are the octave, perfect fifth, and perfect fourth. These harmonics can also be observed noticeably in string and wind instruments. A violin string, when lightly touched to produce a harmonic (string allowed to vibrate on both sides rather than as a stopped string), testifies to the validity of these intervals. Touched at the halfway mark, the string produces a tone an octave higher than the original. Touched at the two-thirds length position, the string produces a perfect fifth and, at the three-fourths position, a perfect fourth. From there on, as in the overtone series, the harmonics either become weaker or come in proportions proving too complicated or not accurate enough to give solid twelve-tone "equality" (the various major and minor seconds differ greatly in proportion to each other). The vibration of air in a column of pipe has very much the same characteristics.

It *seems* logical that if application of these so-called perfect intervals (octave, fifth, and fourth) were applied in a cyclic manner, a complete twelve-tone system might produce a more equal result. Since the octave would only produce a multiplicity of the same note and the fourth is an inversion and slightly more complicated interval than the fifth, the fifth would seem the best yardstick for tuning. Using the cycle of fifths, however, and keeping each fifth in perfect intonation results in a strong discrepancy (known as the Pythagorean Comma) between the first and last notes: C–G–D–A–E–B–G-flat–D-flat–A-flat–E-flat–B-flat–F–C (the final C is not an exact octave from the original, but indeed higher in pitch).

One solution to this Pythagorean tuning is accomplished by lowering each fifth slightly, not so much as to cause beats, but just enough to account for the sharp C at the end of the cycle of fifths. This solution is called *mean-tone* and leads to a third which is very "pure" in terms of overtone or string vibration techniques. This system works well when performing in major keys nearest in signature to the original tuning tone (e.g., if C were the origin of the slightly flat cycle of fifths, then C major, F major, and G major would be suitable for performance). However, once removed from the central system, chromaticism becomes a tuning nightmare and triads vary in intonation quite drastically. *Just intonation* is yet another attempt at solving some of the problems incurred. It attempts *both* a perfect fifth and a pure third. While working substantially well if only the tonic, subdominant, and dominant triads are performed (these are in tune in correlation with the harmonic series), the remainder of the pitches, triads, keys, and such are divergent from any semblance of purity. A number of other systems exist, along with a concomitant list of reform systems for each, as well as a vast number of wholly different systems not based in the slightest on overtone series ideals or twelve-note concepts. However, most of these have been put aside as instrument builders and performers have helped establish an intonation vocabulary which today is somewhat standard.

Equal temperament seems to most composers and performers today the best solution to the problem. If the "natural" materials of harmonics and overtone derivatives fall short of giving equality to the intervals of twelve notes within the octave, a division of the octave into twelve equal parts will. This forced approach first of all achieves a perfect octave. Once found, it parcels the remaining eleven intervals into equal shares. In a quite accurate sense, equal temperament means that all intervals except the octave are out of tune. Once each interval is established, a term known as *cents* is applied: 1200 cents to the octave, with 100 therefore for each half step. Cents are useful in comparing intonation systems to discover variances. For example, the Pythagorean major third is eight cents higher than the equal-tempered major third, and twelve cents higher than the more "in tune" just intonation system. Cents are also useful in that they present a way to discuss and evolve other approaches to intonation and will be used later in this chapter. Most current ideas of intonation revolve around this standard piano tuning. However, two major misconceptions have undermined *all* the systems to this point: (1) that somehow there is such a thing as "in tune," and that (2) the number twelve seems to have unwarranted significance. The following addresses itself to each of these matters in turn.

Most instrumentalists capable of varying the intonation of their instruments (violins, trombone, etc.) do so constantly and for a number of reasons. In tonality many tones tend to *lead* or gravitate toward the pitch anticipated by the music's vocabulary. Such "leading tones," whether the seventh degree of the scale (called such) or thirds of secondary dominants, the augmented sixth of augmented sixth chords (which contain tones *leading* outward to the octave), etc., tend in performance to be "sharper" or "flatter" than normal ("normal" in this case meaning the same pitch if it were the fifth of the tonic triad in the key). Triads in orchestras, for instance, (where intonation is flexible) tend to be *just* in temperament ("pure" triads in the natural sense), flowing through a vast number of other intonations (some calculated, others merely intuited) to achieve some "equality" in modulations, altered chords, etc.

Aside from the role tonality has played in producing microtones, acoustics plays a major role, with even the best of halls providing vast differences in the most carefully planned systems. Even an electronically tuned piano is not truly equal in temperament by the time a hall's resonance and reverberation have played havoc with the intonation. Moreover, the inner ear (cochlea, a nonlinear mixer of sounds; see Chapter 15 on electronic music) and the psychological and psychoacoustical aspects of the listener are ever present.

To summarize, then, instruments of varying intonation capabilities combine "systems" and intuition so that they perform microtones constantly (microtones here meaning pitches less than 100 cents from one another), and the best of fixed-pitch instruments are deviate by nature and incapable of even communicating that *nature* accurately. "In tune," then, is merely a very nice-sounding and sophisticated word with only a personal taste definition. "In tune" is what you wish it to be. Even the perfect octaves, fifths, and fourths discussed at the beginning of the chapter are suspect, as many composers now feel that the beats created by their so-called out of tuneness to be excellent source material for works.

The number twelve seems to be a most definite culprit in this mass of calculations, systems, and deviations of such. Though historians have drawn on vast accumulations of data to show man's search for successful tunings with this number, nothing natural (that is, existing in nature) exists which supports such a number as a valid or static value from which to derive intonations. Thus enter microtones as a recognizable factor for compositional processes. If indeed "in tune" is personal taste and social custom, then nearly any tuning may be acceptable. However, strong conditions should be applied at this point. While electronic and computer musics do have the capabilities of parceling out divisions of almost any type, the composer of instrumental musics for live performance must be content to live with a few human frailties. First, if more than twelve notes are to be used within the octave, the various possible numbers—while intriguing—require a great deal of thought and reasoning for moving to such numbers. Many new numbers (notably from 14 to 144) have been proposed, but none suggest any more validity than twelve. Rules of thumb should imply that, first, performability (especially notation and performance on instruments many of which were designed around twelve-note concepts) be considered. Secondly, the ear should be taken into account for its ability to separate microtones: if they should become too small, many ears (even those yet unschooled in "equal" and other tunings) will derive a more simple number than the one upon which the work was based (e.g., 144 divisions of the octave can very easily dissolve into 72, or more probably 36: one third of an equal-tempered half step in our former division of twelve). No concrete answers can be given in either of these cases as human responses to pitch vary so widely. The following suggestions, however, are set forth to possibly help the composer wade through this most complex swamp of mixed values.

Since "systems" in themselves are what led tuning to this point, deriving or attempting to derive further "universal" systems which seek deliverance from the problem will only complicate matters further. *Scales* of varying numbers of pitches, however, can be extremely useful, being (as with any other scale) viable for a single idea, movement, or work without portending systematic change of audience or music values. Examples 95 through 98 show four possibilities which might suggest to the student a multitude of other ideas for exploration. Example 95 is a quarter-tone (or 24-division) example with notation (see Chapter 22) traditional in nature for such. Fairly easily performed on the violin, it will, to the untrained ear (i.e., the Western world's traditionally trained ear), seem "out of tune." Continued performances of this and other quarter-tone works can be most enlightening, as aesthetics can change from hostile earbending experiences to quite lovely colorings of pitch in often very short periods of time. The quarter tones here imply halving equal-tempered half steps.

Example 95
Quarter-tone excerpt with notation.

Example 96 is for two pianos tuned an eighth tone apart (48 divisions per octave, though only 24 possibilities per octave appear here in the two pianos). Note the lack of need for new notations: only the performance directions need explain the tuning. Visual contact with the score alone does not even slightly suggest new intonations.

Example 96
Excerpt for two pianos tuned 1/8th tone apart.

In example 97 the positions of a trombone part have been altered on the same note at different points. Such alterations (color settings or fingerings in the case of other wind instruments) produce a variety of intonations, most of which can only be measured by cents if measuring is needed at all.

Example 97
Excerpt for trombone showing positions for different available intonations (microtones).

Example 98 shows a very complex (as complex, in fact, as most need get) passage for cello. Above and below a number of the notes are numbers representing cents (50 cents being one quarter of a whole step in equal temperament, or a quarter tone). In this notation, if the number is placed above the note, it should be raised by that amount; if below the note, it should be lowered. The passage is based on equal temperament as the base from which the microtones are formed. The last note of the example has a 48 placed above it to show an unrealistic approach that could be applied. Performance and aural comprehension here would merely suggest 50 cents, and such subtleties, though interesting to imagine, rarely are possible or successful.

Example 98
Short passage for cello in which numerical figures above or below represent 'cents' for microtonal division of the half step (100 cents).

Another approach to performing microtonal music is to create a set division of the octave on an equal-tempered basis (other than twelve) and provide the performer with scales, fingerings, and such for practicing the work. Example 99 shows first a seventeen-note equal-tempered scale with clef such that both the outer notes are Cs an octave apart. Through scale practice and observation of the new visual separation of the octave, the performer can fairly accurately perform the excerpt at the right in the example with the result being a consistent new microtonal composition. This can be as successful and in some cases more successful than the intricate cent notation described before.

Example 99
New clef and seventeen note (division of the octave) equal tempered scale and short excerpt using such.

Possibly the most potential resides in existing instruments of set pitch tunings (e.g., piano, harp) and new instruments tuned or retuned, as the case may be, to microtonal ideals with which the composer wishes to work. This eliminates the problem of notation (which can indeed be completely traditional) and leaves the performer with little new to cope with except the resulting sound. The microtonal results have thus been guaranteed by the tuning of the instrument. Again, the only problem confronting the composer is the listener's perception of the intervallic relations present. It is with this possibility that most composers tend to feel the most potential lies, since all too often microtonal works composed for instruments of variable intonation lay unplayed for many years, if indeed performed at all.

No matter what the decision the composer derives from these possibilities, he should no longer be able to compose just a "note" without at least *thinking* through its tuning potentials. Even if the result be traditionally notated common-practice tunings, the composer might have at least composed the work with a new insight into what the performer may do with certain notes in terms of intonation systems and intuition.

The significant reality present here is that microtones present a tremendous new vocabulary which can be utilized for defined new musical languages. Once it is realized that "in-tuneness" is a learned social/historical/personal concept, only performance credibility and aural perception remain as obstacles for the composer interested in microtones.

ASSIGNMENTS

1. Retune two instruments of variable intonations to become a quarter tone apart. Using standard notation for each, compose a short work starting with wide intervals in which the quarter tones are not as noticeable, and work slowly to a climax based on smaller intervals.

2. Retune a string instrument to have its open strings (scordatura) lowered a microtonal distance of your choice, keeping the open fifths perfect. Compose a work for that instrument and normally tuned piano, again using traditional notation for both instruments. Emphasize the contrasting microtonal differences throughout.

3. Compose a line for an available instrument in traditional notation but use the notation in example 95 for quarter tones. The work should be of some length and the quarter tones used only where they seem appropriate to the lyric "leadings" of the line.

4. Work out a set of variable fingerings for a single note on a wind instrument. Then compose a work which builds to that note. Employ the "color" fingers at this climactic point for variation.

5. Construct a "scale" of fifteen notes per octave along with a set of performing and practice suggestions to the performer (string instrument preferably) and follow with a brief example utilizing the new microtonal scale.

6. Compose a work for three available instruments using the cents notation of example 98. Use as realistic and performable choices as possible and do not indicate microtonal differences on each note.

7. Accompany the violin line in example 100 as appropriately as possible. Use any previous technique discussed in the book, but the result must be analyzed in both melodic and harmonic terms.

Example 100

8. With three voices, begin a work with all three on a unison pitch. Slowly bend one and then another of the voices from the unison (no more than an equal-tempered half step) and compose with the resultant "beats" as a basic ingredient of the work.

9. Write three phrases for a traditional instrument (one available) but not a piano. Each phrase should be in traditional notation but above each should be marked "just intonation," "equal-tempered intonation," or "Pythagorean intonation." Try to utilize predicted vocabularies of each for successful melodic results.

10. Create a small instrument of more than twelve striking surfaces and make a microtonal scale by shaping and reshaping each surface. Compose a brief work with traditional notation with very simple techniques. Utilize the microtones as they seem best suited. Choice of "scale" is left to you.

WORKS FOR ANALYSIS

Consult the most recent Schwann Catalog for current in-print recordings of these works. Publishers are usually found through libraries, music stores, or distributors of music. This list is not meant to be comprehensive, only suggestive of further study.

Bartók, Béla: *Concerto for Violin and Orchestra* (utilizes a number of quarter tones, especially in the solo violin part).

Carrillo, Julian: *The Thirteenth Sound* (breaks the octave into 95 tones; for chamber ensemble of flexible-intonation instruments).

Eaton, John: *Concert Piece for Synket and Symphony Orchestra* (as do most of Eaton's works, this explores the realm of many different microtonal possibilities both in electronics and live instrumental music).

Gaburo, Kenneth: *Lingua II* (as do many of Gaburo's works, this explores microtones as well as new timbres).

Hába, Alois: (nearly all of this composer's music works with quarter tones, notably *Trio* for violin, cello, and quarter-tone piano, and *Three Instructive Duos* for two violins).

Ives, Charles: *Three Quartertone Piano Pieces* (excellent example of piano tuning for quarter tone production).

Johnston, Ben: *String Quartet No. 3* (most of Johnston's string quartets are exploratory of a variable set of tones per octave; all seem very performable).

Lybbert, Donald: *Lines for the Fallen* (good use of microtones).

Macero, Teo: *One-Three Quarters* (interesting work exploring the potentials of quarter tones in a chamber ensemble situation).

Partch, Harry: *Delusion of the Fury* (this, as do most of Partch's works, uses new instruments to create new timbres within a 43-note-to-the-octave system).

Penderecki, Krzysztof: *The Passion According to St. Luke* (includes a few quarter tones in the Polish school of notation as does the *Threnody*).

Takemitsu, Toru: *Voice* (effective use of quarter tones for solo flute).

9

Percussion and the Prepared Piano

While a certain comfortable standardization existed in orchestras and ensembles for at least the latter half of the common-practice period, one group of instruments, surprisingly nurtured by this same conservative era, sought constant expansion and creative development. The percussion ensemble, now as much a separate body from the orchestra as it once was an integral part, is one of the most potent resources the composer has for non-electronic timbre combinations. Due to the somewhat static nature of the wind and string sections of orchestras and the winds of bands, virtually every new or non-Western-world instrument receives percussion identification. Much to the delight of most percussionists and the horror of those who wish to codify the ensemble, every type of instrument has found its way to increase this exploding rate of growth. Using the scientific classification system to group the various instruments (however, not string, wind, brass, etc., which is too limiting), one can easily see, with just this brief introduction, the vast variety present in even the simplest arrangements.

Membranophones (stretched-skin sound-producing instruments) include the entire drum family and are the most common of the percussion section (timpani, snare drum, timbales, tambourine, bass drum, congas, tablas, etc.).

Aerophones (column-of-air sound-producing instruments) include the smallest number of members at the present time, but the list is growing (slide whistle, siren, wind machine, bird calls, etc.).

Idiophones (vibrations-of-entire-body sound-producing instruments) are a large part of the percussion ensemble (cymbals, triangle, gong, tam-tams, vibraphones, etc.).

Chordophones (vibration-of-strings sound-producing instruments) include a wide variety of surprisingly traditional instruments placed here for lack of other identification (piano, harpsichord, cimbalon, Gascony drum, etc.).

Even the newer classification of *electrophones* (acoustical vibrations resulting from electrical means or amplification) has found its way into percussion ensembles (Theremin, Trautonium, chromatic kettledrums, synthesizers, etc.).

These lists, of course, just hint at what instruments exist in the ensemble and the potential inclusion of non-Western-world instruments (already often standardized in their own systems) and the increasing growth of free acceptance of any sound-producing object. Notably, wooden drums (Congo) and Buddhist slit drums fit into the former category, while automobile brake drums (in various scales and intonations) fit the latter. With this wide-open concept, not only do different instruments increase the size of percussion ensembles, but immense varieties of the same instrument make virtually any subtlety and nuance of sound possible. For example, one can never really complete a list of just the varieties of wind chimes, not only in terms of glass, metal, wood, etc., but their tunings and performing techniques as well.

It is vitally important to notate and/or be aware of the type of beater used in a given composition as well as its placement upon the instrument in the act of striking. Example 101 shows a gong in three different situations.

Example 101
Gong with three different performance situations.

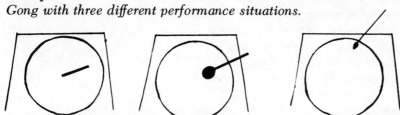

The first is a triangle beater striking the center of the instrument, the second a bass drum mallet at the halfway point, and the third a snare stick at the rim. Each of these presents a strikingly different sound, due not only to the mallet used but placement as well. Motion can produce further differences even with the same mallet in the same place (much as rhythm animates a vertical chord though the chord remains the same). Example 102 illustrates exactly the same gong/triangle beater arrangement as in the first illustration of example 101. Now, however, the beater is rattled across the crown (dome) of the gong, producing a variety of yet different sounds, depending on where struck. A quick staccato scream into the gong will produce an array of overtone resonance vibrations (ring-off) which can be very effective (and with no mallet present at all).

Example 102
Motion of a triangle beater on gong surface.

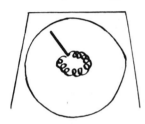

Dampening can be extremely useful on many instruments (e.g., folded cloth on one portion of a timpani head), as is glissando (pedal timpani, elbow pressure on drum head, etc.) and combinations of instruments, one aiding the other. Example 103 shows a popular use of striking a large suspended cymbal just above the head of a timpani. Using the pedal of the timpani for glissando, a neoelectronic sound is produced. Since the timpani is not struck in any way, one discovers the sound being produced by the cymbal resonation (sympathetic vibration) within the body of the timpani thus being controlled by the glissandi of the pedaling.

Example 103
Suspended cymbal—timpani glissando effect.

Applying other nonpercussion techniques and instruments to the section can produce further useful sounds: bowing cymbals, blowing horns into tam-tams, bowing vibraphones, etc. None of this is meant to be in any way comprehensive but only an introduction to the incredibly versatile world of percussion timbres, effects, and potentials. With all of these one must leave the composer to evolve his own unique contributions. Correct and absolutely complete notation is required, however, if a controlled and predictable sound is desired (see Chapter 22).

To this intense and limitless variety one can bring a few composition suggestions pertaining to some of their effective uses. Timbre is indeed only one aspect of the parameters of composition. Often percussion composition, even when couched in orchestral works, dizzies even the most trained listener with an overkill of new sounds. Like rhythm, harmony, dynamics, line, etc., timbre must possess some semblance of *organization, direction,* and *drama.* One procedure to *organization* is to vow that only one or two instruments be used, slowly giving in and allowing others to creep in as they are necessary to create variety. This minimal approach often avoids the complete disclosure of sounds within the first part of the composition, leaving the composer with little but a timbre anticlimax as the composition proceeds. Timbre motives work well for organization (often associated with rhythmic motives). Repetition, like all organizing procedures, is a significant feature of successful percussion writing. It is often associated with timbre modulation (slow transition of one sound to another with as little traceable evidence as necessary of the change itself; see Chapter 21). In large ensembles where percussion is only a small part of the whole composition, decisions must be made as to the role it plays—accompanying, highlighting, or equality with other sections—before organization can take place. While neither accompaniment, highlighting, nor equality is right or wrong, percussion organization is usually most effective when it is at one time or another all three. It is important to note, in all forms of composition, that it is not so much *what* you do as *when* you do it.

Direction is a vital aspect of percussion writing. Often one is led to believe that a triangle highlight here and there along with a "heartbeating" bass drum serve in themselves as effective use of the timbre potential of the percussion section or ensemble. Direction implies a growth, a development of available resources which can be achieved in a number of ways. Additive textures are effective though obvious ways to achieve direction (fugal in a sense). Example 104 shows a short passage for percussion where addition is the vital direction and motivation. Dynamics added would increase the validity and strength of direction as well.

Example 104
Short additive passage for percussion.

Since a great many percussion instruments are tuned or tunable, all the melodic growth and harmonic rationale described in Chapters 1 and 3 are quite useful. Example 105 shows first a melodic line analyzed as per Chapter 3 with a xylophone as the instrument in use. Second is a short progression in the vibraphone with concomitant analysis.

Example 105
a. Melodic line for xylophone with analysis; b. homophonic chorale for vibraphone with analysis.

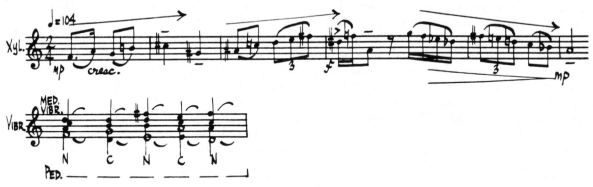

Dramatic uses of percussion can range from obvious rhythmic quotes from known military marches and fortissimo bass drum shots in an otherwise soft continuous texture to subtle uses of harmonics on vibraphone and long-breathed repetitions of soft chimes overlaying a soft mallet-stroked gong (pianissimo). These uses are "events" and portend sonic "intermedia" without image.

Offset isorhythms are also effective continuous dramatic techniques as shown in example 106:

Example 106
Use of isorhythmic technique in percussion composition.

Here each of the instruments has a different-type motive which
implies continuous variation. However, this example should be
considered as having a context of much preceding material which
climaxes here in the last measure when all motives correspond for
two beats. The motives are shown at the left. Indeed, this dramatic
effect of motion can be achieved by merely sketching five or six
short rhythms on a blackboard and having a set of existing,
self-constructed, or available instruments (e.g., chairs, feet, hands,
etc.) performing each motive in any order and for any length of
repetitions. It is necessary for some of the motives to be of different
lengths for the overlay and continuous variation to work. This
concept provides a simple format for composition process and with
a steady beat can be most dramatic (moreover, a texture and dynamic
increase can add to the drama).

Timbre and motivic interplay are indeed most important and
viable sources for drama in percussion writing. Example 107 shows
a very dramatic ten seconds indeed. The opening gong and soft use
of the vibraphone with sustain pedal down is suddenly interrupted
by a blast from the snare drum rimshot. This drama, though very
effective, again verges on overkill. A second hearing would be
predictable (unless some indeterminacy were present) and, moreover, it would be difficult to top the drama here as the work
progresses.

Example 107
Dramatic use of percussion.

Important, therefore, is the concept that the everpresent potential for drama of dynamics and timbre in percussion ensembles must be used most carefully, and should be governed (as always) by analysis of climax, direction, and organization.

The piano (as well as the harp, which will be discussed at various points as the book progresses) possesses an incredible variety of sounds within its frame, many of which make it an extension of percussion techniques. Indeed, many composers use it directly as a percussion instrument, striking its body, strings, or metal crossbars with various mallets, knuckles, hands, etc., and stroking the strings with pencils, fingernails, wire brushes, and other implements. The piano is often played by touching harmonic nodes on inner strings (with damper pedal down, creating harmonics like those produced on other stringed instruments), plucking strings (with fingernails, guitar picks; often marked by means of the note name on tape attached to soundboard nearest the string), damping (muting: touching with some force the area of the string struck by hammer just between the endpin closest to the performer and the dampers), and the like. As well, screeching fingernail sweeps on one of the lower strings and palm clusters (especially effective on the lower strings with sustaining pedal down) for near gonglike sounds, as well as singing or playing an instrument into the piano (with damper pedal down) for amazing like-timbred ringoffs add to this vast array of available sounds.

One of the most significant uses of twentieth-century piano techniques, however, is the "prepared piano." Virtually a percussion section in itself, this often-maligned (and unjustly so) technique is almost limitless in possibilities. By the use of wood (pencils stuck between strings, books laid flat across strings while performing on the keyboard, etc.), metal (coins angled under the middle of the three strings available for each note in the upper registers, bolts and screws placed vertically between strings, etc.), rubber (e.g., thick washers placed between strings, rubber bands intertwined with strings and tied for tension), and cloth (felt, especially, wound and/or stuffed in and around the strings), each string can potentially become a different timbre and often a new pitch as well.

The use of various materials is hampered only by their potential danger to the instrument. If strings are carefully separated to pinion an object, if the felt of the dampers is left untouched and items such as screws carefully inserted and removed, there is very little danger to the instrument. Often even intonation is left with only a "normal" maladjustment (no more "out of tune" than would occur with any ordinary performance situation). Finding nodes and exact placement of the preparation is very important. If a resonant body (e.g., a bolt) is placed at a node (harmonic point), usually a more resonant sound is heard with greater ringoff potential. Felt stuffed heavily in between all three strings at a non-node position would not produce resonance or ringoff (and often not produce discernible pitch). Performing with the damper pedal down or up often produces a doubling of the timbre possibilities. Striking an object (and objects mentioned above just begin a list of materials only the mind can limit) already placed as preparation in the piano with another object of like or different makeup provides yet another sound (e.g., striking an upright pencil between strings with another pencil with damper pedal down). The list, as with percussion, could go on and on. The compositional hazards are obviously as numerous. Organization, direction, and drama are important factors to compositional processes, and a fully prepared piano—as delightful as the sounds at first may be—is in itself no guarantee of anything but a host of different timbres. Along with the procedures discussed with percussion are a few new observations, as the prepared piano is *more* than an instrument; it is instrument*s*. As well, its dramatic potential is very strong, as the visual image does not give predicted outcomes for the listener/observer.

Example 108 shows a short passage in which only three notes are prepared (the ones shown to the left with type of preparation and location on the string shown). Note that the notation remains the same here, as with microtones, for both the unprepared and the prepared sections. If a long prior section of unprepared performance is added to the passage, the drama and timbre have a greatly added effect that complete preparation of the entire instrument would not. Again, however, whatever the medium, timbre, in and of itself, is not exclusive of other compositional techniques. Indeed, if anything, more care must be applied than ordinarily, as the temptation to be satisfied with first-heard timbres is often inordinately strong.

As well, if pitch is microtonal (as it often is in prepared pianos) or hidden behind timbre, rhythm must become a strong force to obtain the necessary development for other than a soundpiece going nowhere. The prepared piano is a most significant concept. It not only provides a single performer with an "orchestra" at his fingertips, but it also gives credence to the further potential of effects on other traditional instruments (without damage) and thus opens a door of nearly unlimited sound sources (see Chapter 14).

Example 108
Excerpt for partially prepared piano.

ASSIGNMENTS

1. Compose a short work for three available *membranophones* achieving a rhythmic counterpoint. Also, explore the uses of at least five different mallets on each instrument (to be changed during performance; allow time!).

2. In a fairly long work for solo timpani (and without the use of the pedal for pitch change), create interest through mallet change and placement as well as composer-created effects.

3. For a particular gong or tam-tam, create a work for solo voice using syllables sung directly into the gong. The ringoff should be an integral part of the work and rests should be many for ringoff to be heard.

4. Compose a short work for any available keyboard-type percussion instrument (vibraphone, chimes, etc.). Use both harmonic and melodic possibilities of the instrument and write with cognizance of the harmonic and melodic procedures of Chapters 1 and 3. Analyze the work.

5. Compose a set of motives of different length. Experiment with their potential success until a best version exists. Create a short work with the instruments being single-pitched but of any kind. Make sure that the piece has strong organization, direction, and drama.

6. Write a short work around example 107, making it effective from a traditional viewpoint in terms of climax, direction, development, etc.

7. Begin a work with only one instrument playing. Add new instruments only when it becomes absolutely necessary for variation. Grow to a complete climax of all available instruments (percussion).

8. Prepare as much of a piano as is possible. Carefully notate all the preparations. Compose a work in which the prepared notes do not become tiresome on second hearing. Analyze the results in terms of rhythm, motive, and direction.

9. Create a work for piano insides in which only the hands can create sounds (plucking, palm clusters, etc.). Notate as accurately as possible (additional information is available in Chapter 22). Use drama as the basic ideal and organize as well as possible. Repetition should be a strong base for the work.

10. Compose a work for prepared piano using materials not mentioned in this chapter. Notate the placement, etc., of these materials at the beginning of the work, which will involve rhythm as the basic parameter, as well as timbre. Use the process of minimalization as much as possible so that all notes are not exposed until the climax. Use complex rhythms.

11. In a work for prepared piano and all available percussion instruments, create mood and drama from silence as well as sound, melody as well as timbre, and harmony as well as combinations of timbre.

12. Write a work for persons performing on nontraditional instruments (walls, chairs, floors, etc.). Retain organization, direction, and drama while scoring the primarily rhythmic patterns necessary for composition.

WORKS FOR ANALYSIS

Consult the most recent Schwann Catalog for current in-print recordings of these works. Publishers are usually found through libraries, music stores, or distributors of music. This list is not meant to be comprehensive, only suggestive of further study.

Antheil, George: *Ballet Mécanique* (interesting use of bizarre instruments such as an airplane engine).

Cage, John: *Amores for Prepared Piano and Percussion* (interesting combination of the various topics of this chapter by the real inventor of the prepared piano).

————: *Concerto for Prepared Piano and Chamber Orchestra* (excellent combination of two contrasting-timbre instrumental bodies).

————: *Perilous Night, Suite for Prepared Piano* (again, very effective use of the instrument, this time in solo situation).

Chavez, Carlos: *Toccata for Percussion* (use of a wide variety of instruments in a pure percussion ensemble work with *direction*).

Colgrass, Michael: *Variations for Four Drums and Viola* (interesting use of percussion with live solo instrument with little timbre potential).

Cope, David: *Iceberg Meadow* (traditional use of the piano keyboard for the most part, except for a set of prepared notes used dramatically near the end).

Cowell, Henry: *The Banshee* (classic work of use of stroking and scratching the strings of the piano; no preparation or keyboard use at all; extraordinary in that it rarely sounds like piano).

Crumb, George: *Ancient Voices of Children* (effective use of percussion and amplified piano guts).

Erb, Donald: *Concerto for Solo Percussionist and Orchestra* (strong use of percussion quite sustaining its own against the orchestra).

Harrison, Lou: *Fugue for Percussion* (one of many works for percussion by this composer and an interesting formal application).

Johnston, Ben: *Knocking Piece* (work which employs nothing but the rhythms of knocking on various parts of the outside of the piano).

Kraft, William: *Triangles* (effective use of percussion by a professional percussionist).

McPhee, Colin: *Tabuh-Tabuhan* (extremely large percussion ensemble with orchestra; very interesting *gamelon* influence as well as correlation with many prepared-piano sounds).

Messiaen, Oliver: *Oiseaux Exotiques* (interesting use of bird calls and imitative bird motives).

Stockhausen, Karlheinz: *Zyklus* (long work for one percussionist moving from one group of instruments to another).

Varèse, Edgard: *Ionisation* (one of the first major works for full percussion ensemble with many diverse instruments: percussion orchestra).

10

Rhythm and Meter

In discussing aspects of rhythm and meter one is inevitably led to that division which separates their intents: the *bar line*. For centuries tactus marks served to identify breathing points, but music survived without bar lines and often with clearly defined implied meter. With the increase in the size of ensembles (e.g., growth of orchestras), the complexity of rhythmic ideas, and the emphasis on strong-beat/weak-beat forms (dance movements, etc.), the bar line became a necessity. Example 109, for instance, shows a short segment for piano *without* bar lines. Note the near impossibility of retaining any semblance of rhythmic order, even though only one performer is involved. Amplify this to include a large orchestra and the need for some organizing factor becomes more than apparent.

Example 109
Excerpt for piano without bar lines.

Concomitant with the development of the bar line, however, were beat patterns, metrical pulses (weak beats, strong beats, depending on placement in the meter), and difficulty crossing bar lines which have made many contemporary composers turn to new possibilities (since meter often imposed arbitrary limitations upon their creativity), some with, some without bar lines. Example 110 shows the passage of example 109 with bar lines. Note the much easier performability but as well a tendency toward strong downbeats and a feeling that the composer worked within the "bars" and was not free to expound the full breadth of his ideas.

Example 110
Example 109 with bar lines.

The examples are very different, though both show the same notes. Both have strong and weak points. Contemporary techniques have worked at bringing out the strong points and destroying the weak of each. Music need not necessarily be tied to barred structures, inviting implied accents and a semiconstant attempt to begin "on the beat" and/or end there (or, worse, tied to a one-and-two-and-three-and framework of rhythmic idea). This, like tonality, is historic, stylistic, and subjective, and a concept which most composers today feel is starving rhythmic exploration and freedom.

Meter changes and composite meters are two of the most obvious methods of aiding the situation. Example 111 shows an example of both. Note, however, that the tendency of emphasizing *down* beats, as well as inner beats, to keep order in the ensemble has not been alleviated; only the aspect of metric monotony has been temporarily relieved.

Isorhythmic ideas help to cross bar lines and weaken their hold on "barring" concepts, yet still allow them to function in holding a group together. Example 112 shows isorhythm (each line is a long rhythmic idea overlapping both the bar lines and the other rhythms). This type of composition leads one to contrapuntal procedures almost exclusively, however.

Example 111
Examples of meter changes and composite rhythms.

Example 112
Isorhythm to help break bar line structures.

Cross-rhythms (polyrhythms) are successful in many times effecting relief from internal implied accents. Example 113 shows three cross-rhythms. The first is an example of 6/8 meter in which the lower idea is, in reality, 3/4 and the upper a true 6/8 division. The metric accents are either destroyed or interestingly contrasted, depending on style considerations and context. The second example involves three meters simultaneously with the beat (quarter note equal to 102) equal for all three. Note the necessary displacement of barlines due to the varying lengths of the meters. The feeling of each meter is implied in this notation and, while expanding rhythmic vocabulary, it also makes thrice complex the contribution of the bar line to structured performance. The third example is in 4/4 time

Example 113
Three types of cross rhythms.

with the two ideas achieving independence by accents placed in different spots. In this example, the performers are more often than not so intent on getting the accents correct that the meter loses all gravitation (and thus the implied accents) toward sedentary beats, and the ideas are free to follow their own intent.

Hemiola (in general, the concept of two against three) helps destroy the potency of the bar line yet allows it to function as a strong element in keeping ensembles together. In example 114, the first excerpt is pure hemiola in its traditional sense. Note the ties across the bar lines. The second excerpt goes one further and allows everything to be tied across the bar line and beat alike (not traditional hemiola but a concept derived from it).

Example 114
Types of hemiola.

Note here again the ability of the bar line to function for performability yet not disturb the freedom of lines or chords in free rhythmic flow.

Avoidance of beats works as effectively as do ties. In example 115, a string quartet—through the use of ties and silence in combination—avoids any metric interference with the material present. As well, note the use of a great many beat subdivisions other than the standard two, three, and four. Here exist five, seven, nine, and eleven, helping yet further to free rhythm from the bar-line structure.

Example 115
Avoidance of metric accents.

Example 116 still keeps the beat and meter intact, but opens up the beat (in a very slow quarter note equals 36) and allows a great deal of internal freedom, rupturing the beat so that it does little but hold the group together.

Example 116
Beat widening for intact meter but lack of metric accents.

Metric modulation is another device to curb a constant flow of steady beats which strangle lines from free flow. Example 117 shows five measures in which the tempo and the meter is changed (modulated) in hopes that the flow of music will not be hampered by the bar lines, yet at the same time the bar lines will be allowed to help the performer/conductor to maintain a vertical grasp of rhythmic development through meter.

Example 117
Excerpt using metric modulation.

All of these methods, and many more, have been utilized constantly by composers to keep the bar line without its maintaining abstract control over rhythmic freedom, motion, and direction. Possibly popular music must maintain a simplified beat and metric pulse for its dance and other conventions, but serious musics need never rely exclusively on such implications. How many compositions have ended as in the first excerpt of example 118 merely because the down beat provided the easiest and simplest route for accent and performability? How many have avoided the off beat ending of the second excerpt for reasons of ease of performance?

Example 118
a. Strong down beat ending; b. mid-measure off beat ending.

Proportional musics allow less control over the rhythm of a given section, but at the same time avoid the bar line entirely. Time equals space, and usually material is placed approximately where desired in a time frame of a set number of seconds (see Chapter 22 for more notation information). Example 119 shows a passage for piano in proportional notation. Here the notes last as long as the lines following them do in proportion to the whole time frame. The entire section lasts twelve seconds. While perfect performance rhythmically (in terms of the composer's ideal) is not possible (if it ever is, anyway), great flexibility is achieved and the beat, implied accents, etc., have all but vanished (although certain performers will force such on the music due to strong "metered" backgrounds).

Example 119
Passage for piano in proportional notation.

In large ensembles, however, the risks of variability of performance become higher. Often in these circumstances, important lines are cued by second markings above or below the score (with vertical dotted lines connecting them) in order to keep closer accuracy in large time frames. At the same time these second markings can, if care is not taken, be construed as beats and the avoidance of beat implications is no longer successful. In extremely large time frames (especially those without "click-track" seconds marked), improvisation and indeed indeterminacy is approached (not so much in regard to *what* will occur but *when* it will occur: a mobile structure often quite different from performance to performance).

Sometimes a single line will need to be (and indeed *will* be) metrical in nature, while others occurring simultaneously must have freedom of rhythmic drive. Example 120 shows two approaches to this problem. In each, the first (top) line is given a strong metric pad from which it can derive desired patterns. In the first excerpt, however, the accompaniment achieves beat independence by use of ties, lack of struck beats, and odd subdivisions of the beat. The second excerpt shows a group of notes within brackets from which emphasis on completely free improvisation evolves (a type of proportionality within the metric system).

Example 120
Two approaches to metric/non-metric simultaneity.

A further development utilizes both proportional concepts and metered ideas whenever the need arises. In example 121 there is a free interchange between metric and proportional sections. The result is an excerpt which achieves whatever the composer wishes: from the strictest beat-dominated idea to the freest-flowing rhythmic lines conceivable. Note the notational need to be very concise in marking tempo marks in metered sections and the *senza tempo* mark to differentiate the proportional sections. This combinational approach is very successful in that it does not rule out any possible rhythm or rhythmic grouping a composer might wish to use.

Example 121
Combination of metric and proportional notations in linear compo-sition.

Many of the previous ways of skirting metric bar lines also invite extremes of other types of composer convention (i.e., they become just other "standards" from which yet newer rhythmic prisons come into existence). With *metriportional* techniques, the composer is truly free to explore the vast possibilities of one of the least expanded aspects of musical potential: rhythm.

Utilizing any of these concepts compositionally is, as with timbre, a very difficult job indeed. Freedom is nothing more than freedom. It does not imply growth or anything new in and of itself. With our surrounding Muzaks and the programming of traditional theory, the unyoking of rhythm may at first seem a long-awaited field day. Yet new and unorganized rhythm can be as overkilled as constantly applied new sounds. Structured and nonstructured rhythm must be bound together if anything but rhythmic chaos is to be the end result. Analysis of how to use these two extremes can be very useful. A few of the potentials are explored below as obviously no "rules" per se can be stated.

Example 122 shows a compositional overview of a work from a rhythmic vantage point. Note the very metrical beginning, slowly becoming free as the climax is reached and receding again as the rhythmic archlike form is completed:

Example 122
Sample rhythmic overview of work.

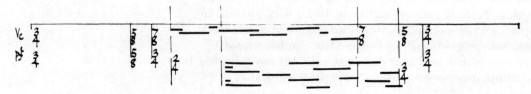

Example 123 is a closer view of a phrase and how rhythm can be applied in a reverse fashion from the above. Note that the contrapuntal opening and density of offbeat and tied rhythms contribute to a free rhythmic texture. This is modulated to a more and more metrical (almost static) climax aided by dynamics. The phrase closes by returning to the freer rhythmic texture of the beginning.

Example 123
Excerpt of rhythmic modulation in metered music.

In example 124 yet another approach is taken with slashing simultaneous chords attacked in the upper register, interrupting a freely improvised section quite opposite in nature below.

Example 124
Improvisation with sudden interruptions.

The ability of rhythmic densities to form thick textures, very much like swarming orchestral clusters, is also useful in compositional process for climax, and can create a climax with many less instruments. Example 125 shows a "straight" cluster for string quartet at the left and a "beehive" rhythmic cluster at the right. Note the great density increase in the second example with nevertheless the same number of instruments:

Example 125
Examples of static cluster and motion clusters for string quartet.

This "density" involvement of rhythm can very much expand cluster creativity and be involved in yet another aspect of compositional development.

In general, the concept of extremes presented herein is very similar to that in any aspect of composition: direction, climax, etc., all leading to successful results. Though any possible combination of free and strict rhythmic concepts is potentially right for a given context, careful combination of these ideas with pitch, dynamics, articulation, and timbre help to form direction, organization, and drama. In general, summation can suffice in terms of rhythmic extremes (metric vs. free): they are generally modulated (slow change, one to the other), contrasted, or combined. Each of these has significant contextual place in music but only in relation to formal overview and integral balance with the other aspects of composition.

ASSIGNMENTS

1. In a brief work for four single-pitched instruments, use isorhythm, cross-rhythms (polyrhythms), and composite meters to maintain interest (meter and bar lines must be continued throughout).

2. Create a work for piano in a moderate 4/4 meter in which rhythmic freedom is achieved by never striking a note "on the beat" (avoid doing so by ties and rests). Then translate the exact work into as best a "re-creation" in proportional notation as possible.

3. Compose a brief work for voice and piano in which each is in a completely different meter with bar lines overlapped. Rewrite the work using single bar lines and metric modulation, trying to achieve the same results. Choose the most performable version.

4. For all available instruments (including piano or pianos and voices), write a work in proportional notation of large time frames. Use the score as the "part" for all performers. Do not use a "second" time track or any other device for guaranteeing more exact entrances.

5. Write a short work for small ensemble (excluding piano) of available instruments using metriportional techniques. Involve microtones in the piece.

6. Compose a work for prepared piano in which simultaneous use of metric bars and free rhythmic structure is obtained using complex rhythms to obtain the latter. Clearly correlate the timbre and rhythm through use of motivic ideas.

7. Analyze example 126 for its use of rhythm (free or controlled by given meter) and then compose an equal-length phrase of exactly opposite usage. Use the same techniques in the composed piece as those in example 126, but different notes and ideas.

Example 126

8. Compose an excerpt for as many available instruments and voices as possible, trying to obtain rhythmic clusters through the use of ties, beat avoidance, and nonstandard beat divisions in a completely metered example.

9. In a short piece for two pianos, explore the potentials of each part in different meters as well as different tempos (held to as strictly as possible). Use of recognizable styles (e.g., waltz, march) can be employed for reference points but is not necessary. Modulate the

two "voices" one to the other slowly during the course of the piece so that each has the other's beginning idea, meter, and tempo.

10. Create a complete rhythmic overview of a composition of short duration. Then compose the work (for two available instruments and piano) having every available aspect of the parameters (timbre, dynamics, etc.) be in complete conjunction at as many points as possible.

WORKS FOR ANALYSIS

Consult the most recent Schwann Catalog for current in-print recordings of these works. Publishers are usually found through libraries, music stores, or distributors of music. This list is not meant to be comprehensive, only suggestive of further study.

Bartók, Béla: *String Quartet No. 6* (cross-metrical patterns without necessarily different measure lengths; as in a great deal of his music, an integral use of meter changes and multiple divisions of complex meters).

Berio, Luciano: *Circles* (use of improvisational "boxes" to free the percussion from metrical implications).

Boulez, Pierre: *Sonata No. 3 for Piano* (this "never completed" work has endless complex metered and nonmetered rhythms avoiding the beat constantly with ties and complex rhythms).

Carter, Elliott: *Double Concerto for Harpsichord, Piano and Two Chamber Orchestras* (very good example of metric modulation by a man who has used it extensively).

Davidovsky, Mario: *Synchronisms No. 1 for Flute and Tape* (semi-metered flute against free taped sounds; good use of staggered entrances and open proportionality in which the notes have value but without meter).

Feldman, Morton: *Durations* (interesting use of rhythm which does not become overly complex yet retains no semblance of beat organization).

Ives, Charles: *Symphony No. 4* (vast use of cross-meters calling for two conductors at times, though successful performances with only one have occurred).

Ligeti, György: *Atmosphères* (extremely effective use of rhythmic clusters and beat avoidance in completely metered structure).

Ligeti, György: *Aventures* (primary example of metriportional notation using metered and proportional notations freely interposed).

Lutoslawski, Witold: *Livre Pour Orchestra* (utilizes improvisational units in often otherwise metered ones; as well, the very free sections contrasting with very metered ones).

Messiaen, Oliver: *Nativité du Seigneur* (example of one of many works by this composer involved with highly complex and personal rhythmic procedures as strict in concept as metered ones, yet resulting in a free form).

Penderecki, Krzysztof: *Devils of Loudon* (completely proportional notation throughout).

Stockhausen, Karlheinz: *Momente* (very free structure with variable form and an example of a total lack of strict rhythmic structure).

Stravinsky, Igor: *L'Histoire du Soldat* (strong evidence here, as in all of Stravinsky's works, of careful analysis of cross-metrical accents and meter used for variable free rhythms; a key to his style).

11

Indeterminacy

Indeterminate music (unpredictable outcome at one point or another in the process of creating sounds) may at first glance seem drastically removed from the concepts discussed up to this point. It has, however, been alluded to in discussions concerning cluster chords (in the lack of "determination" necessary for inner notes) and semi-random pitch production in many percussion instruments and the prepared piano. Moreover, extremely complex dissonant and consonant polytonality as well as rhythmically created clusters often are very random-sounding.

No matter what the compositional process, the end result is analyzable in the manners presented in earlier chapters. Interestingly enough, the problems surrounding indeterminacy are psychosomatic. If the listener is unaware of compositional process (in this case "chance") he will tend to judge the composition more or less as any other, depending on background and experience. On the other hand, if he is aware of the act of indeterminacy his whole set of aesthetics is jarred and judgment is tied to a completely different set of aesthetics according to personal bias.

The compositional problem with indeterminacy is the concept of "chance." Unfortunately, more often than not the composer/performer or audience is the victim: *chance music* very often tends to sound like *chance music*. While to some this is beneficial, to a great majority enough of art is indeterminate as it is and there is no need to inject more. It is with this that a "determined" study of indeterminacy must begin.

There are five basic categories of indeterminate processes:

1. graphic or indeterminate notations on the part of the composer;
2. composer indeterminacy but written out in traditional or semitraditional notations;
3. performer indeterminacy (more closely related to improvisation with little notation "ground work");
4. composer determinacy of events but random selection of the order of these events (mobile structure);
5. stochastic methods wherein basic parameters are determined but material enclosed is basically chosen by random selection.

As well, there are numerous subgroups of each of these classifications, making the term *indeterminacy* very broad-based and not at all the simple term it may first seem to be. Following is a discussion of each of these classifications in more detail, with examples of each and some possible subgroups.

Example 127 is a completely graphic score made from flicking ink randomly from a pen across the page. For sake of extremism, here nothing but the title *Henge* and the instrumentation (prepared piano) are supplied. At first glance the visual image supplies little hint of the musical parameters one is so used to seeing. Careful consideration brings a creative mind, however, to more potentials, and before long one might begin to interpret longer lines as legato and points as very short notes. Verticality might become pitch range and the horizontal aspect a proportional duration frame. At first it may be difficult to seriously involve oneself in such machinations, as the composition and its process is obvious and the lack of care in such bothersome. Indeed, why should a performer spend so much time interpreting something which probably took the composer less than half a minute to create? Yet if one determines that all sound (and silence) is music no matter what its source, motivation, or constructive principle, then the root of these questions is only qualitative or egocentric. Proponents of chance music might argue that, in the first place, if it ends up being good music then what matter the procedure involved? The only qualm might be as to whose name, in fact, goes in the composer's slot on programs: the composer's or the performer's? Often this latter point generates the most conflict.

Further examination into example 127 could guide the interpreter to begin preparations based on random selection of numbers (i.e., if 24 markings, then 24 notes) and specifics of classifications within the numberings (e.g., six long, eight medium and ten short markings can establish type of preparation; e.g., long=resonant preparations, etc.). The list of performer "determinations" is, of course, endless and the inclusion of just letting whatever happens happen (a combination of composer/performer indeterminacy) is certainly possible.

Example 127
Complete graphic score.

HENGE (PREPARED PIANO)

Many first category indeterminate compositions provide more suggestions for performer interpretation and thus more determinacy. Example 128 is a work entitled *Square.* At a quick glance one is no doubt shaken by the fact that the entire work is nothing but a circle. Performance instructions give the work more concrete identity. The work is for voice (female) and piano. Further notes read: "This work is in three short movements. The first implies an imagined square within the circle, the second with the square outside the circle, and the last with the square and circle overlapped. In each case, the square is the object interfering with the progress of the cyclical and lyrical vocal line (the square becoming the piano). All articulations and other musical inferences are derived from the attractions and intersections of the two (one real and one imagined) objects. Nothing should rise above a *mezzo piano* and text should be logical vowel sounds." In *Square,* the work,

though still indeterminate by definition, is moderately determinate
as to articulation, very determinate in regard to dynamics and
timbre, and still quite indeterminate in terms of pitch choice and
direction (though the dynamic instruction suggests lack of such). In
both examples 127 and 128, the results are determined to a great
extent by the interpreter with varying degrees of influence by the
composer. Whatever the "bastard" concept of category 1 is, the
results are as important as in any traditional music: if they are good
then they are good, no matter what the process; if they are poor,
likewise. The chances again, however, at least to some, seem to be
less for success with indeterminacy than with "composed" results.

Example 128
Work entitled Square.

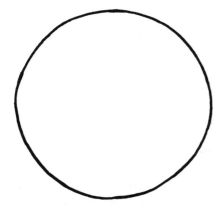

Example 129 is category 2 indeterminacy and may be more
shocking than example 128. There is nothing but traditional notation here (for piano alone) and nothing to even suggest indeterminacy except perhaps the sound (and many might argue that point, for
the clear *klangfarbenmelodien* qualities of this example could easily
lead one to assume a great deal of composer control existed during
composition).

The compositional process employed here was that of tossing
dice. With each parameter shown in example 129 drawn out to
twelve, each note and its accompanying usage was painstakingly
drawn from five tosses of the dice (pitch, dynamics, articulation,
duration, and register). This is probably the purest form of indeterminacy. Only the dice-throwing "talents" of the composer and
natural laws of probability resist *total* indeterminacy. Note that the
example is analyzed according to the concepts raised in earlier
chapters, as all these examples can be (though many must be done
by ear as no notation for analysis exists).

Example 129
Fully notated indeterminacy.

Before progressing to category 3, one might certainly be puzzled by the value this may have to the creation of controlled musics. While mentioning many more later in the chapter, the author thought it best to stop at this point and mention at least four uses to avoid negligence on the part of unsympathetic readers in tackling the *most* necessary problems of this chapter.

First, composers are often wont to get into stylistic ruts, becoming comfortable with reusing past proven successes and not being very clear as to new possibilities. Indeterminacy is a most important and fascinating way to clear the senses and let the sounds freely exist. Such non-ego approaches can lead one not only to new ideas for sound within his own style, but possibly a quite real discovery of (possibly unwanted) old habits.

Secondly, it is a very intriguing proving ground for performer/composer communication. What one may have taken for granted as easy communicative notation may be quite the opposite. Watching performers interact with graphic notations is highly successful feedback in the process of evaluating one's own possibly more, possibly less sophisticated systems. Many new notations (see Chapter 22) were a direct result of some type of applied indeterminate concept.

Thirdly, it is possibly very important to conceive of the freedom implied in indeterminate music and, though one may shy from its oftentimes overdone thoroughness, it can be observed that such freedom (especially in terms of rhythm) might found a very substantial structure when applied to one's own style.

Lastly, and probably most obviously, indeterminacy needs no reason or syntax to exist. Like all other forms of life, it exists, and, regardless of its value to one's own habits and ideas, it should not be overlooked. If nothing else, from personal bias, listening and observing indeterminacy may very well give a necessary reaffirmation of one's own music, shaking doubts away.

Category 3 indeterminacy is closely linked with improvisation (as, to some extent—depending on performer—is category 1). Groups of notes, or areas, are often supplied. Example 130 is very much category 3 indeterminacy. Note the vertical stacking of notes, areas of dynamics to be used, three notated articulations, and set of durations located within the circle. While this work could be for any instrumental ensemble, it implies performer ability to make something of the notes based on his past experience and background. Though each performance will net a quite different result, the "sharing" of compositional process between composer and performer is self-evident and the result the least indeterminate of examples shown thus far.

Example 130
Category 3 indeterminacy.

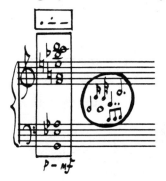

Example 131 is of the fourth category as listed near the beginning of the chapter, and is indeterminate only in regard to form and dynamics. Each "event" (for solo voice) is to be performed in any order for as many times as the performer feels the need. Selections of one of the three dynamics before each event is based on what event preceded the new one chosen, and the direction the piece may or may not be taking at any given point.

Example 132 shows two possible versions of example 131 (both short due to space limitations) demonstrating the still vast variation present within the structure even though every event is written out in extreme detail.

Example 131
Work of 4th category indeterminacy.

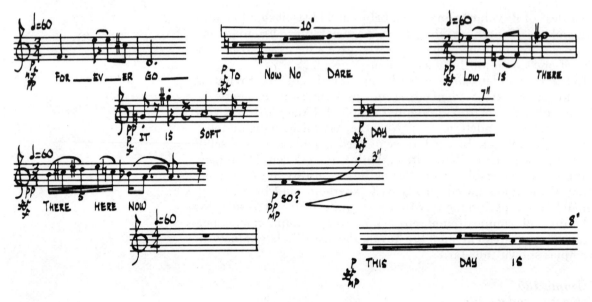

Example 132
Two possible versions of example 131.

The resultant mobile effect can make for an extremely large number of possible works and, if work duration is completely free, the possibilities are infinite.

Category 5 indeterminacy is the least indeterminate and represents a close tie to the earlier reference to rhythmic cluster techniques. Stochastic concepts are those referring to chance events so numerous that the end result is predictable under most circumstances. Example 133 is stochastic chance in operation. Nothing is stated except that the voices (no less than forty) be evenly distributed (SATB) and should sing a note on the vowel *ah* and stick to it, trying not to duplicate the note of any other singer. Repeated efforts would produce results not much different from the tempo fluctuations of various performances of a Mozart sonata. The effect is widely spaced clusters with predictability strengthened if more voices are used. With the built-in spacing (soprano to bass with obviously no overlap except with neighboring voices), only a minimal chance exists that an "accidental" triad might occur and mar the otherwise easily performed example.

Example 133
Stochastic indeterminacy

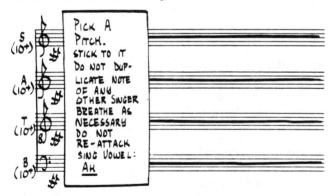

Note the transition from category 1 through 5 with the slow development from near pure chance to "controllable" indeterminacy. While many composers stick to their guns, feeling that only the purity of one system will serve their purposes, the composer bent on using any and all available materials for compositional style and process can gain a great deal of material from each of these categories. Immaculate versions such as examples 127 and 128, while at first seeming unusable, could serve useful purposes in an otherwise different stylistic context. Climaxes, for example, explode many times with nondefined clarity and design, only to again resolve into the frame of the work. Utilizing very free-form graphic category 1 markings can often imply and communicate such explosions better to the performer than well-practiced straight solutions. Traditionally notated indeterminacy as in category 2 is an excellent way to hide category 1 formats from the possibly hostile performer accustomed to only the strictest of musical notation grammars. The same climax may be achieved with a "do anything you want as long as it is as loud and fast as possible" category 3 usage. Category 4 can provide variation from performance to performance of some or all of the events of a climax, and category 5 has obvious stochastic potential for guaranteeing climactic ends through texture. These are just the possible uses for *climax.* They may be applied to any aspect of composition, not only formally but in terms of the simplest parameters of dynamics or articulation, for example.

It is always important to reevaluate one's style as well as evaluate new ones regardless of their seeming inconsequentiality. Indeed indeterminacy, no matter what form it takes, is as valid as any other music. Whether it is good music or bad music is a question that individuals may wish to ponder (and probably will) for years to come. Without question, however, its uses to the open and creative mind are nearly endless.

ASSIGNMENTS

1. Compose a category 1 indeterminate composition using wet blots of ink randomly placed and smeared by slapping a second blank sheet against the first. Have as many performers as possible interpret the score. Record each and compare the results. Note similarities and differences, quality and lack of it.

2. Using a deck of cards, carefully assign to each card a designated note, duration, dynamic, or articulation. Compose a work for three available instruments using completely random card selection for each parameter of each line in succession.

3. Place groupings of notes, articulations, dynamics, durations, and possible registers in five separate locations on a single sheet. Using as many players as available, perform the work. Contrast this with performance by a single performer. Using proportional notation, transcribe the latter into communicative notation.

4. Compose six "events" in traditional notation, each of which should exemplify a technique of a previous chapter. Separate each event (for piano) by space and allow one parameter to be selective (e.g., four registers, three articulations, or the like).

5. Compose a stochastic indeterminate phrase for as many voices as possible. Set general limits (e.g., all loud, all glissandi, all ascending, all long). Perform many times and note the differences.

6. Construct a verbal overview of a work which uses basically standard techniques discussed so far, but as well at least two indeterminate techniques at places other than climax. Work should be for two instruments and piano.

7. Analyze example 134 and determine whether its composition is determinate or indeterminate. Use analytical procedures from earlier chapters to help. If example is other than indeterminate, define techniques used. If indeterminate, compose an equal-length excerpt using similar chance techniques.

Example 134

8. Reevaluate any one of your previous assignments in terms of possible usage of an indeterminate technique at one point to achieve a better result. Consider openings, climaxes, endings, and sections of transition as possible sources of change.

9. Begin a work with category 3 (improvisatory) techniques. The opening (for five instruments, at least three of which should be of different timbres) should be very soft, moving to a louder but not overpowering section. The indeterminacy should slowly modulate to completely determinate music without noticeable point of change. Experiment for successful results.

10. End a work which has been occurring for about five minutes in totally category 1 indeterminacy. Compose this ending (for piano) convincingly in traditional notation and techniques discussed earlier in the book. Perform the work with the performer playing from any graphic source at hand (inclusive of assignment 1 interpretation).

WORKS FOR ANALYSIS

Consult the most recent Schwann Catalog for current in-print recordings of these works. Publishers are usually found through libraries, music stores, or distributors of music. This list is not meant to be comprehensive, only suggestive of further study.

Ashley, Robert: *In Memoriam Crazy Horse* (category 1 indeterminacy with graphic score in quite simple-appearing designs).

Brown, Earle: *Available Forms I* (good example of category 4 mobile structure for orchestra with the score projected and conductor choice).

———: *December 1951* (a classic example of category 1 indeterminate graphic music of thin lines of differing lengths).

Cage, John: *Music of Changes* (a complete category 2 indeterminate work for orchestra in which parameters were worked out in detail through chance procedures but written in generally traditional notation).

———: *Cartridge Music* (category 1 with variations in that the see-through overlays present an ever-changing graphic to determine sound).

———: *Concert for Piano and Orchestra* (a combination of categories, though primarily category 3, as many notes as well as parameters are written out).

Childs, Barney: *Mr. T. His Fancy* (includes interchangeable pages, etc. and is category 4 indeterminacy primarily).

Foss, Lukas: *Time Cycle* (though now in traditional notation, this work evolved out of creative category 3 improvisatory techniques done by the composer at U.C.L.A. in years previous to its creation).

Higgins, Dick: *Thousand Symphonies* (category 1 indeterminacy; the work was created by "machine-gunning" score paper. The end result may, as some suggest, be a combination of categories 1 and 2 due to the use of scores).

Kagel, Mauricio: *Sonant* (a combination of categories with emphasis on the mobile structure of 4).

Oliveros, Pauline: *Outline, for Flute, Percussion, and String Bass* (a category 3 improvisation chart).

Stockhausen, Karlheinz: *Stop* (a combination of categories but more emphasis on the mobile and especially the stochastic ideals of categories 4 and 5).

Xenakis, Iannis: *Duel* (a combination of categories 4 and 5 by this protagonist and first to apply the term *stochastic* to music).

12
Multimedia

In general definition, multimedia expresses that combination of art forms which is predominantly indeterminate in nature. The forms themselves need not necessarily be indeterminate, but the resultant combination of forms is at least loose, if not chance, in concept. In multimedia, none of the art forms present are dependent upon one another for success as is the case with mixed-media (somewhat dependent) and inter-media (completely dependent). Any one of the arts represented can (and often are intended to) stand alone and be successful with no necessary intimation of multimedia context.

The concept of multiple art forms is not particularly new in itself (e.g., opera, the Greek chorus in drama, ballet, have existed for centuries) and indeed there are many current popular examples (e.g., television, musical comedy, motion pictures). The development of new electronic vehicles for media productions has obviously contributed greatly to its increased sophistication and growing usage. However, the importance of multimedia is the aspect of noncorrelation of the art forms used. The variety of reasons is nearly as numerous as works written, yet there do seem to be at least three recognizable "themes" present in most multimedia events:

1. happenings: here the art forms are as completely independent as possible, with the participants in no way "fixing" an end result or predictable outcome; the joy of an unexpected correlation or absurdity can be, and often is, the motivation;

2. theatre pieces: here a message is a product of the combination of forms (yet each could still stand on its own merits); it is often a collage of dadaistic visual and aural images;
3. light shows: here the elements generally correlate in some fashion yet again allow each a successful identity if need be (these vary from simplistic light imitations of sound to extremely complex laser-beam productions).

The elaboration of each of these themes is described in more detail as follows: happenings can (and often do) include a wide variety of art forms. Example 135 shows the input of a sample happening though it should be noted that happenings often imply no prior knowledge of materials to be used (totally unplanned). A most effective approach (as used here) is to have all participants be aware of the general form of each contribution without specifics. This allows for the least interaction between art forms and the most chance without total chaos (though this latter is certainly a happening form as well). The resultant indeterminate combinations may never have occurred if the situation of the happening had not been created.

Example 135
Happening—multimedia.

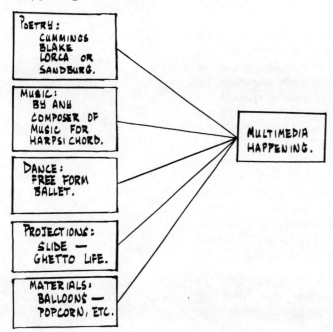

The semiplanned situation does allow for free choice of material while suggesting types of works for poetry (poems of any of the four poets listed), music (works by any composer of music for harpsichord), dance (free-form ballet), projections (slides dealing with any aspect of ghetto life), and materials (any size and shape of balloons in great numbers). The choice of exact poem, music, slides, etc., remains up to the performers, who may make decisions preferably *without* foreknowledge of other participants' exact decisions but with an overview of the "score" in its entirety. The *materials* used in happening environments can often affect audience participation (quite frequently an important factor in happening situations).

Example 136 is less verbose and more defined in activity. The probable effect here of humor and/or frustration demonstrates the dramatic aspects of happening formats (a more than redeemable feature). It consists of a hallway the sides of which are dotted with framed minimal-art forms. The observer must obviously get very close to each of these art objects for clear observance, yet the hallway has been strung with recording tape and partially filled with balloons. Obviously any quick movement will send the participant ripping and popping his way to the floor. Yet no hung print (actually less than one inch square) can be seen comfortably (i.e., without standing precariously at extremely awkward angles, often on one foot or straddling from wall to wall). Compounding the situation, the hall is filled with the sound of spliced-together versions of contrasting musics, from slow recognizable hymn tunes to extremely brittle and fast electronic sounds (the tape is to be made independently with no attempt at growth or shape, only total disarray of sound). Each of the minimal-art objects is either a mirror or one single color without shadings (except those resulting from the lighting of the hall).

Example 136
More defined happening (see text).

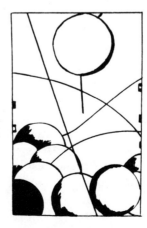

From a composer's viewpoint, the exact or particular nature of the happening situations of the above examples and the thousands of others that exist must be considered to be an independent decision based on whether knowledge of other art forms is present and to what degree such knowledge is disclosed. In general, the more knowledge each creator possesses of the whole, the less freedom he will have in contributing his art form (whether this lesser freedom is conscious or unconscious, it will exist no matter what he is instructed to disregard).

Example 136 involves less indeterminacy but more audience participation and contribution than example 135. In both cases it is the *unexpected* that is desired, and not the predicted. As with indeterminacy, the obvious, the usual is not desired, but rather that illogical and often incomprehensible candid act which is the mark of success (the partial reasons for desiring such are given to some extent in the last chapter, and will be covered in more depth later in this chapter).

Example 137 is a short theatre piece in which the art forms are thrust together in a more determinate manner in terms of general frames of reference. *Ready* is a work requiring about twenty actors dressed as soldiers who, marching to a known or unknown (composed by the participant) military-sounding music, come to a strict formation on a brightly lit stage. The commands shown in the example are given very slowly and, should any of the audience remain by the time "fire" is screamed, they would be showered by a multitude of corks filling the hall.

Example 137
Theatre piece: Ready!

READY!

$$\left. \begin{array}{l} \text{READY} \\ \text{AIM} \end{array} \right] 20'' \\ \text{FIRE} \left. \right] 20''$$

Again, as with happenings, both the music and the staging could be effective in its own right. The results seem here to be a bit more predictable, yet the actual media format is still very loose, allowing for free choice of musics (comic to dread: each having a quite different effect on the audience) and acting (again, from comic obviousness to intense reality).

The compositional process in writing theatre pieces is to clearly define the role the aural activity is to play and what freedoms are allowed within that framework. Again, while no specifics can be given, a general rule of thumb is to allow the dramatic concept to pose the situation and derive compositional techniques from resulting choices. Since theatre always requires certain expected audience responses, theatre pieces and their chance elements can often create confused reactions, especially if completely defined theatrical control over musics is not allowed (the opposite becomes not a theatre piece but merely a drama with musical accompaniment).

Example 138
Multimedia light show.

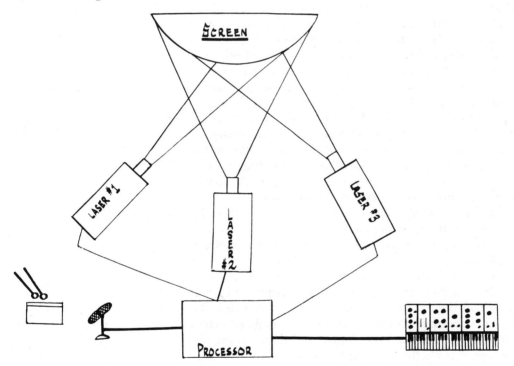

In example 138, a set of three different colored lasers have been connected through electronic adapters which enables live sound-producers (conventional instruments, voices, or electronics) to control their intensity and direction. The visual light show can then be controlled by a third element, sometimes allowing the obvious sound control of visuals, and sometimes not (or even possibly delaying the sound so that a canon of sorts exists between light and sound). With the current state of laser development and combinations of such with sound, the end result can be highly effective and sophisticated. While quality must enter into any discussion of what indeed can stand on its own, it is apparent that the visual aspect of laser shows can certainly do without sound accompaniment and, since the composition involved can be freely chosen or composed, one must assume that it too can exist apart from the projections. The predictability here can usually be measured by the number of rehearsals which have occurred (as it can be in most multimedia), for with each ensuing rehearsal more and more successful-appearing combinations occur and there is a growing dependence of one art form upon the other.

There are obviously lesser degrees of complexity, and often one confronts a light source (colored lights diffused by grained glass) reacting to varying electric impulses from a sound source (e.g., a radio or record player). These latter barely can fit the definition of multimedia in that predictability is quite often obtained within a few minutes or less, and no chance is available for further accidents.

The process in composing music for light shows is determined exclusively by the obvious relationship which is to occur between sight and sound. On the one extreme, if few sound sources are available and the correlation direct and constant, the more compositional variety the more acceptable the result as multimedia. At the other extreme, if many sound sources exist and alternating correlation between sound source and image is available, the fewer techniques used the more correlated the media form; the more techniques used the more abstract and incredible becomes the diversity and variety of the multimedia form.

Through all of this discussion there remain at least two significant questions regarding the use of multimedia: "Why?" and "Is it music?" Addressing the former, one might refer to the expansion of ideas expressed in regard to indeterminacy: the possible revelation of something extraordinary. Besides this, however, remains the constant media question in its entirety. While concerts do present a kind of interesting visual correlation of sound and sight (as one can see an up-bow agree with the hearing of such), many find this tedious. Concerts of electronic music demonstrate this in the extreme when the audience is often forced to view the circling reels for the duration of the piece (indeed, many have felt that this particular situation may have given direct rise to the media movement). Moreover, one cannot completely divorce the effects of other stimuli upon the body while attending a concert or even listening to a recording at home. Many diversities exist in the realm of visual activity, as well as other aural phenomena not at all relevant to the concert at hand, extraneous physical problems, etc. While it might seem easy to dismiss them, it is probably true that these and more are occurring even as this passage is being read. Multimedia does not seek to *correlate* these extraneous events, but attempts to *control* some or all of them in one form or another. In most simple terms, *all events are noncontrolled multimedia* to begin with. The listener, in the case of music, has just attempted (and the term *attempted* is well-advised here, as often the attempt fails) to disregard all the peripheral effects in order to focus upon one. The creator of multimedia, in its multitude of forms, tends to markedly force the mind not to disregard, but rather begin a *gestalt* concept of the arts and activities of man: to not allow the avoidance of what might at first seem out of context with the desired situation.

In reply to "Is it music?" one can only respond by noting the destruction of so many ideas by categorization. Many act as if art were a definitive slot into which only one size and shape of activity may fit; music into one, art another, etc. When a larger size delivers itself upon the observer, either the definition must change or the newcomer be dismissed (usually not in terms of quality but singularly because of description). The idea of "Is it music?" is truly beside the point, as definitions should be flexible enough to grant admittance to the senses with or without formal designation or the observer's past experience. The question should instead be posed, "Is it good?" or "Does it fulfill its creator's wishes?" or "Can I use it constructively?" or "Does it really need classification?"

For the composer of multimedia there exist few of the problems inherent in mixed-media and inter-media (where he is faced with direct correlation with the other art forms). In general, multimedia is a group activity inviting other artists to participate with possibly a guiding principle or focal point in mind. Regardless, with the exception of theatre pieces (in which the composer is usually the creator of the entire work), the composer is allowed the luxury of going his own way, utilizing any technique or process at his disposal and using the sound-producing forces available. If he is to be "controller" as in theatre pieces (and some light shows of sophistication), he must have command of all the techniques of the other art forms used or employ another person to execute the desired activities. Multimedia suggests that a multitude of individuals combine to form the work, without (or with only some) knowledge of the resultant outcome; this then becomes the model for the indeterminate combinations of art forms.

To some, the simplest of multimedia happenings are the most pregnant source of attractive materials. If truly immaculate and noncorrelated events are staged without imposing cleverness, many fascinating simultaneities can occur amid the obviously often tedious wading through the mire of uninteresting "accidents." To others, the light show is a new form of art, defined and ready for Webster codification. Whatever the aesthetic or prognostication, the antagonist or protagonist, multimedia forms continue to contribute possibilities for the unbiased observer. Its analysis must be dramatic in overview and formalistic internally (e.g., distinctly sound as one element, drama another, etc.). Its techniques in terms of music are those of any within this volume, and the resultant hybrids of such techniques. The processes are as limitless as the works themselves, hampered only by definitions imposed not for restriction but to enable further exploration into the more consonant forms of mixed-media (see Chapter 23) and inter-media (see Chapter 25), where correlation between art forms becomes of increased importance.

ASSIGNMENTS

1. Create (in words) the elements of a happening involving art, drama, dance, and music. Dispense the overview framework (as loose as possible in restrictions) to three other people (versed or not in the areas above) and then compose a short work for piano in any style given to this point except indeterminacy. Perform and observe the correlations.

2. Compose music for example 135. Deliver the example to other available "creators" so that performance can take place. N.B.: the composer here becomes a composer for harpsichord and may or may not wish to create "in the style of. . . ."

3. Using as many performers as possible, create a collage of overlapped recognizable musics (all of which should be carefully notated). Given one actor, create (through words) a situation in which he cannot (or must not) react in any way to the sounds occurring.

4. Randomly select twenty-five slides from any available source. Select five different sound sources (e.g., radio, television, etc.) and perform such with no rehearsal, with the projections in a dark hall. Note occasional accidents as well as more often complete lack of direction.

5. Compose a complete theatre piece in which anyone in a set area (known only to you) inadvertently (or eventually advertently) becomes a performer. Create the work by "selection" of aural, visual, and other instruments present within the performance area (these may be traditional or completely nontraditional, as would be the case with, for instance, chairs, light bulbs, etc.). The less obvious the performance area chosen the better.

6. With available resources, set up a light show in which in some way correlation is arranged between sight and sound (e.g., projector slide change equals note change, etc. as simple solutions; if more sophisticated, examples are not available). Write a work for solo voice in which no correlation with the end multimedia is anticipated, yet perform the work with both sources.

7. Analyze the musical example in example 139 in traditional terms expressed earlier in the text. Sketch a dramatic sequence of like duration in which there is no observable correlation. Sketch a second one in which all the features are as correlated as possible. Sketch verbally. Perform each.

Example 139

8. Gather every conceivable object, person, instrument, etc., available and, within the confines of a room, signal each to perform (individually and without correlation to any other person present). Record the performance and note any successful surprises present.

9. Taking any one of the previous assignments, analyze for any and all successful ideas. Compose a work or create a multimedia event which attempts to utilize these successes to create direction and notably all the traditional aspects of artistic creation. Note the change occurring from the loose framework to the structured.

10. Perform any traditional piece of chamber music. Divert your attention from the music to every other phenomenon present in the existing environment. Structure a multimedia piece in much the same manner (i.e., concert situation in which the abstract and irrelevant activities present are allowed to overtake the senses of the observer). Notation may be any that presents the best solution.

WORKS FOR ANALYSIS

Consult the most recent Schwann Catalog for current in-print recordings of these works (note that recordings alone do not give the entirety of multimedia performance, though many do contain information and materials for performance). Publishers are usually found through libraries, music stores, or distributors of music. This list is not meant to be comprehensive, only suggestive of further study.

Austin, Larry: *Accidents* (work for amplified piano and projections in which the performer tries not to strike the keyboard; notes struck—accidents—are the only sonic events of the work).

Cage, John: *Water Music* (as with many of Cage's multimedia works this includes short instructions as to what to do; many include theatrical and media involvement).

————: *Variations IV* (while only being sound in the recorded version, it was during its live performance in Los Angeles a collage of radios, live electronics and such for sound and interaction of lights and people and visuals and theatre; all by pure indeterminacy).

Hiller, Lejaren, and John Cage: *HPSCHD* (full performance involves a huge number of projections, taped and harpsichord sounds, and is one of the largest multimedia events in existence).

Kagel, Mauricio: *Match* (includes traditional instruments and notation as well as gymnastic activity by the performers and birds).

Martirano, Salvatore: *L'sGA* (based on Lincoln's Gettysburg Address, this is a mass of sight and sound coming from every direction with no apparent correlation save the underlying but barely distingishable text).

Moran, Robert: *Bethlehem* (work written for the entire city of Bethlehem, Pennsylvania; includes a mass of sounds, sights, and materials that no one could begin to correlate; highly inventive multimedia).

Scriabin, Alexander: *Prometheus* (originally written for orchestra and light show and performed that way today, though lacking the instrument for projections which the composer intended: clavier à lumières).

Varèse, Edgard: *Poème Electronique* (originally written for the Brussels World's Fair of 1958; intended for the Philips pavilion in the shape of a cow's stomach with many projections and paintings on the walls; no correlation was intended between any of the art forms present).

13

Electronic Music I: Musique Concrète

Musique concrète is that form of electronic music which involves manipulation (usually with tape recorder and splicing block) and composition using non-electronic sound sources (i.e., electronic only in process of composition). These non-electronic sources involve a wide spread of sounds inclusive of natural sounds of the environment, man-made sounds not ordinarily considered musical in traditional terms, as well as traditional and nontraditional instrumental sounds. The process is fourfold: seeking/finding sources, recording sources, manipulating sources, and composition. Though it is possibly best to start with composition, as will be pointed out later in the chapter, the discussion here will follow the above order.

The list below can serve as a springboard for further sources of *musique concrète:*

wind	jet plane	scratched balloons
thunder	cello solo	chorus sounds
street sounds	organ cluster	night sounds
gunfire	radio static	clock ticking
waterfalls	children playing	piano insides
percussion ensemble	plucked rubber	car horns
human voice	bands	guitar
heartbeat		

All of the above have been used in one way or another in successful *concrète* compositions and could serve again in different contexts. As well, they should suggest an immense variety of other available sounds for use. Once one has become familiar with the multiplicity of sounds from a percussion ensemble or prepared piano, the above should not be too remote as raw materials for music composition.

Obviously, in seeking sound sources, some present rather consonant sounds while others are quite dissonant. *Musique concrète* does not impose the necessity of using one or the other, both, or any combination. Source consideration is very important as it will greatly influence eventual choices in compositional process and thus should be considered and reconsidered continually in seeking and finding sounds.

The recording of sources involves at least a basic understanding of tape machines and techniques of operation. Example 140 shows two basic microphone patterns, each designed for a particular reason. Though many more patterns exist, these are the most common.

Example 140
Cardioid and omnidirectional microphone patterns.

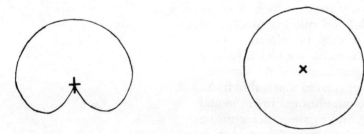

The cardioid pattern is very directional and should be used when sound behind the microphone might disturb the source or interrupt the recording. The omnidirectional pattern picks up sounds from all directions equally, and is especially useful when the complete "presence" or live quality of a hall or location is desired as well as sounds from all directions. The reasons for using one or the other should be obvious from their descriptions (important to note, however, is the careful placement of microphones to avoid ground or floor disturbance through vibrations, as well as use of microphones in the intended way: e.g., it would be rather useless to point an omnidirectional microphone at an object, for its coverage then would include a large portion of ground and sky, and not so much the object intended). If recording in stereo, microphone placement should depend on the pattern and situation. In general, mikes should not be placed very far apart unless the so-called ping-pong effect is desired. A seven-inch-wide human head hears stereo, so wide separation is not needed in most cases. Widely spaced mikes (ten feet and more apart) pick up material from such diverse directions that the process becomes an effect rather than a *real* quality of sound. However, the microphones should be as far from the tape recorder as possible to avoid extra noise from the operation of the machine.

Example 141 shows a standard three-head tape recorder. Note the order of the heads (erase, record, playback: E R P in abbreviation) and the various input/output sections, as well as gain (volume) meters (known as VU or volume unit meters) and gain knobs (often called *pots* for potentiometers or variable resistors), all of which become very important in the process of recording and eventually manipulation.

Example 141
Standard three head tape recorder; plug types.

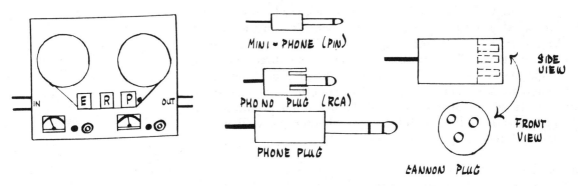

It is important to note here that many machines have just two heads: E and RP, the erase head usually pinpointed by its bland singular color facing. Connectors are a very confusing aspect of tape recorder operation (note that four types are shown in example 141). The pin plug (miniphone) is usually used with cassette machines and the like (not recommended for *concrète* recording). The phono plug (often referred to as the RCA) is very common between speakers and amplifiers and in adapting one source to another. The phone plug (note the obvious similarity in name to, and thus the common confusion with, the phono designation) is the most standard for microphone and headphone inputs. The cannon plug is most often used with professional tape recorders for microphone connection as well as mixer to tape deck.

Heads on a tape recorder (whether two or three) have a variety of track (channel) arrangements. Example 142 shows a number of these. It is imperative to know exactly which type will be used before taping begins. The full-track mono is usually not found except in older recorders or extremely expensive models for professional use. The half-track monophonic machine is useful for mono only, but does allow for recording both directions, thus doubling the use of tape. The half-track stereo machine is the standard machine for recording most semiprofessional and professional concerts, etc. This machine is well advised if one can afford it. Quarter-track machines (stereo) are the most common and almost all decks or recorders costing less than $1,000 today are of this variety. It is possible to record tracks one and three in one direction and then, by reversing the reels, record tracks two and four, thus getting twice as much on the tape. This, however, poses two problems: crosstalk (or leakage of sound from one channel to another, made more possible due to the greater number of channels involved and their closer proximity to one another) and the possibility of accidental playback on a half-track machine, the result being all four tracks sounding simultaneously (two forward, two backward). Though this latter "reversed" sound can be a *concrète* device, it is suggested that recording in only one direction on quarter-track stereo is best. There also exist four-track machines (four channels in one direction only), eight-track machines, etc., but these represent more and more expense and are rarely at the disposal of any but the better electronic studios. More will be discussed about the use and manipulation of these channels at a later point in this chapter (as well as the potentials of three- and two-head machines).

Example 142
Channel arrangements for various tape recorders.

Speeds usually vary from $3^3/_4$ to $7^1/_2$ or $7^1/_2$ to 15 inches per second (ips) with the former the most common among popular machines. Generally, the higher the speed the better the fidelity (15 ips is usually the limit, as tape passing the head at faster speeds tends to increase background noise). In *musique concrète,* one should note carefully that recording speed suggests potentials for speeding up and slowing down recorded sounds (discussed later in the chapter). In general, however, the higher speed should be chosen, for fidelity at $3^3/_4$ ips is very poor.

Meters are complicated and space does not provide for full discussion here. It is important to note that the red portion (dangerous distortion-level area) is not always a completely poor area in which to record. It is possible to nearly "pin" needles to the right on some machines without distortion, while on others distortion occurs immediately upon entering the area. A good deal of experimentation should take place to gauge an individual machine before recording. As well, it is not always necessary for a needle to move for the recorder to be recording. Constant "riding" of the gain controls during recording will result in a middle-of-the-road general dynamic very uncharacteristic of the source recorded. In general, there should be one or two settings for a given situation to retain dynamic integrity.

Choice of tape is extremely important, with 1.5-mil. polyester (high level, low noise) being the best to date. One should avoid being fooled by the extra tape that comes with lesser thicknesses of tape, as these only contribute to higher levels of print-through (magnetic particles [domains] influencing each other from one layer of tape on the spool to another). The only possible reason for using 1.0-mil. or 0.5-mil. tape would be extraordinarily long continuous recording times, which one would question from the outset in any event.

It is advisable when recording a variety of events to make special notations from the meter readings (always beginning the tape at zero) in a notebook so that it will be easy in manipulation to find the right spot. Much further advice can be obtained from the tape recorder manual and is so peculiar to each machine that further discussion at this point would be too specific and confusing.

There are an enormous number of tape manipulations one can make once sounds have been collected. The most common ones are listed below and then, in turn, discussed in detail:

1. splicing
2. speed changes
3. reversing sounds
4. sound with sound, sound on sound
5. tape loops
6. panning and gain control
7. processing and mixing

Splicing should be done with a professional splicing block as shown in example 143.

Example 143
Professional splicing block; splicing tape (⁷/₃₂-inch wide) on recording tape.

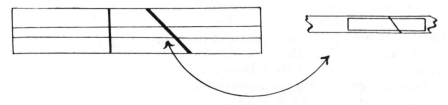

Most splices should be done at the angle so that more tape contacts more tape for surer binding. ⁷/₃₂-inch splicing tape (plenty: one to two inches) should be used so that glue does not bleed from one layer of tape to the next. Quarter-inch splicing tape (matching the electronic tape width) very frequently bleeds glue not only due to its equal width but to accidental angular mishaps in applying. Most professional blocks have instructions so that further information is not necessary here except to caution the composer against using the "chopper" type of splicer which produces an hourglass form from which glue bleeding is a severe problem:

Example 144
Hourglass splice (very poor) from chopping type splicers.

The first splice should be to attach at least ten winds of paper (if possible) leader to the head of the tape. From this point it should be noted that any sound one wishes placed after another should be spliced and not just rerecorded from another recorder, as the latter often produces clicks as well as different gain levels (very noticeable). A well-done splice in the proper place should not be noticed at all. Splicing can produce a wide variety of diverse and unique alterations of sounds. Abrupt changes of sound can be achieved by splicing, with the result an immense variety of juxtapositions of collected sounds. Distortions of sound by splitting its envelope (natural dynamic shape) can be very effective, rendering recognizable sounds often completely unrecognizable. In general, the act of splicing can be the basic tool for composition as each note, passage, movement, etc., is welded into place. In all cases it is important to pinpoint the exact splicing place. If the machine in use does not have a switch allowing the tape to remain in contact with heads without being in play position (which allows "rocking" the reels to hear exactly where the sound is), it is advisable to play the tape, stop at the approximate point of splicing, and mark with a grease pencil (N.B. mark at the playback head). Replay across the spot and make special note of the accuracy of the marking. Remark closer to the point of the sound and replay again. With usually four or five plays an accurate splicing place is reached on the tape.

Speed changes can be very effective. At least two machines are required, but obviously one can be used for experimentation (just play back a tape recorded at $7^{1}/_{2}$ ips at $3^{3}/_{4}$ to see the results). Multiple uses of this technique can be accomplished fairly rapidly by first playing a $7^{1}/_{2}$ ips tape at $3^{3}/_{4}$ speed and recording on another machine at $7^{1}/_{2}$ ips. The second machine should then be turned to $3^{3}/_{4}$ ips and played, recording back into the first machine as before, continuing the process until the desired result is obtained. Speeding up sounds can be very effective as well. Play the sounds on recorder one at $7^{1}/_{2}$ ips and record on the second machine at $3^{3}/_{4}$. Then play machine two at $7^{1}/_{2}$ ips while recording on recorder one at $3^{3}/_{4}$, and so on. It should be noted, however, that with each of these rerecordings the SNR (signal to noise ratio, or recorded signal in reference to background noise) gets worse and usually four or five times becomes the limit where noise becomes intolerable. However, four or five speed changes in one direction can turn a simple flute line, for example, into an extremely high (if audible) rip of quick sounds or a slow tuba-type sound with vibrato slower than the notes in the original.

Machines which allow the tape to remain in contact with the tape heads when not in play position can be an extraordinary source for sound manipulation; in essence, one has a variable-speed recorder of infinite variations. Just a quick "fast forward," "fast reverse," or hand swiveling of the tape reels will invite an incredible number of potentials for the creative mind.

Reversing sounds is quite easily accomplished but varies from machine to machine due to track alignment. For point of reference, the half-track machine has been chosen for examples here (quarter-track reversal is possible only in machines where head contact with tape can be maintained in other than the play position). The process is to have the recorder play the tape to a tails position, reverse the reels, and every sound should be in reverse. This can be a very effective manipulation, though at times, like speed changes, it can become a bit obvious when using recognizable sounds such as the human voice, and often becomes more theatre than music. Playing a fully recorded (both directions) quarter-track tape on a half-track machine nets an interesting result in that both forward and backward channels are heard simultaneously.

Sound *with* sound is accomplished by first recording one track, returning to the point of origin, and recording separately the second track. Two problems can exist in regard to sound with sound. Some machines are not capable of separate-track recording and the channel not in use is automatically erased. As well, in a three-head machine the playback head is a slight distance from the record head and exact synchronization is very difficult if it is desired (this does not occur in two-head machines due to the fact that the record and playback head are one and the same; however, this fact should not persuade the composer to assume that two-head machines are superior: the best solution is a three-head machine with some form of selective synchronization; see Appendix). Sound with sound does enable one to achieve at least a two-voice texture (or more, depending on how many voices exist on each channel to begin with), with independence of directions and very interesting potential for combining sounds into complex textures.

Sound *on* sound is quite a bit more difficult unless the machine in use has built-in capabilities (many do). Sound on sound is the ability of a recorder to tape more than one sound on one channel (i.e., defeating the erase head). If the recorder does not have this advantage, it can be approached by placing a nonconductor between the tape and the erase head. Experimentation with this should be quite involved as no set approach can be advised.

Tape loops are single strips of tape the two ends of which are spliced together to produce one circle or loop of tape. It is then usually placed in playing position against the recorder heads and then tightened to the desired tension by using a microphone stand (or the equivalent) as shown in example 145. Such loops produce ostinati of varying lengths, depending on the length of the loop and the speed of the tape recorder. These can be used for rhythmic repetitions or as a way to achieve a continuous sound from one which was possibly too short in its previous environment. Multiple tape loops (or taping first a loop of one length on one channel and a loop of a differing length on another channel) can be most effective.

Example 145
Tape loop setup.

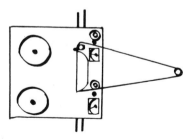

When one is recording a stereo *concrète* sound, it is not necessary (not even desirable) to try and match VU meter levels, for one important effect of stereo is sound movement (panning); recording gain levels should, in general, be at the same points. In manipulation, however, it is possible to heighten the sound motion drastically and effect a very creative potential. Panning is usually done by having one recorder play into another which is recording. By turning either the gain levels on the playback machine or the record levels on the recording machine in even but opposite motions for each track, the resultant sound tends to fade from one speaker while increasing in the other, creating this sound movement known as panning (effective, but not to be overdone).

Simple gain adjustments can be equally effective. By playing through a tape, one can allow sounds to burst from silence (gain on zero, suddenly moving to high level), fade (slow turning down of gain), etc. Programmed crescendos and diminuendos become in reality—as does silence—an integral part of the composition. While adjustments of gain in the recording process are usually as accurate as possible, the gain levels in the studio can quickly become tools for compositional process.

Processing sound through other devices (namely synthesizers) is still in the realm of *musique concrète,* though it must wait for extended discussion until Chapter 17. Sounds can be transformed through a vast array of equipment and finalized in totally different guises, depending on units used. Mixing of sounds to create many simultaneously can add to (or replace) sound on sound to such an extent that one can readily say that the limit of sounds together is only as restricted as the composer's ability to desire or create such. Both mixing and sound processing have been brought up at this point to acquaint the reader with the potential *concrète* uses of the electronic studio and with the hope that one will not consider *concrète* and electronic sources as immaculately separate but as useful tools together for the creation of music.

Besides the techniques mentioned in more detail, there exist a large number of other techniques for *musique concrète* quite as viable and often as easy to use: echo, reverberation, channeling (nonstereo effect), etc. *Most* important is the possibility of using more than one technique to achieve a desired sound. It is quite possible for one to use splicing, reverse speed, and panning in combination and in the creation of a tape loop. The multiplications of various techniques applied simultaneously is truly incredible and with only a bare minimum of materials one can create a voluminous supply of totally different sounds for use in composition.

Certainly a large part of composition must necessarily begin with collection of sound materials. However, the macroconceptual approach to composition can be effective in *musique concrète* (though it is advised that in first compositions it should not be applied first, as the composer is just not sure enough as to what his manipulations can accomplish). The experienced composer in this genre should be able to gain at least a compositional overview *before* collecting sounds or be constantly at the mercy of materials he may soon discover offer no purposeful direction.

Example 146 is a basic overview of a potential *musique concrète* work. Note that the basic constructs of direction, balance, climax, etc., have not been abandoned. In fact, in this fragile world of very complex sounds, these basics are often more important than ever for a successful composition (though indeterminacy has not been discarded; "successful" here refers only to attempts at creating directed compositions, compositions that go somewhere or work).

Example 146
Overview of possible musique concrète *work.*

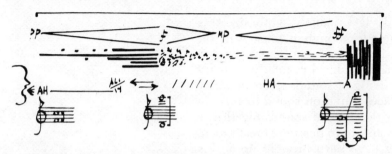

Example 147 shows a clearer close-up of the opening of the work, showing the detail of the techniques in use.

Example 147
Opening of example 146 in more detail.

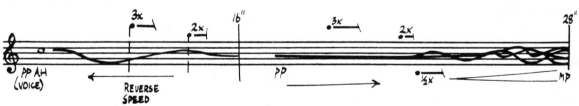

Two major points are important at this juncture:

(1) Any of the techniques used to this point can successfully be used in *musique concrète* composition. In some cases, broadening of terms is necessary, such as *polytonality* to *polychannelity* or *cross-rhythms* to *loop-rhythms.* Other techniques such as pointillism, microtones, and indeterminacy are subject only to choice of sound material and its resultant manipulation.

(2) As with percussion and prepared piano, new sounds get old sooner than one is aware (as involved as one can be in the mechanical processes of creating a sound), and it is important always to be able to become separated from the labors of the field and studio and listen as if neither of these were important, as if it were for the very first time with only the musical results remaining significant. So often works run away with their own techniques, creating a vast mass of effects contributing to little but disarray. Audience fascination with "trade secrets" and gimmickry is quickly lost (if observed at all) and most successful works are concise, balanced, and have only a few of the incredible array of potential sounds available.

In general, one must reaffirm the concept of evolutionary processes and constantly realize that this apparently "new" music has the very same governing ideals and directions of traditional musics; only the palette has changed.

ASSIGNMENTS

1. Record only one minute of *concrète* sounds, concentrating on only one sound. Utilize the manipulative techniques described herein to create a short unified work (with direction, climax, etc.) seeming to be made up of a large selection of different sounds.

2. Record a large number of quite different sounds, logging the numbers and type of each in a separate notebook. Use only splicing to create a unified and directed work of short duration.

3. Using tapes of only the human voice (singing and/or speaking), use speed changes to create sounds not recognizable as human. Along with sound on sound, or sound with sound, create a work from this material.

4. Record a set of different but highly rhythmic ideas. Make loops of varying lengths and, using sound with sound (or sound on sound), create a short isorhythmic work which grows through gain control during manipulation.

5. Compose a work for flute solo. Record the work and, through processes of speed change, reversing sounds, and/or splicing, create a tape to go along with the flute part played live (use leader for spots of silence in the tape part).

6. Using a stereo machine, record effects from the inside of a piano. Create a work by the use of splicing and speed changes only such that it contains concise direction, balance, and climax.

7. Collect as many sources as possible on one tape. Segregate each type of sound on a different reel and then cut each into a collection of small different-length tapes. Create a composition by arbitrarily splicing a number of these together. Be as indeterminate as possible (do, however, if the tape is quarter-track, note which end is forward by marking with a grease pencil). Add silence in the form of leader at will, and note the end results compared to other completed assignments.

8. Take one recorded scream of about ten-seconds duration and splice it so that no two (and there should be at least twenty cuts) tapes meet in original fashion. Note the effect. Create a piece from nothing but this tape by using speed changes, panning, and silence.

9. Compose a twelve-tone work for piano which is very lyrical. Record it intact but make at least two copies at different speeds. By speed manipulation and silent leader, keep the twelve-tone aspect but make the work *klangfarbenmelodien.*

10. Compose an overview of a potential *musique concrète* work. Collect the sounds and begin manipulation. Change the overview as any new possibility seems successful. When completed, make an overview of the final product and compare it with the original.

WORKS FOR ANALYSIS

Consult the most recent Schwann Catalog for current in-print recordings of these works. Publishers are usually found through libraries, music stores, or distributors of music. This list is not meant to be comprehensive, only suggestive of further study.

Berio, Luciano: *Thema (Ommagio a Joyce)* (a work primarily composed of many voices on tape; along with his *Visage,* most effective *musique concrète*).

Cage, John: *Variations IV* (collected random sounds spliced together in somewhat the same manner).

Cope, David: *K* (many traditional works by the composer fed and processed through a synthesizer and hardly recognizable).

Erb, Donald: *". . . And Then Towards the End . . ."* (work for solo trombone and trombone on tape with a huge amount of intricate *concrète* techniques).

Erickson, Robert: *Ricercar à 5* (work for live trombone and four on tape).

Henry, Pierre: *Le Voyage* (one of many *concrète* masterworks by this composer whose output is almost totally *concrète* in nature).

Kupferman, Meyer: *Superflute* (for flute and flutes on tape).

Luening, Otto: *Legend* (one of many early *concrète* tape works by this composer dedicated to this genre; many of the early pieces are simplistic but very useful to beginners).

————: *A Poem in Cycles and Bells* (composed with Ussachevsky and is a most fascinating work with skilled *concrète* techniques).

Schwartz, Elliott: *Interruptions* (for woodwind quintet and tape loop).

Stockhausen, Karlheinz: *Gesang der Jünglinge* (fascinating combination of electronic and *concrète* sounds with a minimal use of materials: a boy's voice and an incredible assortment of manipulations used).

Ussachevsky, Vladimir: *Of Wood and Brass* (a classic study of limited materials and effective use of them with tape loops and processing).

Varèse, Edgard: *Poème Electronique* (masterwork of combination of *concrète* and electronic sounds spliced together for musical effect and direction).

Wilson, Galen: *Applications* (excellent use of speed change and splicing as a route to achieve completely new materials from original sound sources).

14

New "Traditional" Instrument Resources

There exist within the framework of traditional instrument designations (brass, woodwind, string, voice, and harp, with piano and percussion discussed earlier) numerous new techniques for creating timbres quite unlike those previously explored. While Chapter 22 designates notations for many of the effects listed herein, the definition and performance of each new source in this chapter will be arranged by type of effect rather than by section. The reason for this approach is that many composers look toward combinational structures from many different instruments at once (e.g., percussive sounds from an ensemble of violin, flute, and trombone) rather than just seeking a new effect from one instrument for the sake of it. Therefore, rather than proceeding section by section (except under each sound classification), these effects will be listed together under separate headings as follows:

1. percussive effects
2. multiphonics
3. muting effects
4. extensions of traditional techniques
5. dramatic effects

Each of these general areas will be covered in the next few pages in the above order with the listing of instruments discussed within each area being: brass, woodwinds, strings, voice, and harp in each

150

case except drama, which is allied to all in somewhat the same degree.

Percussive effects on brass instruments include rapping, tapping, and knocking on the instrument with fingernails, mutes and, more rarely (due to possible damage), mouthpieces. Location of the activity can bring a variety of different timbres: bell (inside and outside), valves, conical bore section, etc. As well, rattling valves (key clicks) produces a rustle of sound and blowing through the instrument without pitch produces an effective rush of air quite magnified and different from just blowing without the instrument. Hand pops on open mouthpieces are effective (with even pitch being altered with different fingerings or slide positions); however, care must be taken to avoid pounding. For best hand pops, the palm must *slap* (not *push*) the mouthpiece, avoiding the otherwise necessary maneuver of having to pry the mouthpiece from the instrument at a later time. Rattling mutes inside the bell in either regular or irregular tremolo is effective, and timbre can be controlled by type of mute used and especially the material used for its construction (e.g., metal, cardboard, fiberglass).

Woodwind instruments incorporate much the same rapping and tapping effects, fingering without blowing, etc., as do brass instruments. Knocking and rapping music stands, finger clicks, foot stomps (though often coming under the heading of drama) can be used by any player—woodwind or not—to obtain yet further percussive sounds.

String instruments have an immense vocabulary for percussive effects. Aside from the rapping, tapping, and slapping by fingernails, pads of fingers, and palm of hand, there is a great distinction between one area of the instrument and another (ribs, top, back) as well as high, low, and middle spots in these areas. Important to note is that the cello and bass respond best and with most clarity to these effects, and with smaller string instruments (violin, viola) the effects are not nearly so resonant or loud. The bow can be used in traditional *col legno* (wood of bow) on strings, on the bridge, tailpiece, end-pin, strings between bridge and tailpiece, etc. These *battuto* effects, if done carefully, do no harm to either the bow or the instrument (however, composers often have to point out the use of a poorer bow for such passages, or even the substitution of an object of wood like a pencil). All struck areas, as well as object used, show well-defined timbres and even variations of pitch are quite noticeable.

Vocal percussive effects include short bursts of sounds in normal fashion but with little of the vowel or syllable audible, tongue trills, tongue clucks, lip smacks, kissing effects, panting, etc. The list is as long as one wishes to make it, with composer creativity being the only limit. It should be noted that the quicker and harsher the activity the more percussive it will be. Moreover, any other instrumentalist can effectively use vocal effects simultaneously with his instrumental performance. Many vocal percussive effects can be considered dramatic (inclusive of humor) as well, and one must be careful to note the intended effect in proper contexts.

The harp is very much like the piano, with numerous varieties of percussive effects similar in nature. Other effects include rapping and tapping of fingernails, pads of fingers, tuning keys and other objects against the body of the instrument. As well, very short (muted) slaps of the strings with the palm of the hand (hand remaining on the strings) can produce a very percussive effect with little pitch. Knocking, etc., on the body will (in most harps), because of the inner construction, produce a strong resonance much like the hitting of the crossbar on the inside of a piano with the damper pedal down. Example 148 is for voice, violin, French horn, and bassoon with the emphasis on percussive effects alone. Note the use of vocal effects in the instruments as well. Here, too, extra rapping on other objects (e.g., floor, music stands) adds to the overall materials.

Example 148
Traditional instrument percussive effects.

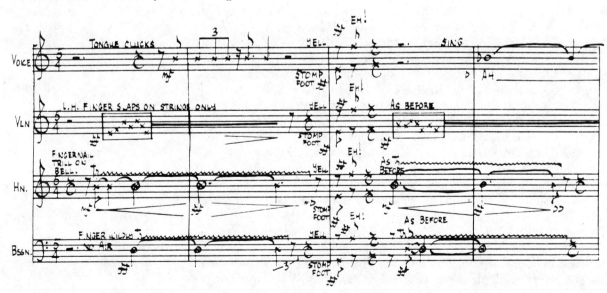

The general effect will be a flourish of soft percussive sounds such that probably even the most schooled of listeners would not be able to correctly establish the instrumentation. Of course, this is not a contest, and it is the extension of sound sources for musical context which is desired. It is also important to note that a great variety of near-orchestral effects become available in the combinations of sounds now possible (a point especially important when orchestral textures may be desired but the orchestra is not available for one reason or another).

Multiphonics (more than one pitch audible simultaneously from one instrument) in brass instruments is usually limited to singing while playing. Note that around unisons and, to a lesser degree, around fourths and fifths (as was discussed in Chapter 1), there are "beats" and, as these become faster and faster, a third pitch is produced (usually very low). With such effects, it is possible while singing and playing at the same time for more than two notes to sound. It is difficult to control or even notate these other pitches. The notation and performance of multiphonics—considering only the two directly produced pitches—is growing in popularity among performers and is not extremely difficult except when exact pitches from both the singing and playing is desired. Glissandi and relative pitch for the voice part is fairly easy, but two-part counterpoint requires extensive training for accurate performance.

Woodwind multiphonics are created by bringing out strong overtone resonances by certain fingerings and embouchures thought in the past to be ugly and unmusical. To the contrary, many three-, four-, and five-note chords are quite harmonious even in the traditional framework. All woodwind instruments now have published charts for the various fingerings (which should be placed above the note; see Chapter 22). Some woodwind multiphonics are quite easily produced, while others take a great deal of time to produce effectively and under exacting performance conditions. A thorough review of the available multiphonics on any given instrument in notation and sound is suggested before proceeding with composition. Notation may show a very consonant vertical structure, but resultant sound may be extremely dissonant due to microtones present and internal timbre conflicts.

Color fingerings are also effective (as they are to some extent in the brass) and involve the concept that upper range notes have many different fingering possibilities. Each of these has a somewhat different timbre, inflection, and pitch (microtone separations). In past musics, the performer chose the fingering based on the syntax of the work, composer, and period. In new music the composer has the option to alter fingerings for a variety of reasons: microtones, different timbres with a line or on a single pitch, etc. Example 149 shows a single note for oboe in which the fingering is changed with a given rhythm. The effect will be a flowing modulation of microtonal variations of pitch, timbre nuances and subtle envelope changes of the sound. The performer should not reattack any of the new fingerings.

Example 149
Color fingerings for oboe with rhythms for accurate performance.

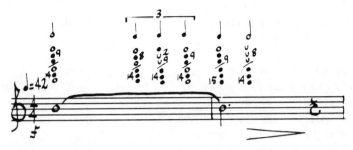

String instruments have a built-in multiphonic capability in performance of double and triple stops. Singing with the instrument provides another possibility, but since the timbres are so different in most cases (depending on the voice), this provides little advantage.

The voice can obtain multiphonics by gutturally forcing sounds. This can be quite effective but is not at all common practice and, when used, it seems more effective in its dramatic impact than in its multiple pitch possibilities. The separate pitches produced are not at all clear and only the effect of multiphonics is produced.

The harp follows the string classification with multiphonics as a natural phenomenon of the instrument. Various ways of plucking chords, however, do produce a variety of timbres (fingernails, pads of fingers, etc.).

Example 150 shows a clarinet, trumpet, and cello in a multiphonic environment of slowly (and overlapping) changing textures and vertical pitch structures. The excerpt begins fairly consonantly but builds tension by both choice of multiphonics and pitches used.

Muting effects in most instruments have become much more carefully noted (and notated: see Chapter 22) in the past few years, with a host of new timbres resulting. Clarifying exactly which mute to use in brass instruments is very important (e.g., harmon, straight, whisper, plunger, cup, etc.), as each has its own unique timbre. As well, with harmon mutes, the exact location of the stem is vital, as the timbre can be altered quite dramatically by different stem positioning. Mutes can effectively be removed and put in slowly, often creating a nuance on a single note that could not be achieved in other manners. Quick muting is effective (especially in trumpets and horns) with different notes then having different timbres as well.

Example 150
Multiphonic environment (as many as 9 vertical sounds for a trio of usually 3-5 potential).

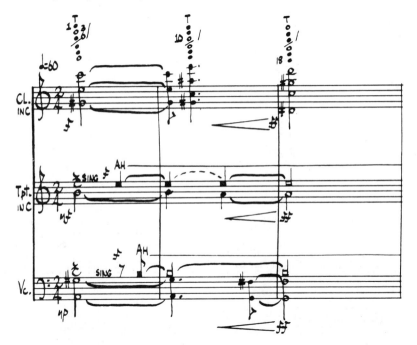

Muting in woodwinds *can* be accomplished in a number of ways, all of which, however, often become more theatre than timbre change. Performing into a deep bucket with cloth pile lining so that the open holes releasing air will be muted can dampen the sound to some extent. Performing offstage will certainly quiet (mute) a woodwind instrument. Some have resorted to placing part of the instrument in water for muting. The result is more humorous than effective in terms of muting.

Muting in string instruments can effectively use many harp and piano muting techniques. The traditional wood mute on the bridge is only a beginning. Hand-stopping the strings while bowing or plucking is quite unusual and effective, with the timbre and resonance established by the amount of hand pressure used (variable mute). The bow can be used as a muting device with left-hand pizzicati again allowing certain amounts of ringoff selected by the bow's pressure on the string. Clothespins, paper clips, and numerous other devices have been used to stop the bridge in one way or another with varying degrees of success. In this case, whatever the object used, the manner of application and density of the material will affect the dampening process; experimentation with the instrument is highly advised.

Vocal muting is usually done with the hand covering the mouth. This can be heightened by approaching slowly and leaving in like manner, producing a slow modulating sound. Humming can be considered a natural muting technique.

Example 151 shows a lyrical passage for two instruments (trumpet and viola in duet) with contrasting unmuted, nearly percussive effects in the string bass. Note the ——+——o slowly modulating mute effect in the trumpet line, giving a whole new subtlety to the melodies in counterpoint. As well, note the exact identification of even the string (Bach) mute (an important identification).

Example 151
Trio with contrasting effects on traditional instruments.

The extension of traditional techniques is manifold in all instruments under discussion, so no attempt at complete compilation is used, only some unique concepts which would lead the reader to further exploration. Brass and woodwind extensions are very similar and especially evolve from removal of mouthpiece for performances on either the mouthpiece itself or the open bore of the instrument. These get varieties of squeaks and squacks (particularly on the oboe and bassoon) to very controllable pitches (on brass instruments). Glissandi (as well as jazz rips, fall-offs, etc.), pedal tones (fundamental tones on—especially—brass instruments), flutter tongues (especially used now with varying speeds from very fast to near-triple-tonguing), circular breathing (a technique in which the performer breathes in through his nose while expelling air through controlled embouchure, producing a continuous sound for minutes at a time), varying speeds of vibrato (none to slow to fast, with all the subtleties in between), and harmonics are just a few of the extensions of traditional techniques on wind instruments. A number of these vary from player to player, and it is always best to consult a performer before expecting him to produce something which he has never heard.

New string instrument techniques include tremolo pizzicati (right-hand fingers one and two alternating fast back and forth tripping of string), glissandi (especially to the top extremes of the instrument, beyond the fingerboard), irregular tremolo, fingering without bowing (also an excellent percussive effect), bowing unique places (e.g., across the bridge, on strings between bridge and tailpiece, wood of instrument), circular bowing (a way of avoiding a real bow direction change, creating a constant flow of modulating timbres), harmonics (especially in glissandi), undertones (produced by bowing with great pressure, producing pitches often well below the lowest open string on the instrument), etc., are all effective in given contexts.

Vocal extensions are so numerous that one can only scratch the surface. Laughing, crying, screaming, whispering, whistling, talking, and mumbling, along with effects such as kissing, clucking, smacking, trilling, etc., present just a few of the more often used effects (often, again, more dramatic than for timbre alone).

Harp extensions include the wide variety of effects established by Carlos Salzedo (c. 1918) which can hardly be called new. One can only call these to the attention of the composer by suggesting that he read source books by Salzedo and others. The harp, being a sort of diatonic upright piano without the "clutterance" of crossbars, has most of the potential that the innards of the piano do (except preparation, which gets a bit difficult due to string spacing and the tendency for such preparations to fall off the upright instrument; some, however, are possible and effective). It also hosts a variety of performance techniques (besides the unique types of glissandi offered by Salzedo) inclusive of plucking *près de la table* (near the sound board) with various plectra such as fingernails, guitar picks, finger pads, coins, etc.

Example 152 shows a short passage for clarinet, trombone, and violin showing a few of the techniques described herein.

Example 152
Excerpt of many effects, contrasting and unified.

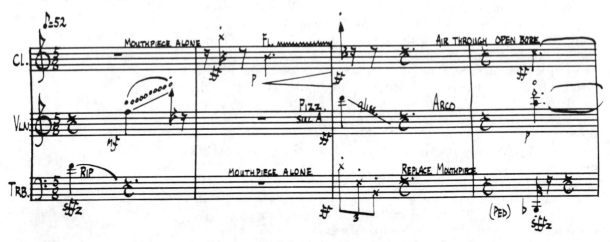

Dramatic effects are quite common in the music of today. It should be noted immediately that by "drama" here, the author refers to *all* aspects inclusive of humor. So often the element of humor is lacking in music of the twentieth century, as it is indeed lacking in audience reaction to the *intended* humor of traditional scherzi, divertimenti, etc. Slowly, however, humor is beginning to find its needed place in the concert hall.

Singing, talking, or whispering instead of (or while) playing during a work can be very effective in that each cuts the traditional concert ritual of actions expected by the audience. Moving about or leaving the stage during traditional performances is often used for all the instruments discussed in this chapter. Masks or unusual attire during traditional concert rites as well as different lighting are all very effective in context but border on multimedia techniques. In general, audiences of traditional posture are at the mercy of the composer of new music. Dramatic effects have little lasting value in most cases, however, in that second performances too often provide highly predictable results (this is particularly true in lighting and costuming effects). If the effect (e.g., whispering) is an integral part of the work, it will still be effective even after the initial shock value has worn off. This dramatic balance is a very difficult one to manage if a carefully constructed composition is desired.

Skillful use of effects is like all new timbres: if used correctly and without overkill they can be most contributive to the significance and musicality of the work. Example 153 shows at least one of each of the technique categories in an overview of a single movement composition.

Example 153
Overview of movement using traditional instrumental effects.

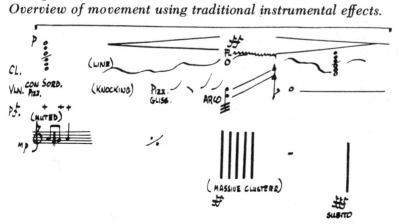

Note in this particular example the three uses of effects: (1) like effects clumped together for timbre soundmass; (2) the sparing uses of unusual effects with *line* holding phrase and direction together, and (3) the *klangfarbenmelodien* use of effects for contrast.

Example 154 shows each of these in written-out form for clarification.

Example 154
a. Like effects; b. sparing use of unusual effects; c. contrasting effects.

As seen in example 155, effects in this chapter can be used to contrast or promote techniques discussed in other chapters. In the first excerpt, interval exploration in the piano, though dissonant, is contrasted by a wide variety of effects in the violin (polytextures). In the second excerpt the four horns use mutes in and out, bending, and a final simultaneous rip-up to have the effects help the line, idea, and potential of the music's direction (a combination of polytonality and twelve-tone processes).

Example 155
Two excerpts of effects used with other techniques of previous chapters.

ASSIGNMENTS

1. Compose a passage for available instruments of quite different timbres (with no piano or percussion included) with emphasis on percussive techniques. Begin with all effects and slowly introduce a long lyrical line in twelve-tone technique.

2. In a work for solo instrument (not piano or percussion) use a number of percussive effects which do not jar other musical considerations of line, direction, climax, etc. Make notations at points where the effects work especially well.

3. Find and study the multiphonic chart of any available woodwind instrument. Have an available performer (or use a recording) to determine which multiphonics on this instrument are consonant. Compose a short work using primarily consonant multiphonics, saving dissonance for climax.

4. Compose a short movement for as many brass and string instruments as available. Select as many possible muting techniques and mutes as available and compose these into the work as an integral (not extramural) part of the piece (include slow insertions, quick alternations of mute and nonmute, etc.). The movement should begin very slowly and accelerate to extreme speed. Pitch should be based on interval exploration.

5. Create a list of ten extensions of traditional techniques and apply them as successfully as possible to any previously composed assignment.

6. Using as many available voices as possible create a work using as many vocal techniques as possible (though traditional materials can be used as well). Utilize them in large masses of similar sounds (e.g., laughing) as well as pointillistic techniques of scattering. Find a viable text for the thus created drama.

7. Research the work of Carlos Salzedo on the harp and compose a short work utilizing some of his effects and notations. Have it performed if possible.

8. Create an overview of a work for three instruments of contrasting timbres (exclusive of piano and percussion), verbally noting the types of effects used and where and for what purpose. Compose one of the major passages in detail for performance (include the climax of the entire work).

9. List at least fifty effects for as many instruments other than piano and percussion available on a single sheet. Make Xerox copies for each performer and improvise a work using these effects exclusively. Note the useful surprises and whether the work gets tedious.

10. Analyze example 156 for type of instrument used (as expressed in the techniques) and effectiveness of the effects for this short a work. Recompose the effects only for a better result. Options include leaving out any effect or effects as well as replacement. Perform if possible both versions.

Example 156

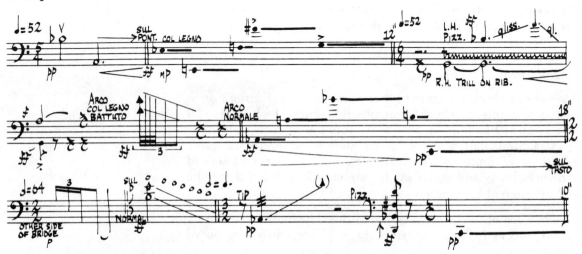

WORKS FOR ANALYSIS

Consult the most recent Schwann Catalog for current in-print recordings of these works. Publishers are usually found through libraries, music stores, or distributors of music. This list is not meant to be comprehensive, only suggestive of further study.

Bamert, Matthias: *Septuria Lunaris* (includes a variety of effects used quite musically; for full orchestra).

Cope, David: *Margins* (uses a large number of effects from every aspect of this chapter: trumpet, cello, piano, and percussion).

Crumb, George: *Echoes of Time and the River* (in addition to effects, uses the drama of players moving about on the stage; for orchestra).

Erb, Donald: *The Seventh Trumpet* (uses frequent timbral masses effectively throughout the orchestra).

Henze, Hans Werner: *Versuch über Schweine* (incredible use of vocal multiphonics and dramatic use of vocal effects).

Husa, Karel: *Apotheosis of this Earth* (uses effects sparingly but constantly, and they become so much a part of the music that they are not noticeable separately; particular exact muting in the brass).

Ligeti, György: *Atmosphères* (like most of his works, especially *Aventures,* full of effects of every conceivable kind used musically; for orchestra).

Oliveros, Pauline: *Sound Patterns* (excellent use of vocal effects in sound-mass fashion; for choir).

Penderecki, Krzysztof: *De Natura Sonoris* (full of effects used in almost every way imaginable; for orchestra).

Salzedo, Carlos: *Chanson dans la Nuit* (interesting work for harp, exploring a few of his own inventions).

Stockhausen, Karlheinz: *Gruppen* (for three orchestras; uses a number of effects in a wide variety of ways along with space separation).

Xenakis, Iannis: *Pithoprakta* (uses interesting effects for string orchestra, as does *Akrata* for brass).

15

Electronic Music II: Synthesizer Techniques

While a number of important considerations of electronic music were examined in Chapter 13, the elements of sounds created by pure electronic means will be studied here. Note that not only are many of the ideas discussed in Chapter 13 *necessary* here (e.g., tape recording and splicing), but others quite relevant. It is important to note that *musique concrète* is not the *opposite* of "electronic music" but indeed can be used in conjunction with it and the compositional techniques applied equally to both.

A brief amount of acoustical information is necessary to understand the concepts which follow. Sound is produced electronically by varying amounts of alternating current (AC). In a speaker, the back and forth motion of the AC is translated into magnetic energy which in turn pushes a speaker cone forward and backward (this then affects air vibrations, in turn affecting the ear drum, etc.). If the speaker cone is moved back and forth twenty times per second, a barely audible low sound is heard. If the vibrations are sped up to twenty thousand times (or cycles per second, now known as Hz after Hertz) in one second, a very high sound will occur (the human hearing range is usually considered from around 20 to 20,000 Hz, but is flexible according to the person). At 440 Hz the music standard of concert A will sound. At 880 Hz the A an octave above will sound, and at 220 Hz the A an octave below will occur. Once it is understood that any sound emanating from any electronic machine with speakers (such as radios, televisions, and output speakers from amplified synthesizers) is basically the sophisticated forward and backward motion of a paper cone (advanced as most are, they still form this basic concept) and that this motion is measured in Hz, the elements creating the AC (or electronic flow) can be considered.

Oscillators are the basic sound sources of electronic music and usually produce a standard set of waveforms (note that the output at this point is in terms of AC electronic current, not sound *per se*). The sine wave is produced aurally by an oscillator when it causes the speaker cone to move in a smooth back and forth motion. The waveform and the cone movement are shown in example 157:

Example 157
Sine wave speaker cone movement.

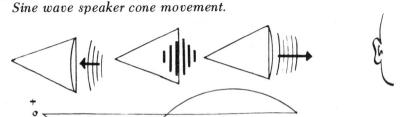

Note that the waveform is in reality a visual translation of exactly what the cone is doing.

The sawtooth waveform is shown in example 158:

Example 158
Sawtooth wave form.

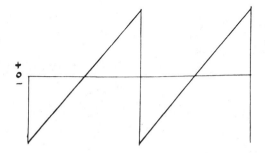

Note here the smooth and even forward movement with a quick snap back to the original position. Example 159 shows the other standard formats, the triangle wave and the rectangular or pulse waveform:

Example 159
Triangle and rectangle wave forms.

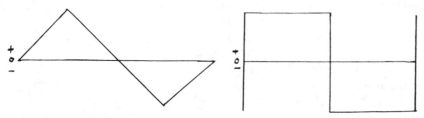

What is so significant about each of these is that they each provide a different set of overtone contents and thus different timbres. The sine wave (in the best of circumstances) produces no overtones, the sawtooth wave all overtones, the triangle wave every other overtone, and the rectangular wave a variable number, depending on the ratio of the forward position (+ portion of the waveform, called the duty cycle) to the back position of the speaker cone. Each of these formats (there are more, but these bespeak the necessary fundamentals) provide basic raw materials for the synthesizer to vary and control (i.e., manipulate). Note that oscillators usually have one or more *pots* to control their frequencies throughout the entire audio spectrum.

White and pink sound (often referred to as *noise*) are also very useful sound sources. White sound contains literally all of the audible frequencies simultaneously and produces a hiss much like steam escaping from a boiling steam kettle. Pink sound (as in the visual spectrum) is the lower portion of white sound (below 1,000 Hz usually). These add further to the collection of sound sources. Though at this point the comparison with *concrète* sources seems meager, the *control* of the sources is much more secure. Moreover, the electronic manipulation in synthesizers is much more complex and controllable than with tape recorder splicing techniques alone.

Usually the types of sounds found on the synthesizer are so limited that further timbre variation is required. Filters accomplish this by merely screening unwanted overtones from a particular sound while allowing others through. This is variable through pots, and the composer can control the timbre until he gets exactly what he wishes. The basic filters are *low-pass, high-pass, band-pass* (in each, the word before *pass* represents the Hz area being passed), *band-reject* (which is the opposite of band-pass in that it *rejects* a select band of frequencies), and the *filter bank* (which is a number of dials [pots] each set to cover an area of the audible spectrum of sounds). By using one of these types of filters one can eliminate unwanted frequencies while allowing wanted ones to pass, thus altering the overtone content of a sound and its resultant timbre. Example 160 shows the effect each of the filters mentioned above would have on the overtone content (timbre) of a sawtooth waveform (most useful due to the number of overtones the composer can work with).

Example 160
Various filtering of a sawtooth wave form.

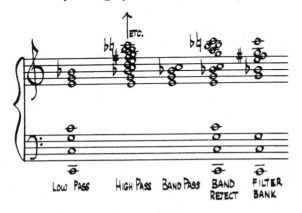

These filters are capable of controlling the overtones of any given fundamental for any conceivable timbre as well as controlling the passage of louder multiples of sounds such as a number of different frequencies (chords) and especially white and pink sound.

Dynamics need control as well, and this is accomplished by an envelope generator. The envelope of a sound in its simplest terms is shown in example 161, with attack, initial decay, sustain, and final decay being the major functions.

Example 161
Sound envelope and amplitude characteristics in simplified terms.

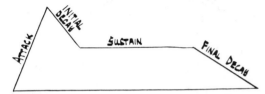

Most synthesizers work with these basic functions, though, to be sure, sounds generally go through much more complex dynamic structures. Envelope is an aspect of the dynamics of a given sound as overtone control is to timbre and Hz to pitch. Sophisticated control of each of the above "dynamics" of a pitch in terms of envelope gives the composer yet another tool for control of sound.

An envelope generator is usually a set of variable voltage outputs which need to be applied to a sound through its dynamic aspect only. Therefore, they are usually fed through what is known as a voltage controlled amplifier (VCA) and this brings to the fore the extremely important concept—in fact the binding concept—of synthesizer operation: voltage control principles. To avoid complicated definition, voltage control is an alternate or "automated" way to turn a pot rather than having to do the process manually. A voltage controlled amplifier is merely the tool that allows set timings of the envelope generator to control dynamics of a sound. Indeed, attack, decay, etc., could all be done by hand at any gain portion of the synthesizer or amplifier but can be done much more easily by presetting the controls of the envelope generator (thus producing small measured control currents) and controlling the amplitude (dynamics) of a sound passing through the VCA.

Another example of voltage control on the synthesizer is frequency modulation. Example 162 shows a pot being turned back and forth to give the sound a bit of slow vibrato. To avoid the task of manually having to do this, a sine wave of very slow Hz can be fed into a voltage controlled oscillator (VCO) and, as shown in the example, the same result is achieved. The hands and mind are then free to explore other possibilities of the sound and composition.

Example 162
Frequency modulation: vibrato.

Voltage control in terms of frequency modulation (FM) can produce yet further varieties of unique sounds other than vibrato. With other wave forms used at slow Hz, each form becomes an aural counterpart to its visual aspect (i.e., each waveform is heard slowly and clearly as a glissando of frequency [pitch]). As the frequency of the program wave (the intruding slow waveform) increases in Hz, it takes on audible frequency and the two sounds (the original one being frequency modulated and the modulating frequency) now present a whole new set of frequencies called sidebands (see Appendix III) which offer yet further manipulation and construction of sounds. The sounds become incredibly diverse and usable for filtering, envelope, etc. Voltage control can be applied to amplitude (dynamic) as well, creating amplitude modulation (AM).

This is usually accomplished by applying a "program" signal from an oscillator through the VCA and the result is tremolo of the sound. In example 163 tremolo is obtained by varying the gain control on an amplifier. This gain control can again be "automated" by the incoming voltage of a slow sine wave producing the same results (though more accurate and again leaving the hands free for other things).

Example 163
Amplitude modulation: tremolo.

Voltage control principles thus allow automation of instruments (theoretically any apparatus on the synthesizer with voltage control inputs can be then automated by various waveforms) which would otherwise take many technicians and a great many hours to handle. Through sequencers (complex units which permit settings of many notes to control any aspects of an incoming sound: pitch, timbre, rhythm, etc.) the synthesizer becomes indeed an instrument capable of performing extremely long passages of sounds without any hand for performance but that used for the "on" switch. At this point, vast potential for incredible combinations of instruments capable of nearly any sound imaginable is quite apparent.

Silence, however, is an equal and integral aspect of music composition and it is valuable to have something to control *when* a sound should occur: in synthesizer operation these are known as "triggers." A keyboard is a multiple set of triggers and is usually connected to the envelope generator (so that the keyboard trigger can set the attack of the sound in motion) and to the trigger input on the oscillator in use to control the pitch of sound desired. Thus silence occurs unless the keyboard is performed, thereby initiating the dynamic and pitch of a sound (already possibly fixed in timbre by filters, etc.). The composer at this point is the performer as well.

When a sound is created (by an oscillator), timbre selected (by filter control), given dynamic shape (envelope control), given warmth or denser texture (FM or AM), it can be "turned off" and performed staccato, legato, etc. on the keyboard by the use of the envelope controls with silence created as the composer wishes. He may then record and manipulate further in accordance with those techniques discussed under *musique concrète*.

Mixers allow sounds to be "on" but not necessarily sounding, as well as combine sounds. Example 164 shows a four-channel mixer (four in and two channels out). Note the inputs of synthesizer, previously taped sounds, voice (fed through a filter bank), and white sound (continuous as opposed to the synthesizer input which is keyboard controlled).

Example 164
Mixer usage.

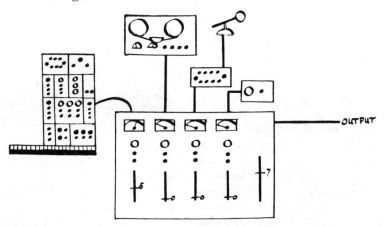

In this example, only the sounds of the synthesizer (keyboard controlled) will be heard since the pots (gain controls) of the other three channels are off. The white sound could pour in over the synthesizer notes if the respective pot were turned up. Mixers represent vast potential for combining sounds in various dynamic relations to one another. As well, mixers permit a sound on sound situation before recording and offer the extra potential of many sources in use at the same time, always at the control of the composer.

Most synthesizers effect all these manipulations of sound through one instrument, then another, etc. by using modular construction. Each instrument is independent of the others (excepting the common power supply source) and can be removed for repair without causing any of the other modules to be unusable. The connection between modules is then accomplished through patchcords (many use phone or phono patchcords to connect the output of one module to the input of another by use of jacks in each) or pin or matrix setups. Example 165 shows a sample oscillator with jacks for various inputs and outputs.

Example 165
Simple oscillator.

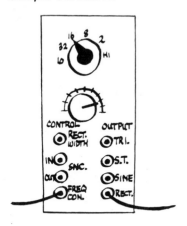

A wide variety of other sound sources (inclusive of all *concrète* sources fed through the synthesizer, usually with some amplification), sound manipulation (notably the ring modulator which separates sidebands from incoming modulated signals and rejects the signals), and keyboards (notably the touch capacitance keyboards which allow for dynamic control by the fingers themselves bypassing the envelope necessity to a degree, as well as the ribbon controller) exist, and many will continue to be developed. However, no matter how sophisticated the equipment, the artistic responsibility remains entirely with the composer.

At this point a number of compositional ideas should be brought to the attention of the reader. The concept of the "classical" studio is an important one. "Classical" electronic music is basically non-keyboard oriented (some definitions avoid even voltage control of any kind, but—excepting sequencers, etc.—these seem arbitrary and needless limitations). Sounds are created (*concrète* or electronic) and manipulated (particularly by splicing rather than by using any synthesizer component for creating more than one sound horizontally) to create the work. The process is extremely time-consuming with literally thousands of splices necessary to create a single work. The opposite of this is using keyboards, sequencers, etc. to lay more than one sound on tape at a time (without splicing) to evolve literally the possibility of programming a composition and performing it in the same time it takes to record it.

There are indeed good points and bad to each of these approaches. In "classical" studios, the composer has the opportunity to think and rethink each sound he wishes (for indeed it takes some time to splice and exactly time the material). While this may produce a more thought-out work, it is extremely expensive in terms of time and work. In voltage control situations time is really not such a factor, as indeed with sequencers and sample holds (see Appendix III) one can compose, perform, and record a composition of thirty minutes duration in thirty minutes of time (though this is obviously an extreme). The gain with voltage control and triggering devices is time, the loss is that of the composer becoming a performer on an instrument hardly in existence for twenty years (an enigmatic problem indeed). Most composers of electronic music choose a middle of the road procedure, not spending endless hours on a passage splicing together each individual note when it would take minutes on a keyboard at the synthesizer, yet at the same time not allowing a classic sonata (just played on a similar keyboard) to influence a passage needing care and deliberation only "classical" techniques can provide. Certainly a ten-fingered set of hands at a keyboard are no match for the infinitesimal possibilities of the mind.

Like any other music, synthesizer-electronic music cannot produce anything but sounds, and in the end it is the composer who must *compose.* Temptations of new timbres, new controls, and incredibly complicated patching techniques often lure the beginner away from music and into a certain realm of technical lunacy. Indeed if one tangible *new* concept is a result of synthesizer and *concrète* composition, it is the ability of the composer to structure *time* without the need of meters or even notatable rhythms. This newfound freedom is both a blessing and a conflict. More often than not it is this (and not the new timbres) which most listeners find difficult to comprehend about electronic music (though they very frequently cannot articulate the problem). In general, it should be noted that the human body and mind respond to sound as a physical property (which it is). When sounds occur so quickly or so abstractly in terms of this physical approach to listening, correlation must diminish or the listener must find new ways to establish viable ties with the communicative process.

Many composers confronted with a studio, no matter how simple or complex it may be (from a tape recorder and a few oscillators to a half-million dollar complex), seem to feel that every technique previously learned is obsolete and a totally new spectrum of techniques must be acquired. Nothing could be further from the truth. While rhythm has the capability to be "freer" (discussed in Chapter 10), any of the techniques used so far (as well as those to be discussed) can successfully be applied. The synthesizer is just another instrument for the application of techniques for creating music. Some of these techniques lend themselves more easily to synthesizer operation (pointillism, *klangfarbenmelodien,* microtones, indeterminacy, etc.) while others seem less mobile for composition with electronic sounds (polytonality, interval exploration, etc.). The ideas are not only just as valid, they often seem *more* valid. Tools which present literally any sound and combination of sounds in any time framework are tools with no frame of reference but their own internal exercises in sound production. Unless the composer can cope with the synthesizer as an extension of instruments with which his learned techniques have significant meaning, his works will be little more than sonic masturbations lacking in all the elements that make music that works.

As with all discussions of timbre, new sound overkill is often the first obstacle to overcome. New procedures, *once learned,* can often be utilized best by applying an advance overview to a work to determine what will successfully contribute to organization, direction, climax, etc. Example 166 shows just such a sample overview.

Example 166
Sample movement for electronic tape.

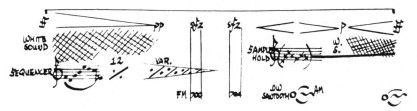

ASSIGNMENTS

A special note here should be made: studios and equipment facilities vary a great deal so that exacting assignments are not feasible. The author has made a special attempt here to make each assignment adaptable to a wide variety of studio situations.

1. Compose a twelve-tone work for synthesizer in a classical manner (i.e., each sound is separately put on the tape and spliced to the next). Make the work short and use pointillism freely.

2. With *klangfarbenmelodien* as a beginning frame (but not twelve-tone concepts), create a work on tape in a continuous fashion (i.e., the work is to be practiced in some manner so that one taping is all that is required for the work to exist; "real-time" composition).

3. Make an overview of a long synthesizer work on paper, including techniques to be used and creating direction, climax, and organization. Realize at least the opening, climax, and ending of the work in a combination of classical, voltage control and triggering techniques.

4. Using only one waveform from any source (radio static would do in cases where no synthesizer is available), create a composition by variance of timbre only. Allow no silence but just a continuous flow of varying sounds. Note the most effective length.

5. Using every electronic instrument available, create a work in which no two sounds anywhere in the piece resemble another (as much as possible create this divergence). Compose elements of direction and organization through use of dynamics and rhythm only.

6. With whatever synthesizer instruments are available, create a completely indeterminate montage of sounds. Make no attempt whatever to organize or structure anything. With the resultant tape of the work, create an entirely new work by splicing and tape loops. This time apply all the elements of organization, direction, climax, etc. available.

7. Using white-type sound of any kind (*concrète* examples are possible), use envelope (generator or splicing) and filtering techniques and especially silence to create a short and fast work. Note the capability of filtered white sound in short bursts to resemble percussive sounds and work with this element.

8. Using any form of programmed material (preferably sample-holds or sequencers, but tape loops if the former are not available), create a work using slowly changing and modulating ostinati (especially overlapped isorhythmic ideas between two channels on the tape recorder). Develop the material as strongly in traditional terms as possible.

9. Explore microtonal possibilities in oscillator sound production and create a work which uses primarily one timbre but achieves variety through microtonal inflections (bends, glissandi all included).

10. Using any mix-down device available, create an extremely dense texture of at least twenty-five separate entities. Listen and relisten to the tape and develop some aesthetic concerning the potential listener receptability. Use as many synthesizer techniques as you have at your disposal.

16

New Instruments

Creation of new instruments is much like that of new notations: do the advantages outweigh the problems? Looking at the problems first, one finds most significant the disadvantage of "practice time." One assumes with standard instruments that the performer has spent years learning his instrument and that adding a few new techniques for new sounds will not be overly difficult. Such assumptions are indeed idyllic for new instruments. The solution to this problem can be achieved in a number of ways; however, each of these poses a probable lessening of ideals in terms of the new instrument's sophistication and musical potential. Most obviously, new instruments can be constructed whose performance problems are minimal (that is, they are extremely simple to perform). While this does often solve the problem, one usually finds the simplicity of practice and performance often limits composition to the same parameters.

Another solution is to involve the new instrument in an indeterminate way so that no skill is required, no new notation systems, and yet a diverse sound is achieved (many percussion instruments serve as examples, though each does require musical ears and some technique: wind chimes, bird calls, whip, etc.). The major problem here is the level of techniques the composer has at his disposal, namely two: effects and indeterminacy. Some composers construct instruments which do not require human performers but rather perform themselves (or have other nonhuman performers). Wind-

WORKS FOR ANALYSIS

Consult the most recent Schwann Catalog for current in-print recordings of these works. Publishers are usually obtained through libraries, music stores, or distributors of music. This list is not meant to be comprehensive, only suggestive of further study.

Babbitt, Milton: *Composition for Synthesizer* (effective use of the synthesizer in a very controlled way, not using every sound available).

Blacher, Boris: *Electronic Impulses* (uses mixing and frequency modulated sounds with direction and balance).

Davidovsky, Mario: *Electronic Study No. 1* (as with most of this composer's works, this is done classically; an amazing virtuoso work).

Leedy, Douglas: *Entropical Paradise* (long real-time work with great amounts of slowly changing voltage control and trigger devices).

Ligeti, György: *Articulation* (a notated electronic work which is a combination of classical and trigger techniques).

McLean, Priscilla: *Dance of Dawn* (work very involved with sequencer techniques and other elements of voltage control).

Mimaroglu, Ilhan: *Wings of the Delirious Demon* (versatile combination of studio techniques).

Subotnick, Morton: *The Wild Bull* (composed for two sides of a long-play record, this work utilizes constantly the effect of modulating sequencers and other real-time instruments).

————: *Silver Apples of the Moon* (as with *The Wild Bull,* this work explores the vast densities and complexities of rhythm and timbre of composite real-time performance for a recording).

Stockhausen, Karlheinz: *Kontakte* (effective panning as well as distinct uses of both classical and triggering effects, though more of the former).

Wuorinen, Charles: *Time's Encomium* (work realized on the Mark IV Synthesizer with digital inputs for control of oscillators, etc.).

sound sculptures, fire-sound sculptures, water-sound sculptures are such examples, with the first word of the name being the "performer." As well, machines with balls moving with the energy of gravity can effect not only one sound but often an incredible array of sounds. Example 167 shows examples of each of the above mentioned instrument types.

Example 167
Examples of new instruments (see text).

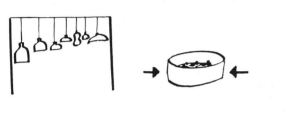
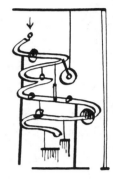

First is shown an instrument of hanging tuned jars and bottles severed at various points for timbre and intonation (a good example of simplicity of performance but lacking in sophisticated solo-ensemble potential). Second is shown a bucket filled with broken glass and, while based on a similar premise as the gourd, it has a dramatic new sound (though, again, indeterminate performance or use for effect is generally the end result). Third is shown a water-sound structure where an electric pump recycles the water so that it continually flows down, over, and into the various sound-producing devices. The last example is of an instrument of various channels, dips, and falls for a ball bearing which, when placed at the top, moves through the areas of the instrument setting off various bells, chimes, and occasionally multiple complexes of sound.

A newer idea is that born of the concept of *trigger delay* from electronic music synthesizers. Though not a great deal of work has been done to date, it would be possible to preset electronic sources to set off activities on a non-electronic instrument. This counteracts the problem of practice, as one can take as long as needed to preset the triggers for timing of the activities before actuation. This closely approximates the processes of computers in music (see Chapter 19) and, since all timbre construction is possible with computers, one might wonder (except for the visual complement) why the complicated new instruments were constructed in the first place. An incredible list of new instrumental situations exists with performers working with electronic equipment in live situations, but this is saved for the next chapter.

Standardization is a second major problem of new instruments. Certainly thousands of new instruments have come into existence during the past few centuries, no matter how "common" our practice may have seemed. Most of these disappeared as quickly as they were constructed with a few possibly still residing as "part-time" members of today's percussion ensemble. If one assumes that standardization is not necessary, then a possible solution is to have each work accompanied by instructions as to the construction of the new instrument. This too, however, snags in complex problems of what type of person would do the construction and what quality the results would be. As well, the end produces (even in the best of circumstances) no more than a circle back to the problem of practice.

At this point one must seriously question the reasons or advantages new instruments provide if the odds against their success seem so great. New tunings (with possibly traditional notations), new timbres, new techniques of composition, extreme personalization of style (new instruments, though possibly of limited technique, can provide completely new frames of reference and stylistic designations), extensions of standard techniques (the valve trumpet undoubtedly founded many value changes, but the result seemed worth the trouble), evolutions of new performance techniques (to avoid often shopworn habits of performance of many of today's instruments, limiting composer freedom and often—if the composer is the performer—limiting his own creativity), etc., are but a few of the possible advantages. Any one of these could be enough for a composer to attack the problem of performability and standardization (or just ignore them completely) and become a champion of new instruments and their techniques.

With both problems and advantages examined to some extent, the matter of active solution and prospects can be considered. At least one substantial reference point exists in favor of success: instruments, no matter how standard they may seem to be at any given point in time, have, throughout history, evolved and changed constantly. The prepared piano is, in essence, a *new* instrument (and a successful one in constant use) and shall serve here as an example of possible success in new instrument construction. It provides the composer with substantial premises on which to base his own construction:

1. use at least one major familiar part of a traditional instrument in construction (including the potential of using the entire instrument, avoiding any destruction of its normal functioning);
2. retain at least the hint that this part or parts shall be used in a traditional manner;

3. avoid immense constructions of wood and/or metal and secure standard musical materials or at least easily found and used objects of the human and natural environment;
4. retain a traditional notation, allowing the resultant sound to bespeak the advantage of the instrument;
5. develop variants and possibly families of these instruments so that one is not limited to a constant solo or concerto situation.

It is important to note that the above five ideas are not rules but rather suggestions; any one or more in combination might provide successful construction. One might very well choose a completely different formula and achieve success.

With these five concepts in mind, however, the author will describe through word and example the process for two such conceived instruments.

Example 168 is a cugaphone. It contains a familiar part of a traditional instrument (the trumpet mouthpiece), the hint of traditional usage (nonvalved bugle-type sound production), an easily purchased set of materials (length of 3/8-inch bore Plexiglas tubing and a household funnel for the bell), and the potential of families easily constructed by varying the length of tubing with a pair of scissors.

Example 168
Cugaphone.

The instrument can be used in a number of diverse ways with the greatest new advantage (aside from different timbre and easily changed fundamentals) being *direction.* The instrument may be played with the funnel (bell) in hand, slowly modulating the direction toward the audience back and forth, muting into the clothing of the performer, skyward projection, and so forth. Moreover, the instrument can be twirled above the head for a Doppler effect which is quite spectacular in both sound and visual complement. Families of cugaphones can be built to create ensembles of such without the need for any other instruments to be present. Each of the instruments can be constructed from varying lengths of tubings and, with composer knowledge of the overtone series and brass performance techniques, the instruments can easily be accommodated by traditional notations.

A second example is slightly more complex in nature but still follows the basic concepts for possible successful performance and usage. Using a harpsichord as both the familiar instrument and the hint to the performer that it might function in a traditional way, a large section of light wood stock is cut just large enough to cover the entire area above the plectra. With the knowledge that on the harpsichord the plectra move upward when a key is depressed, a new instrument is conceived with these plectra no longer being used as plucking devices on the strings but striking devices on objects attached to the piece of wood. The objects in this case are suspended by nails with their heads off-line from the plectra so as not to damage the plectra during performance. Example 169 shows the harpsichord, a large heavy blanket to dampen the strings, and the board in place for performance. The objects struck by the plectra can be different for each member of this family of *microchords,* with possibilities including: bells hung, finger cymbals of like circular metal objects which ring, suspended glass tubing, suspended metal tubing which rings, other items, or a combination of any of these. Tuning becomes a simple matter of choosing various sizes of the chosen object. It is possible for the strings to be used along with the object (i.e., no blanket) either tuned with the struck material or tuned in another manner. As well, the plucking surface could be removed entirely so that the strings would not be touched at all.

Example 169
Microchord.

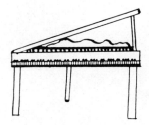

The board shown in example 169 could be tilted so that room could be made for the longer, lower-pitched objects. Performance could use exact traditional notation with the tuning so flexible that literally any microtonal system could be employed. If care is taken in the choice of material, construction, etc., no damage would be done to the harpsichord, yet the new microchord could be a viable instrument. Note that the wood is portable and that it can be removed and stored (once constructed) for later use and does not disable the instrument in any way. Unlike the prepared piano, the microchord does not require extensive redoing for each performance (a factor which is very time-consuming) or great knowledge of the internal structure of the instrument. Performance merely requires correct placement of the wood on the top of the instrument and a muting (or possibly nonmuting) of the strings in one of the aforementioned manners. Example 170 shows a sample wood structure for suspended glass rods. Tuning could be accomplished by trimming the rods as needed. Amplification of the obvious soft sounds can be accomplished by either contact microphones attached to the top (back) of the wood at specific intervals or acoustic mikes placed within the body of the instrument.

Example 170
Portable glass rod wood frame for microchord.

While the microchord is merely a simplified drawing board potential, it does demonstrate possibilities for the creative mind exploring new instruments. The cugaphone is a new instrument already in limited use in compositions. While tape provides secure control over sound, it does not supply very adequate performance situations. New instruments such as these mentioned, with their ease of performance and usage, can achieve a live concert atmosphere and even contribute to media presentations. While each of these new instruments seems a more modified traditional one, it would seem that for most purposes this is a compatible way to proceed, allowing electronic devices to produce further and much more complicated extensions to this list (see next chapter).

Compositional process depends greatly on the source, control, sophistication, and limits of the invented instrument. Multiplicity, or groups of such instruments, provide a successful air of metamorphic ideas and, though a sextet of varied and amplified microchords may seem a bit farfetched, compositions involving many cugaphones already exist. Each ensemble could provide an incredible source of new tunings, timbres, and combinations of such with performance secure and standardization unnecessary.

It is important to note that the instrument should not control the composer, but the composer the instrument. Often with traditional instruments one is confronted with a host of arbitrarily (or even worse, tonally) influenced limits. If care is taken in new instrument construction, these limits are governed by the composer, and his needs become realities.

Example 171 is a short passage for four microchords, and the beginning of a work. Note the notations for metal, glass, bell, and cymbal types as well as the traditional notation easily read by any keyboard performer. The difficulty for the composer now becomes (besides the necessary instructions for construction at the beginning of the score) the care of compositional detail with the finding of his core structure. If *music* is not the catalyst for new instruments at all times, then—as with the synthesizer—these instruments remain merely unique toys. Every aspect of the aural output must retain the often repeated concepts of direction, motion, balance, etc., if a working piece is to be achieved. While it is certainly possible for a new aesthetic to parallel a new instrument, it is more likely that these created techniques are merely a reordering of importance: instrument first, music second. While either cugaphones or microchords could easily become source material for the later-to-be-discussed "environments" of continuous sounds, one must constantly analyze whether escape from the complexities of understanding the new sounds is the true source of the new aesthetic. If the instrument is created with the new concept in hand as the stated objective, certainly not the least of conservatives could object to the viable reasons for its creation.

Example 171
Short passage for four different microchords.

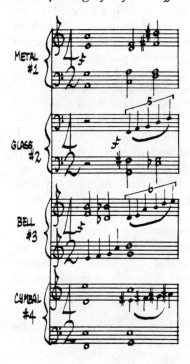

ASSIGNMENTS

1. Create an instrument whose performance problems are minimal (so that anyone reading music could perform it). Use traditional notation and compose a work for this new instrument (not using any traditional musical apparatus) and as many other performers as available (concertino).

2. Create an instrument of any amount of complexity but which is to be played for a single effect or in an indeterminate manner. Write a short work for this and two other instruments (their score to be determinate).

3. Create an instrument which is not performed by a person (except for the possible necessity of getting it going).

4. Compose a solo work for a new instrument which has been built using parts of traditional instruments for making music (e.g., oboe mouthpiece into a trombone). Have the work utilize the best aspects of the new instrument but also work as a piece (having all the characteristics of direction, balance, etc.).

5. Using a simple motive to create a new instrument (i.e., five minutes construction time), make a family of such instruments. Compose a short work for the ensemble using traditional notation. Use pointillism in a framework of *klangfarbenmelodien* (created by diverse approaches to the instrument: new performing techniques on new instruments).

6. Find as many unconventional sound producers as possible. Put these together in such a fashion that they are capable of producing a wide variety of sounds using one approach to sound production (e.g., a mallet). Compose a short work involved with interval exploration and avoiding constant attempts at exploring all the new potentials of the instrument in terms of timbre.

7. Create a cugaphone in B-flat. Write a solo work for it using graphic indeterminate techniques.

8. Describe in detail (on paper) the construction, step by step, of any of the instruments created above. Alter as new sophistications present themselves. Create a new work for the instrument—as structured as possible—and utilize all possible potential sounds available.

9. Create an instrument which has eleven notes to the octave (equal-tempered). Compose a work in a new notation which uses the expanded microtonality of the instrument.

WORKS FOR ANALYSIS

Consult the most recent Schwann Catalog for current in-print recordings of these works. Publishers are usually found through libraries, music stores, or distributors of music. This list is not meant to be comprehensive, only suggestive of further study.

Cope, David: *Margins* (uses the cugaphone at the climax for special emphasis; includes the twirling of the instrument over the head).

Crumb, George: *Ancient Voices of Children* (uses prayer stones and other instruments, such as toy piano, not ordinarily considered standard repertoire).

Erb, Donald: *The Purple Roofed Ethical Suicide Parlor* (for wind orchestra and tape, it also includes the use of coke bottles in soundmass as new instrument resource).

Kagel, Mauricio: *Der Schall* (as do many of Kagel's works, this contains many new and interesting instruments).

Leedy, Douglas: *Usable Music I* (uses a family of very simple wind instruments which can be played almost immediately).

MacKenzie, I. A.: (noted for his wind-sound sculptures, fire-sound sculptures, and water-sound sculptures).

Partch, Harry: *And on the Seventh Day Petals Fell in Petaluma* (as with most of this composer's works, includes not only new instruments but new techniques for performance on those instruments; moreover, the expanded families of instruments are all microtonal, usually forty-four tones per octave).

———: *Delusion of the Fury* (again an excellent example of use of composer-created new instruments in a vast form with practiced techniques necessary).

Varèse, Edgard: *Equatorial* (use of the new instrument *ondes martenot* which, while electronic, is handled with traditional notation and very much as a viable and successful new instrument, one which many composers have since used).

17

Electronic Music III: Further Extensions

A number of electronic music concepts can further aid the composer in search of particular vocabularies and/or live performance situations. In spite of the timbre, texture, and rhythmic complexity and control evident in both the discussions of *musique concrète* and synthesizer techniques, there is usually the problem that a reel of tape provides very little visual complement for the concert situation. While media presentations do present one viable solution to this problem, many composers feel that the elimination of the performer from the stage is a crucial concern. Performer gymnastics, potential mistakes, and particularly (hopefully) their sensitive performances can add intensity to an otherwise potentially stale consistency of tape playbacks. One of the most obvious approaches in solving this is to correlate a traditional performer or ensemble of performers with the tape. While this might seem an easy point to make and solve, there are indeed a number of practical and compositional problems well worth consideration.

One of the problems encountered in tape and solo (or ensemble) situations is the practical solution of how the tape is to be run. The simplest approach is to have the tape turned on and run the complete extent of the work with silences programmed in (usually with leader for careful timings and more complete silences). This can work, but usually leaves the conductor with a stopwatch and the performer(s) with little interpretative possibilities. Tape recorders are notorious for being excellent timekeepers and rather relentless at not allowing the performer any freedoms (thus often making the performance stale with the performer more tied up in trying to keep up with the tape than with making music). A second approach is to have a tape deck "performer" who at leadered points (programmed by the composer) stops the deck and waits for the next cue. This leaves the performer the opportunity of both an occasional freedom and the chance of making a timing error without resulting in a rush to catch up or retard to match the tape playback. At the same time it gives many composers and performers alike the added risk of yet another performer, doing a rather thankless (and usually offstage) job of turning knobs, and the constant nightmare of a poor choice of personnel and a missed cue by the recording technician. Neither approach is offered as best here, but rather both are examined for their possible usage, depending entirely on the context of the work.

Live performer(s) and tape also present the problem of dynamic balance between the musician(s) and tape playback system. Dress rehearsals for not only dynamics but also for speaker placement are a must (and especially in the hall for performance). As a general rule of thumb (unless a particular effect is to be achieved otherwise), speakers (like microphones) should be placed relatively close to one another and not at the ends of the stage (as is so often the arrangement). One-third distance from either wall with speakers facing directly forward often gives the best stereo results for tape playback. Regardless of the material on the tape (*concrète,* electronic, or both), the relationship between tape and solo (or ensemble) in terms of composition is a very sophisticated one indeed. Tapes rarely submit to a role of accompanist. By their very nature, electronic musics are capable of so many sound structures that no matter how large the orchestra or band, none could outdo the tape's *potential* for aural overkill. The composer must therefore be much more aware of the role to be played by each of the two entities: conflict, blend, interaction, and/or a combination of these. As well, he should be constantly aware of the silence potential of both while the other becomes a soloist. Example 172 shows an overview of a composition for solo instrument and tape (this could be telescoped for larger ensemble and tape).

Example 172
Overview of a composition for solo instrument and tape with conflicting materials.

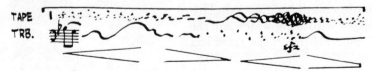

The instrument here is in total conflict with the tape throughout. Though they do change roles as "instigators," the result throughout is much the same: while one is legato the other is pointillistic, and vice versa.

Example 173 shows a blend of entities with each supporting the other with similar material, ideas, and timbres.

Example 173
Tape and instrument supporting each other: integrated.

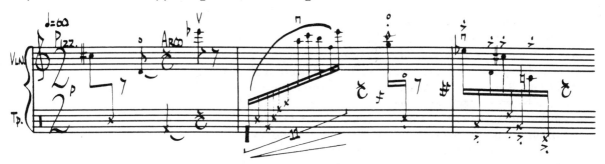

It is not an accident that both example 172 and example 173 represent the extremes—as many compositions do—gaining effective intensity, direction, climax, etc., not from the variation of roles but in the standard musical syntax used. Another overview is shown in example 174. It is a combination of blend, conflict, and interaction, giving the composer a constant source of dialogue from which to draw not only material (tape from instrument/instrument from tape) but a motion, a type of counterpoint, inclusive of stretto, evoking direction.

Example 174
Overview of a work for soloist and tape with blend of elements as well as conflict and interaction.

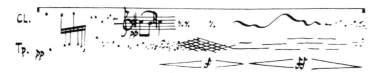

At most points in this example the concept is quite clear as to the delineation between the two "instruments." Choice of extremes is composer directed.

All types of relationships between performer(s) and tape are possible, depending on the context. Many times the choice will depend on a sound source provided by one or the other of the "performers" (e.g., a motive, timbre, rhythm, or articulation of sounds). Regardless of the motivation, careful attention must be paid not to compose one part separate from the other unless some abstract dramatic point is to be made. Often overviews, while being realized in the electronic laboratory, lead the composer to instrumental ideas and vice versa. This compositional interplay is vitally important to a work whose concepts rely on integration between the two sources in one way or another.

As was evident in the chapter on *musique concrète* (in an assignment), not only do a variety of sound sources (synthesizer and *concrète*) exist, but there is as well the possibility of a completely written-out score for multiples of the same instrument on tape—as many as will be in the live performance. From this point all is not as simplified as it may seem. While indeed instrumental canons and imitations between tape and performer can exist, they become somewhat stagnant after repeated hearings. *Concrète* manipulations (e.g., splicing, speed changes, sound on sound, echo, synthesizer processing) can be used effectively in regard to the recorded instrument parts, adding an incredible diversity to the tape, which then might be said to manifest more of its "electronic" potential. It should be noted, however, that works do exist with untouched recordings on tape of the performer doing the various tracks. The advantage to the latter is in increased performance potential (rare to have five tubas available to perform tuba quintets, but easy to have one tubist perform five separate parts onto tape) and economics (ten professional trumpets would indeed require substantial financial backing). An added benefit is the performer's ability to hear himself perform and thus learn more about his musical interpretations.

Example 175 shows a sample of three different types of flute and flute on tape. In the first, note that each of the flutes on tape is without manipulation and each part can be recorded separately by one performer, resulting in a flute quintet performed by only one flutist. A spatial effect of speakers being widely separated could add to the otherwise straightforward flute ensemble treatment.

The second excerpt shows speed manipulation of two channels (accomplished by recording the flute normally and then rerecording with speeds changed). Within this concept the composer can indeed alter the flute to such a degree that it might at times be unrecognizable. An effective way to approach this is to have the process be in stages so that the listener could observe the evolution of sounds, one to another. Modulation and interactions between a normal low live flute with a "tuba-flute" on one track and a whipping-about piercing high flute can also present successful results. The third excerpt has

Example 175
Samples of three types of flute and flute-on-tape composition.

been completely composed on tape by the composer and notation is only suggestive of entrances, etc. In compositional process, the flute performs various traditionally notated ideas onto tape. The composer then uses a wide variety of manipulative techniques so that for at least a part of the time the tape sounds "electronic" in synthesizer terms. Though often the taped flute may become obvious, at other times the complexity, density (clouds of flutes), and completely manipulated sounds give the listener only a suggestion that evolution may have been derived from the flute as original sound source. Choice of which type (or types in combination) of the above techniques to use is composer determined. It should be noted, however, that the first excerpt is the most difficult for performance circumstances, as usually each performer has to take the time to create his own tape (not wishing to have to follow the interpretation of another performer on tape).

"Live electronics" is another solution to the lack of visual counterpart to the concert situation. The simplest forms for "live electronics" are those of amplification and manipulation during live performance. Amplification is usually used for extended soft passages or, in some cases, to achieve an overwhelming mass of sound from a source incapable of achieving it by itself. Linked with manipulation in live circumstances, amplification provides interesting new raw material. Example 176 shows a double-loop setup for delay and dynamic alteration of a string duet during performance.

Example 176
Double tape loop setup for tape delay and dynamic alteration of two violins in live performance situation.

Note that the score in example 177 shows somewhat traditional string duet writing (polytonality), the two loop channels, the delay time applied, and the dynamic (often off), which creates a whole new work beyond that scored for the duet alone (the erase head on both machines has been defeated).

Example 178 shows a solo vocal line which is fed through various modules with trigger delays such that the performer (or composer/ performer if the situation at the synthesizer is improvised) can manipulate the sounds radically before they emanate from the speakers. In live performance and with both performers on stage as equals, the situation can be most effective with the observer aware that the sound processing is being accomplished by a performer in a "duet" with the vocalist.

Example 177
Example 176's violin duet and the two delays and dynamic variation.

Example 178
Live synthesizer sound manipulation (input; manipulation; output).

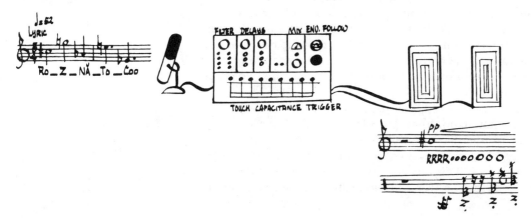

Contact mikes attached to the bridge of stringed instruments, parts of the body, etc., and then linked to reverberation units, ring modulators, and the like, can give a new vocabulary to traditional instrument techniques, sounds, and interplay. In example 179, the performer (a cellist) has a contact microphone attached directly to the bridge of his instrument while performing the lines shown in traditional notation.

Example 179
Live ring modulation of performer (singing and playing).

An electronic synthesizer using only a ring modulator (signal in—sidebands created—sidebands only out) produces a significantly different performance result. While only graphically shown below in example 179, one notes that the cello line is heard somewhat, but also (and much more loudly so as to nearly cover the "live" instrument) the extremely involved manipulated sound becomes the bulk of the sonic environment. The only true way to notate the end result would be to visually record the oscilloscope readouts from a microphone feed (or directly from the ring modulator). In free situations the performer could even be open to interact to the sounds the synthesizer has manipulated, and the two could improvise effectively.

In cases where the synthesizer is performed separately from instrumentalists (not manipulating their material), "live electronics" are subject to at least a degree of improvisation, as even the best of synthesizer performers need time to create the proper patches for exact live performance. This area of "live electronics" extends from a solo performer on synthesizer with orchestra or chamber group to ensembles of synthesizers without any traditional instruments present at all. The spectrum between these two extremes presents the composer with an almost limitless supply of combinations of synthesizer with different ensembles of other performers on traditional instruments or other synthesizers. Example 180 shows three excerpts from the various possible arrangements and samples of the notations (which, in the case of the electronic instruments, necessarily depends on "brand"; thus the obscurity of exact charts and only the presence of graphic hints). The first excerpt is that of a performer on synthesizer and string orchestra. Note the set-up time allowed (here the orchestra amply supplies the continuity so no extended silences occur) for patches and the accurate notation for the synthesizer keyboard. The second excerpt is of a solo performer on synthesizer for live performance. Here the notations remain intact with certain modules remaining "on" to provide materials to cover silences created by patching gaps. In this case a sequencer does the chore well with its diversity of pitch, timbre, and rhythms, changeable with a slight touch to a pot even while patching for another section. This sequencer notation often necessarily becomes somewhat graphic with only a vague outline of the frame of sound desired. Practice becomes ever time consuming, and the composer/performer must be a man of many trades to successfully compose and realize such works in live audience situations.

This need for practice is what usually leads larger groups towards improvisation, the subject of the third excerpt. To the best synthesizer performer the instrument is a beehive of knobs, jacks, switches, etc., so that one has very little potential of really interacting (as in a string quartet) unless the large list of patch sheets and notations for keyboards and the like are lifted (at least in part) from his shoulders. With this third excerpt for five composer/performers, one finds nothing but the embryonic impetus of an idea for which the performers interact freely in a discourse of improvisation. While exactly structured live electronic group performances are possible, the practice and dedication required for exacting performance is usually such that the work rarely lasts longer than the group for which it was written.

Implications of such live interplay can bring about situations in which the synthesizer becomes an entity in its own right: programmed for random triggering of modules so that the performer (often traditional, e.g., voice) is actually unaware of what sounds will or will not be manipulated (or even heard). This "electronic indeterminacy" can be a dramatic extension of the synthesizer operation: a real-time interactive system. A vast number of other interesting uses of synthesizers, amplifiers, etc. in conjunction with

Example 180
Three excerpts of possible arrangements and notation for 'pure' live
electronics.

live sources can produce limitless raw materials. Amplifying natural sources away from the concert hall, allowing audience control through voice, touch, or movement (usually through laser beam interruption), and other such activities just begin these concepts. However, most of these, while electronic, imply compositional processes of mixed- and inter-media, biomusic, and similar expanded concepts so that further inclusion here would grossly overlap other chapters.

One last statement should be made concerning the analysis of electronic music: while it may seem a bit distant since study took place concerning vertical and horizontal structures in music, such information can be applied through harmonic and melodic direction, no matter what the degree of complexity of sounds involved. In some cases, as with linear mixed selections of sine tones, analysis is quite easy; in others (especially *musique concrète*) it becomes possible only by complex and abstract oscilloscope functions. Regardless, however, of how complex a sound may be, analysis is possible, especially in generalities; and it should be realized that abandoning self-appraisal of one's musical rhetoric merely due to manifestations of increased complexity should be done not out of desperation or lack of guides (they are there), but out of the free choice of rational substitutes.

ASSIGNMENTS

1. Compose a short work for available instrument and tape. Program the tape with leader so that it is to be turned off and on at various times during performance, allowing the performer freedom of interpretation. Use *concrète* sounds only. Keep the tape and instrument in conflict throughout.

2. Write a work for three instruments, of which only one is available. Record two of the lines on tape and perform with one live, without the tape stopping during performance.

3. Compose a twelve-tone work for piano. Record it. Use every available process which seems viable to manipulate the tape so that the timbre of the piano is lost but at least some degree of the work's idea remains audible. Play the tape with the original piano live. Create yet another work (short) using excerpts of the best of both the piano work and the resultant tape.

4. Using splicing only, manipulate the recorded sounds of an available instrument (created by improvising from a single motive) while at the same time composing a line for that instrument (with the same motive in mind). Use blend as a relationship between the tape and instrument when completed.

5. Create a tape loop and observe its potential when two machines are combined (i.e., one for record and one for playback; see example 181 below). Compose a short work for three available instruments with tape loop manipulation and variable application of such through volume control.

Example 181

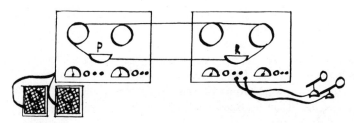

6. With any available electronic source, experiment with a large ensemble of performers on available instruments to obtain some feedback of ideas. Create a work for this ensemble with the electronic instrument as "soloist" in a more or less concerto style (not length). Notate the electronic part and the ensemble's parts as accurately as possible.

7. Compose a work for electronic instrument and solo voice. Freely improvise both parts from a given set of ten motives. The two parts should act and react as directly (but subtly) as possible with each other. The situation should be repeated with someone other than the composer performing.

8. Record a vocal improvisation. Use only speed manipulation to alter the tape. With this new (composed) tape, perform on an electronic instrument live. The live part should be practiced and notated as accurately as possible through patch charts and traditional notation if necessary.

9. Compose a work for as many performers and electronic instruments as are available, with group live electronics in mind. The degree to which determinate notation is used should depend entirely on your decision, after careful consideration, of what combination of notations will work best.

WORKS FOR ANALYSIS

Consult the most recent Schwann Catalog for current in-print recordings of these works. Publishers are usually found through libraries, music stores, or distributors of music. This list is not meant to be comprehensive, only suggestive of further study.

AMM (group of composer/performers actively performing live electronic music in an improvisational framework).

Berio, Luciano: *Visage* (tape and voice; originally a soundtrack for a proposed radio program; extremely dramatic with a great portion of the tape manipulated voice, at times such that it can barely be distinguished).

Chadabe, Joel: *Daisy* (a work for real-time interactive system in which a performer's sounds are fed into the synthesizer with Daisy, the instrument of chance here, choosing what variation and how).

Davidovsky, Mario: *Synchronisms No. 1* (for flute and tape in which the tape is turned on and off during the performance, allowing performer freedom).

Eaton, John: *Concert Piece for Synket and Orchestra* (work for live electronics and orchestra).

Druckman, Jacob: *Animus III* (for clarinet and tape; involves all elements of conflict, blend, and interaction between tape and instrument).

Erb, Donald: *Reconnaissance* (work for ensemble and live Moog synthesizer).

Erickson, Robert: *Ricercar à 5* (for trombone and four tracks of trombone recorded on tape without manipulation).

Korte, Karl: *Remembrances* (for flute and tape, which involves a predominant blend and interaction between tape and instrument).

Musica Elettronica Viva: *MEV* (a group of composer/performers who work with live electronics inclusive of manipulation of traditional instruments).

Varèse, Edgard: *Déserts* (good use of tape and large ensemble with conflict, interplay and blend used at various times for contrast).

18
Total Organization

Total organization is compositional process in which more than one parameter is serialized. The use of the word *total* here is a relative one. Just as indeterminacy can only be approached, "totality" of composer control is only a general frame in which the composer attempts as much control as he can. In general, composers seeking total organization do so by a multitude of methods and systems, many of which allow for intuitive controls as well as intellectual ones. Thus, it is often the case that the use of as few as two parameters under serial control fall under the umbrella term of *total organization.* What is significant here is not the *number,* per se, of elements under organized frames of reference, but the fact that pitch is no longer singled out as a sole potential for serialization.

For centuries composers have used organizational principles for compositions: melodic motives, rhythmic motives, isorhythm, specialized scale systems, and other such devices. Total organization goes one step further in not only combining some of these same concepts, but also in bringing them to a high level of consistency. Though numbers, as will be seen, can play an important role in total organization, for the most part they are not the central feature. While using highly structured raw materials, total organization can foster as significant a result as any other process (in manners not unlike the aforementioned motivic predecessors).

Total organization does not in any way *guarantee* that a composition will work any more than any other technique or process. It does, however, give some composers an extra degree of determinacy and built-in consistency. While theoreticians and those bent on constructing aesthetic systems suggest that total organization and indeterminacy are merely extremes the sum of which is very little, if any, successful music, the frame of this text suggests that anyone prognosticating the success or failure of a work on its compositional process alone is only destroying his own potential for hearing good musics.

Works involving total organization usually have composer control of pitch, rhythm, dynamics, articulations, timbre, tempo, and/or form. Organization of *pitch* is most easily achieved by twelve-tone processes and their variants (as was discussed in Chapter 2). Example 182 shows a row and its resulting box for all versions (original, inversion, retrograde, inversion retrograde, and all possible transpositions).

Example 182
Row and row box.

A	C	B♭	B	C#	D	D#	E	F#	G	F♮	G#
F#	A	G	G#	A#	B	C	C#	D#	E	D	F
G#	B	A	A#	C	C#	D	D#	F	F#	E	G
G	B♭	A♭	A	B	C	D♭	D	E	F	E♭	F#
F	A♭	G♭	G	A	B♭	B	C	D	E♭	D♭	E
E	G	F	F#	G#	A	A#	B	C#	D	C	E♭
E♭	F#	E	F	G	A♭	A	B♭	C	C#	B	D
D	F	E♭	E	F#	G	A♭	A	B	C	B♭	C#
C	E♭	D♭	D	E	F	G♭	G	A	B♭	A♭	B
B	D	C	D♭	E♭	E	F	F#	G#	A	G	B♭
C#	E	D	E♭	F	F#	G	G#	A#	B	A	C
A#	C#	B	C	D	D#	E	F	G	G#	F#	A

Though twelve-tone concepts need not apply to total organization, they lend the consistency of pitch language quite often desired. As well, with the subset constructions observed in Chapter 2, a suitable set of materials for variation is supplied. The row in example 182 is one in which the subset of the hexachord is the transposed retrograde inversion relationship, and will be useful in the coming examples for variation as as well as setting an example for similar relationships for other parameters. This pitch row—like all the other organization rows (rhythm, etc.)—will be used throughout the chapter in all of the examples.

Total organization of *rhythm* can be most effective when the serialization concept is understood. Example 183 shows a set of twelve durations. Note that the durations dovetail into one another to create recognizable units.

Example 183
Duration set.

The dotted-quarter first duration is complemented by an eighth-note second duration, with the third being a quarter note. The second three durations are the same but in diminution (dotted-eighth, sixteenth, and eighth-note durations). This hexachord of durations sets the basic structure for the second subset, with the use of augmentation in the place of diminution. Durations seven, eight, and nine are the same as those of one, two, and three, with the final three durations being augmented (dotted half, quarter, and half note). This presents a sort of "sine wave" view when observed graphically, as the two equivalent duration patterns (trichords one and three) set the gravity for the two variants (diminution and augmentation trichords two and four). The listings in example 184 show first the retrograde, then the inversion, and the inversion retrograde of the duration row. The creation of the retrograde and the inversion retrograde versions can be understood once the principle of the inversion is discovered. The inversion here has been constructed by interweaving the trichords so that the two equal ones (one and three in the original) invert their relationship with their two variant trichords (thus becoming two and four with the variants becoming one and three). The retrograde and the inverted retrograde are then constructed by merely beginning with the twelfth duration and going in the opposite direction.

Example 184
Retrograde, inversion and inverted retrograde versions of duration set.

An example of rhythm and pitch organization using the pitch row in example 182 and the previously discussed durational row is shown in example 185:

Example 185
Pitch (example 182) and duration rows used simultaneously.

It should be noted that the two rows (pitch and duration) can complement each other (moving at the same speed and correlating inversion, original, retrograde, and inversion retrograde with each other) or be layered (each beginning and ending in different spots). Many compositions employ a composite form of complementing and layering to give the composition the unity and variety necessary for "working." Example 185 shows category 1 twelve-tone process used with both of the rows (pitch/duration) in sync, suggesting the often-used profitable consistency provided by correlation.

For rhythmic variety (obviously needed in longer works), duration rows can use metric change, rests of equal duration substituting for notes, total augmentation and diminution of the entire row, and especially translation into other frames than two. Example 186 shows a triplet version of the original row:

Example 186
Triplet version of duration row.

Though these "transfigured" duration rows often involve some hairsplitting in terms of exactness, they do present recognizable rhythmic reference points and motives in new guises.

Dynamic rows can be achieved in much the same manner as duration rows. Example 187 first shows twelve dynamics from *ppp* to *fff*. The resultant row is built from these in trichords, each of which contains similar dynamics so as not to cause great dynamic change except between subsets. Note that the row is a soft-to-loud-to-soft arch form.

Example 187
Set of twelve dynamics and a dynamic row.

$$ppp \quad mppp \quad pp \quad mpp \quad p \quad mp \quad mf \quad f \quad mff \quad ff \quad mfff \quad fff$$

Row: | ppp   pp   mppp | mff   mf   f, | fff   ff   mfff, | mpp   mp   p |

Each subset (trichord) has the most extreme in its direction (loud or soft) first, the least extreme second, and the middle dynamic of the three last (i.e., *ppp* is the softest of the first grouping, *pp* the least soft of the three, and *mppp* the moderate of the group). Example 188 shows the inversion, retrograde, and the inversion retrograde.

Example 188
Retrograde, inversion and inversion retrograde of dynamic row.

R   p mp mpp   mfff ff fff   f mf mff   mppp pp ppp

I   mff mf f   ppp pp mppp   mpp mp p   fff ff mfff

IR   mfff ff fff   p mp mpp   mppp pp ppp   f mf mff

As with rhythmic rows (duration sets), the inverted version is built by interchanging the first and third trichords (the extremes: *ppp* and *fff*) with the second and fourth trichords. The previous second and fourth subsets move back a position to complete the variation. Important here is the fact that while pitch and rhythm must be a note-by-note progression, dynamic need not be such. The actual change from dynamic to dynamic may occur over periods of time set by phrases and often complete formal movements or works (see example 194 for the use of dynamics in this manner). Dynamic rows may occur in a note-by-note manner to help promote *klangfarbenmelodien,* and example 189 shows just such a case.

Example 189
Pitch, duration and dynamic rows together for klangfarbenmelodien.

Note here the rests of exact duration used in place of notes in the duration row of example 183 to help effect the separation; the two arrows show the location. Here all the rows are original in form. Note that the pitch and dynamic rows have not completed their course yet in this example.

A list of *articulations* is shown in example 190. Though twelve can easily be created, only six have been chosen here in order to underline that twelve is not a "divine" number. The row for our purposes is shown below. Again, the trichord gives the other three versions as shown in example 191.

Example 190
Articulation row.

• > — ʌ ÷ ʌ

Example 191
Retrograde, inversion and inversion retrograde versions of articulation row.

R ʌ ÷ ʌ — > •

I ʌ ÷ ʌ • > —

IR — > • ʌ ÷ ʌ

By interchanging the order of the first three notes with the last three notes (456123), the inversion is obtained, with the retrogrades of both the original and the inversion obtained by moving in the reverse direction.

Example 192 shows an excerpt illustrating the use of pitch, rhythm, dynamics, and articulation in total control (note that the dynamic row has just begun at this point; note also the repetition of articulations within the row).

Example 192
Pitch, duration, dynamic and articulation rows used simultaneously.

Tempo and form are both overview structures in that they rarely change in a measure-by-measure fashion. Likewise, they usually go together supportively. To that end, a tempo/form row is shown in example 193. Note that while forms other than the original can exist, they have meaning only in multimovement works (where one movement might be a retrograde, for instance, of another). The invention of a "row" here is significant in that the six parts are a version of the articulation row of example 190 (short being equal to fast; longer being equal to slow).

Example 193
Tempo/form row.

Example 194 shows a very short work using the various parameters so far mentioned with the beginning of an analysis (for completion, see Assignments).

Example 194
Short work of total organization.

All the "rows" of pitch, rhythm, dynamics, articulation, tempo, and form are completely intact throughout, with variation achieved from within the variations of the system and not from without. It should be made clear here that the microscoping of the piece into a very few measures for cello obviously distorts the idea somewhat, and that the potential is far greater than shown. Note that the dynamic row occurs only twice (original and inversion), the tempo/form row only once (less the final tempo), and that there is a very definite correlation established throughout of starting the rows together as well as maintaining as much of a constant one-to-one relationship between versions of the various rows as is possible.

Various combinations of organization of parameters are quite possible with the remaining concepts controlled by composer intuition. On the other hand, further total control can be had in pieces for larger instrumentation by means of *timbre* (timbre or instrumentation rows; not used here simply due to the lack of space for a chamber work to be composed). Example 195 does show two ways in which timbre can be structured (there are, of course, others).

Example 195
Two types of timbre rows.

TROMBONE   VIOLIN   FLUTE   HARP   BASSOON   BASS DRUM

BRIGHT   DULL   DARK   PIERCING   SOMBRE   HARSH

The first row is by instrument to be used in a sextet. The second row is created by timbres separate from instruments (bright, dark, etc.). This latter row is much more flexible, but being so it does lack determinacy from the timbre structuring. Rows of registers to be used (usually by octave, but not necessarily so), module to be used (in electronic music), or indeed any other controllable aspect of sound can be constructed by the composer to achieve more "total determinacy."

One must be very aware that the inversion, retrograde, and inversion retrograde are not the only possible ways for "organization" in music, and that augmentation, diminution, skeletonizing, and other such devices can all be used effectively. In general, the more variable the application or process is, the more it tends to bend the recognizability of organization and the values implied by "total" organization.

For those composers who feel that such consummate organization based on rather limited theories (strictly adhered to) is a poor substitute for their own initiative, one must add that, like the twelve-tone row box, these materials can provide a composer with a vast storehouse of raw material already integrated. He may use it as it appeals to his musical values and whenever he may need or want it. Immaculate processes, devoid of the infinite combinations of processes available, often tend to tire the concepts of direction in music as well as often equate style with a given process. Process is not an end in itself, but merely a means to an end. No composition need be "either/or" but rather can be more constructively "both/and."

ASSIGNMENTS

1. Complete a separate set of rows for pitch and rhythm (durations) with high degrees of subset relationships. Create all versions of the rows and from this compose a small work for three available instruments. The other available parameters should be freely composed as the music demands. A version of the rhythmic row should be used which is altered by constructing it around some other figuration than the original (e.g., if the original is duple, make a variant in triplets). Use rests in the row freely.

2. Analyze example 185. Continue and complete the example using the same rows and attempt direction and climax as well as consistency.

3. Create a dynamic row using twelve different dynamics. From this row create all the standard versions. Now create a dynamic row box. Note that the box is created in the same manner as pitch (the dynamic distance from each horizontal row creates the next: *mf* to *mp* same as *mff* to *f,* etc.).

4. Complete the analysis of example 194, carefully noting the various versions of each row. Using the same rows, begin a new work in a markedly different manner.

5. Compose a work for three available instruments in which all the possible parameters are totally controlled. Try to derive as much relevancy between each of the rows for the various parameters as is possible.

6. Compose a work for as many instruments as are available in which total determinacy plays a large role but does not dominate. Make decisions on when it does not, based on musical ideas. Analyze the totally organized sections in terms of rows.

7. Compose a brief work for piano using totally organized principles of construction. Analyze the work not from the processes used but in terms of Chapter 1 and Chapter 3 principles of strength, direction, etc.

8. Create a row of twelve articulations. Compose a work in which no other parameter is totally organized except the articulations. Use all forms of the row.

9. Create a timbre row based on five available instruments. Compose a brief work for these instruments. Though only five instruments are present, through the use of register, tessitura, etc., create a twelve-timbred row. Control of other aspects is completely up to the composer.

10. Analyze example 196 and, once the areas of organization are discovered, as well as the row structures (all begin together with original), complete the excerpt in similar procedure yet making it consistent and musical.

Example 196

WORKS FOR ANALYSIS

Consult the most recent Schwann Catalog for current in-print recordings of these works. Publishers are usually found through libraries, music stores, or distributors of music. This list is not meant to be comprehensive, only suggestive of further study.

Babbitt, Milton: *Three Compositions for Piano* (control of easily recognizable rows of many possible parameters in the variant forms).

Boulez, Pierre: *Structures* (total organization is evident here to a large degree, especially in rhythm and pitch).

————: *Second Piano Sonata* (highly organized around structured parameters, especially in terms of pitch, rhythm, and articulations).

Cage, John: *Music of Changes* (indeterminate work notated in traditional manner with each parameter "controlled" by an *I Ching* chance operation. With each aspect of a given note attached to a particular "chance," the work is totally organized, though by chance operation; interesting combination of two seemingly opposite procedures).

Messiaen, Olivier: *Quatre Etudes de Rythme* (total organization, yet based on 36 "sounds," 24 durations, 7 dynamics, and 12 articulations. Many of this composer's other works show marked rhythmic organization along with pitch in a most certainly non-atonal framework).

Randall, J. K.: *Quartets in Pairs* (included here because of its connective value with the next chapter. This work is computer generated and totally organized in that the composer is responsible for exact delineation of information on each bit of material; total organization here is particular to timbres: four, to be exact).

Stockhausen, Karlheinz: *Nr. 5 Zeitmasse for Five Woodwinds* (shows careful organization of especially pitch, timbre, and rhythm, though to varying degrees, and with freedoms often allowed).

Webern, Anton: *Symphony for Chamber Orchestra* (totally organized in terms of rows other than just those of pitch; timbre particularly contributes in a row structure to *klangfarbenmelodien,* as do rests in rhythmic structures).

Zimmermann, Bernd Alois: *Perspectives* (this work is for two pianos and is totally controlled from as many aspects and parameters as possible, inclusive of form).

19

Computer Techniques

While computers are technically *capable* of "composing" music, they do not possess any choice capabilities other than those that have been composer programmed or those derived from random selection. The two most promising uses of the computer in composing are computer-generated sound (in which the composer has a potential for "total organization" through programmed data) and computer aid (utilization of the computer's high speed, memory, and/or random selection capabilities).

Computer-generated sound is understood when the concept of digital and analog functions are explained. Digital computers function by data fed usually through keypunching cards or the like. Once a program (a set of limitations imposed on the computer for interpretation of the keypunched information) has been established, any parameter of any subject can be controlled (as long as the program and parameter match). Example 197 shows sample data fed into the computer for establishing the shape of a waveform. The two sets of points show the necessity of complete information in order to accurately describe a waveform. Note that the first set of dots is barely discrete enough to graphically give the impression of the desired sine wave form. Filling in a straight line from each point shown gives more of an "octangle" than a sine function. The second has a much larger sampling of the waveform and connecting the dots with straight lines easily produces a visual sine wave. Thus, the more bits of information supplied about a given parameter (e.g., pitch, timbre), the more exact will be the result. When a given waveform (sine, triangle, composite, and the like) has been fed to the computer—along with its frequency, envelope, modulation, etc.—it is necessary for the information (now in the form of "digital" stages or points) to be converted to some kind of continuous flow for the creation of sound. This is accomplished through a digital-to-analog interface (D/A) which turns these stored points or bits of information (D) into a smooth flow (A).

Example 197
Varying sampling rates of a sine wave.

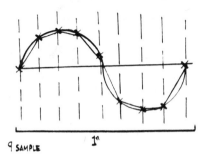
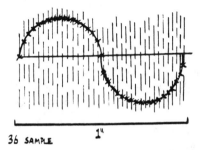

9 SAMPLE   1"   36 SAMPLE   1"

To further examine this concept of digital versus analog information, the simile of an automobile drive shaft may be used. While the gear shift supplies information to the transmission in terms of "stages" or set positions (digital), the steering wheel transmits information to the front axle in a continuous flow (analog). It is easiest for most commercial computer duties to have digital information in use for storage, high speed computations, and retrieval. Therefore, the composer is usually beset with confronting a digital input when in fact he wishes an analog output (in terms of a continuous flow of sound for clean waveform production; note that even the shortest of pitches can have thousands of vibrations or Hz, depending on its frequency). The translation of this digital information into analog information is accomplished through the D/A interface.

Once the digital-to-analog conversion has taken place and the information necessarily "smoothed out" as needed, the analog information can be utilized in terms of electrical current. The analog current can then be applied directly to the record head of a tape recorder and onto tape. The playback sound will be that which was digitally programmed and will have been produced without any oscillators, filters, or other such devices so commonplace with the synthesizer: thus the term computer-*generated* sound.

Example 198 shows the basic units of a computer-generated sound setup. The D/A interface is the object which most computers, destined for mathematical problems or paper grading, do not possess and the reason why there are to date so few works in this genre. As well, time is a great drawback, since digital keypunching does indeed take great amounts of time and effort. Most computer studios contain banks of tapes for the composer to study so that he will not have to wade through endless hours of experimentation (something that possibly a colleague or he himself might have taken up at an earlier date). A sound once found in the tape bank can be punched from the directions or program included (or cross-referenced in the computer if the program is still intact). Once studied and heard, it can be varied to suit the context of the work at hand.

Example 198
Simplified computer-generated sound arrangement.

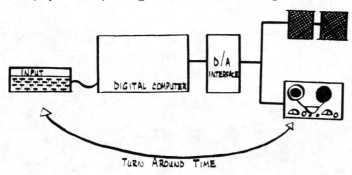

Complex synthesizers hint at potential analog computer design. The problem, however, points up again the difference and reasoning behind digital input. While the analog (gain control or pots on the sequencer) approach is far less time consuming, it offers the composer far less control than if one were to imagine a digital frequency control switch on an oscillator with each click defining but one dot of the wave form in example 197. In the one case, the composer turns dials until the sound he wishes appears (or one close to it); a very experimental sort of wandering. In the digital situation, the composer can define the most intricate relationship imaginable, carrying out complexities of rhythm and pitch that are nearly impossible from any other source. The simile of smooth gain (pot) dials being analog and the switchable frequency choices being digital is yet another viable definition of D and A so necessary to the understanding of the complexities of computer-generated sound.

While this general definition of computer-generated sound is extremely over-simplified, it is not possible within the scope of this book to define it in detail. The generality written above is simply to give the reader a basic orientation and understanding of some of the potentials of computer-generated sound, and show that it is surely a "totally organized" concept which more often than not defines it. One can, of course, shuffle the punched cards at the input stage and produce more or less random results. The computer, once programmed, will react to the input data as instructed and produce as viable an indeterminacy as a toss of a coin.

While there are predictions for CRT (cathode ray tube: television-type picture tubes) light-pen inputs and actual "reading" of music in traditional notation by computers with laser vision, it seems more feasible for the composer without the advantages of computer-generated sound facilities to seek the potential of computer aid as a significant direction in which to pursue computer music.

Though there are many ways in which computers can aid composers, stochastic methods seem one of the more useful. It should be immediately stated that no D/A interface is necessary with computer aid composition and that—while many composers avoid computers due to their seeming hostility or complexity—most of these problems are quite easily solved. First of all, computers (usually without D/A interfaces) exist in nearly every university or sizable business. Smaller schools and businesses still utilize computer potentials through a sharing of computer time by means of telephone connections with one large central computer. Thus, the computer *is* available. Secondly, the expense in many cases (depending on the work and program involved) is relatively small. The work to be discussed in detail here cost $1.81 to run in full (25 computer printout sheets of 1,049 lines printed) and execution time is very short (4/10 of a minute, or 24 seconds). Thirdly, vast programming knowledge is not usually required, as most students and many teachers and programmers take great interest in providing such information for music programming and/or running programs and providing printouts themselves.

With this degree of practicality in mind, the first step to the understanding of the computer aid is to realize that the computer prints out *numbers*. A random piece could, for example, be composed with a printout sheet from any source available (a waste basket at any computer center is quite helpful). Once obtained, each vertical column of numbers could be given a meaning in terms of pitch, timbre, and other musical parameters, and a selective process defined (e.g., 1 = A; 2 = A-sharp, etc.). A work could then be realized in terms of traditional music notation. Example 199 shows a set of numbers from a business program output.

Example 199
Business program output; randomly assigned musical parameters.

(articulation)	(duration)	(pitch)	(texture)	(dynamic)	(timbre)	(performer)
2	49.9	9.0	10.0	−5.0	0.81	61
2	10.1	0.0	0.0	0.0	1.57	32
8	39.8	0.0	0.0	0.0	0.42	29
1	43.8	0.0	0.0	0.0	0.0	28
6	0.0	0.0	0.0	0.0	0.41	45
1	43.2	0.0	0.0	0.0	0.16	39
2	18.3	0.0	0.0	0.0	0.0	33
2	33.3	37.0	14.0	−18.0	0.85	11
3	30.7	15.0	12.0	−8.0	1.53	29
1	0.0	0.0	0.0	0.0	0.91	22
3	43.8	38.0	35.0	19.0	1.26	32
2	0.0	0.0	0.0	0.0	0.68	11
8	0.0	0.0	0.0	6.0	1.95	36
5	0.0	0.0	0.0	0.0	1.40	12
1	40.7	0.0	0.0	0.0	0.22	8
2	22.1	18.0	13.0	9.0	1.02	50

If one were to assign each vertical column with a parameter of sound (as shown here in parentheses above each number), as well as define the limits needed (e.g., if a subsequent column below a number were to show only numbers between one and ten, it might be useful to allow a set of articulations to be assigned each number from one to ten), notes shown in example 200 could be determined:

Example 200
Notes determined by example 199.

While random computer aid in the sense of "pickup" readouts is a simple (though time-consuming) method, there are procedures which allow the composer a good deal of control yet utilize the computer for its speed. Stochastic techniques are the evolutionary basis behind the work to be discussed, which for the sake of continuity has been given the name HAGCOPCOM—computer language for Summers *Hag*erman (a computer technician whose help was enormous), *Cop*e, and *Com*puter; the three elements in the syntax of this work. The procedures described in HAGCOPMOM are certainly not the only ones available, but are used here as an example in order that the chapter not be just an overview of computer technology (a host of books exist on the subject already), but a discussion of how the computer *can* be a viable and active participant in compositional process and technique.

Example 201 is an overview of HAGCOPCOM in terms of form, and graphically in terms of general types of material, dynamics, and textures present in the work.

Example 201
Overview of HAGCOPCOM.

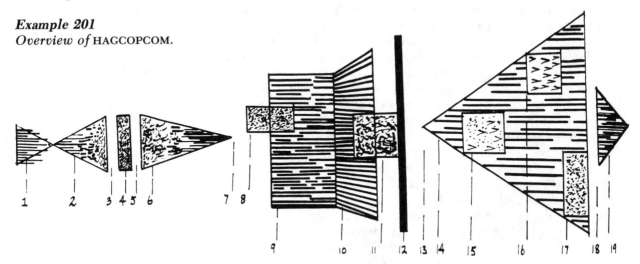

Example 202 shows the basic construct of composer control (utilizing an IBM 370, model 765). Note that the nineteen sequences correspond to the number of different sequences in example 201.

Example 202
19 sequences of HAGCOPCOM *provided to the program.*

```
CHOIR CONTAINS 8 RANGES
WCRK CONSISTS OF 19 MODULES
  12. POSSIBLE DYNAMIC QUALITIES AVAILABLE

CHOIR PARAMETERS SELECTED
RANGE HIGH LOW SNGRS BREATH
    1   62   44    4    10
    2   59   42    4    10
    3   54   38    4    10
    4   54   35    4    10
    5   47   30    4    10
    6   44   30    4    10
    7   40   23    4    10
    8   35   20    4    10
```

SKETCH OF COMPOSITION PROVIDED TO THE PROGRAM:

SEQUENCE NUMBER	START TIME	DURATION	MEAN DENSITY		EVENT DURATION		DYNAMIC VELOCITY		MEAN DYNAMIC		MEAN PITCH		PITCH SPREAD		DYNAMIC /SEC	TEXTURE	CLIP
1	0.0	5.00	0.50/	0.20	5.00/	5.00	-1.00/	-1.00	12.00/	1.00	42./	42.	41./	41.	2.40	32.00	0.
2	5.00	62.00	0.20/	2.00	8.00/	0.50	C.70/	0.70	1.00/	10.00	42./	48.	2./	35.	0.16	0.0	1.
3	67.00	2.00	0.0 /	0.0	0.0 /	0.0	C.C /	0.0	0.0 /	0.0	0./	0.	0./	0.	0.0	0.0	0.
4	69.00	3.00	2.00/	2.00	0.50/	0.50	C.0 /	0.0	12.00/	12.00	30./	30.	41./	41.	0.C	32.00	1.
5	72.00	3.00	0.0 /	0.0	0.0 /	0.0	C.C /	0.0	0.0 /	0.0	0./	0.	0./	0.	0.0	0.0	0.
6	75.00	51.00	2.00/	0.10	0.50/	8.00	-C.80/	-1.00	12.00/	1.00	48./	42.	41./	2.	3.00	32.00	0.
7	126.00	5.00	0.0 /	0.0	0.0 /	0.0	C.0 /	0.0	0.0 /	0.C	C./	C.	0./	0.	0.C	0.0	0.
8	131.00	32.00	0.50/	0.50	2.00/	2.00	-1.C0/	-0.40	3.00/	10.00	23./	35.	1./	5.	2.00	10.00	1.
9	143.00	32.00	0.20/	0.10	8.00/	12.00	C.10/	0.10	1.00/	3.00	30./	30.	50./	50.	8.00	32.00	1.
10	175.00	15.00	0.10/	0.10	12.00/	12.00	1.00/	1.00	3.00/	12.00	30./	42.	50./	50.	8.00	32.00	1.
11	185.00	8.00	0.03/	0.20	5.00/	5.00	C.0 /	0.0	2.00/	2.00	30./	30.	20./	20.	0.0	5.00	1.
12	198.00	1.00	1.00/	1.00	1.00/	0.0	1.C0/	1.00	10.00/	10.00	54./	54.	30./	30.	0.10	32.00	1.
13	199.00	10.00	0.0 /	0.0	0.0 /	0.0	C.0 /	0.0	0.0 /	0.0	0./	0.	0./	0.	0.C	0.0	0.
14	209.00	120.00	0.05/	0.20	10.00/	10.00	0.0 /	1.00	1.00/	12.00	28./	32.	2./	41.	10.00	0.0	1.
15	229.00	20.00	0.50/	0.50	1.00/	1.00	-1.00/	-1.00	12.00/	1.00	59./	59.	12./	16.	1.00	5.00	1.
16	269.00	15.00	0.50/	0.50	1.50/	1.50	1.00/	1.00	1.00/	12.00	35./	35.	10./	14.	1.50	5.00	1.
17	299.00	30.00	3.00/	3.00	0.30/	0.30	1.00/	1.00	12.00/	12.00	30./	30.	20./	40.	0.0	7.00	1.
18	329.00	8.00	0.0 /	0.0	0.0 /	0.0	C.C /	0.0	0.0 /	0.0	0./	0.	0./	0.	0.0	0.0	0.
19	337.00	50.00	0.30/	0.05	3.00/	12.00	-1.00/	-1.00	8.00/	1.00	25./	44.	41./	1.	7.00	32.00	0.

Before progressing to discussion of the vertical columns themselves, it would be appropriate at this point to review some
general stochastic techniques. Probability theory is such that if
enough events occur in similar fashion and circumstances, the result
is very nearly the same in every occurrence. If one were to select ten
thousand ping-pong balls and dump them simultaneously on three
different occasions into an empty room from above and record the
resultant sound events, the three soundmasses would be very
similar, if in fact any aural difference could be detected at all.
Though the ping-pong balls react, reflect, and bounce in different
ways in each of the three "dumps," the number of events tends to
merge the totality into a homogeneous and predictable sound. The
randomness is under stochastic order. Translated to computer
technology, one finds that the computer can be incredibly accurate
in random outputs. It multiplies the ten thousand ping-pong balls
by a sizable number indeed. The composer can, however, limit the
random aspects so that they conform to his own uses and desires.

Looking back at example 202, one finds that for each sequence a
set of limits is set for the computer to choose materials. The
"start time" for each sequence is completely composer-controlled,
as is the duration of each sequence. Under "mean density" the
composer-defined program allows for 1.00 as the complete ensemble
(in this case, 32 voices and instruments total) texture. The left figure
is the beginning density of the sequence and the right figure, the
ending density. Thus, here there is lessening of texture (from 0.50 to
0.20) but the process of selection of how and what voices are left out
is randomly decided by the computer. "Event duration" is in
seconds around which the computer may choose various durations
as long as the tendency of duration is five seconds. At this point it is
appropriate to mention the last two columns. "Clip" tells the
computer (when on "1") to stop all sounds for exact cutoffs (or when
on "0" to allow whatever durations which may have started late in
the sequence and/or have durations longer than the sequence by
computer chance [e.g., ten seconds] to continue to completion). In
effect, "clipping" allows the composer to achieve exact breaks of the
entire ensemble or allow random event durations to overlap into the
next section. "Texture" (second-to-last column) is another "clip"
device used to avoid overkill. When a number is present it gives the
computer the exact number of voices to be present (i.e., even if 32 is
the fullest texture, the computer's random sampling may come up
with 17, and thus "crossing" composer intention for tutti at given
points). Both these last columns allow the composer to set limits on
the computer's random movements to avoid complete destruction of
composer intent for a given section ("clip" in terms of cutoff and

"texture" in terms of the occasional need for exact numbers of voices for effective realization of the score).

"Dynamic velocity" is measured from −1 to +1 (i.e., speed of dynamic change: if dynamics given in next column were 12.00/1.00 at −1 to −1, the change would be slow and even, whereas if the velocity were −1 to +1, the dynamic change would be incredibly drastic: *fff* to *ppp* in possibly fractions of seconds). "Mean dynamic" uses twelve dynamics (see Chapter 18 for an example of this) and shows what dynamic will appear at the beginning of the sequence and what will be present at the end (in this case, *fff* to *ppp,* but evenly measured over the event duration due to constant dynamic velocity). Pitch in this example is keyboard-oriented. Example 203 shows the pitch-numbering used. With this in mind, "mean-pitch" designation shown in example 202 simply means the center pitch area is 42 (or D above middle C) at the beginning and end of the sequence number 1. The computer is then allowed to choose pitches around that 42 within the "pitch spread" (41 here means 20½ up and 20½ down from the given D under mean pitch). Thus, the result of this arrangement should give more than one D, with a random selection of pitches from that D upward and downward twenty or so half steps (i.e., a very large pitch spread). "Dynamic/sec." gives the average in seconds of the mean dynamic velocity (columns six and five). Example 202 is example 201 in the frame of composer control and gives the limits to the computer of what indeed it can "randomly" select. Note that horizontal sequence 5 (Example 202) has but a start time (72 seconds into the work) and a duration time (3 seconds), with all other information being zero. Correlating this with example 201, one will find that sequence 5 is complete silence. There is no computer choice here, only silence.

Example 204 is sequence 1 run with the program. Note how the composer translates the numbers into musical symbols for performance. The first horizontal line states that the voice/instrument begins at the very beginning (0.0) with pitch 22 (F-sharp, the space below

Example 203
Keyboard pitch numbering for example 202.

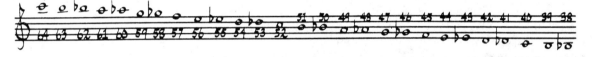

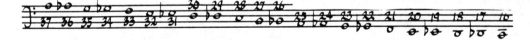

the bass staff). The duration here was randomly chosen at ten seconds, even though the sequence (section) was to last only five seconds. With the "clip" of sequence 1 off, such random selections produce slow transitions and modulations from one section to another. The dynamic begins at 12 (*fff*) and goes to −11 (diminishes to *mppp*), is sung or played by designated performer one in section number 8 (these are freely translatable variables such that the work could be for eight sections with four members in each; for orientation the eight sections were programmed with the ranges of SSAATTBB choral setting, though such need not necessarily be the chosen ensemble):

Example 204
Sequence 1 of HAGCOPCOM *in computer printout.*

```
SEQUENCE NUMBER  1           START TIME     0.0  SECONDS FROM START OF PIECE
       START                     STARTING  CRESC. OR   SUNG BY    IN SECTION
    N  TIME    PITCH  DURATION   DYNAMIC   DIMIN. TO   NUMBER     NUMBER
    1  0.0      22    10.00        12        -11         1           8
    1  0.0      25    10.00        12        -11         1           7
    1  0.0      28    10.00        12        -11         2           7
    1  0.0      55    10.00        12        -11         1           1
    1  0.0      42    10.00        12        -11         1           2
    1  0.0      53     5.35        12          0         2           1
    1  0.0      49     3.06        12          5         3           1
    1  0.0      45     9.71        12        -10         4           1
    1  0.0      55    10.00        12        -11         2           2
    1  0.0      29    10.00        12        -11         3           7
    1  0.0      42     5.01        12          0         3           2
    1  0.0      43     0.93        12         10         4           2
    1  0.0      39     5.36        12          0         1           3
    1  0.0      44     4.06        12          2         2           3
    1  0.0      42    10.00        12        -11         3           3
    1  0.0      52    10.00        12        -11         4           3
    1  0.0      33     0.97        12         10         1           5
    1  0.0      45    10.00        12        -11         1           4
*** TEXTURE INCREASING *** PROGRAM SEARCHING FOR SINGER   PRESENT DENSITY= 0.50
    1  0.0      41     9.79        12        -11         2           4
    1  0.0      39     0.78        12         10         3           4
    1  0.0      49     0.18        12         12         4           4
    1  0.0      33    10.00        12        -11         2           5
    1  0.0      41    10.00        12        -11         3           5
    1  0.0      33     4.78        12          1         4           5
*** TEXTURE INCREASING *** PROGRAM SEARCHING FOR SINGER   PRESENT DENSITY= 0.50
    1  0.0      36     0.27        12         11         1           6
    1  0.0      30     4.75        12          1         2           6
*** TEXTURE INCREASING *** PROGRAM SEARCHING FOR SINGER   PRESENT DENSITY= 0.50
    2  0.10     32     4.68        12          1         3           6
    3  2.77     43     7.83        12         -6         4           2
    4  11.22    42     0.43         6          5         1           2
```

Example 205 shows the opening of HAGCOPCOM and a complete translation of sequence 1 in example 204, excepting complete durations.

While much of this may need rereading for complete digestion, it should prove valuable. Quite skeptical about this form of computer usage before beginning HAGCOPCOM, the author became almost immediately a constant learner of his own style. The first printout of sequence 1 showed ten-second and longer event durations randomly chosen by the computer in what was conceived as a five-second *section*. Before clipping it, the surprise offered the question of why this would not work (overlaying of section endings

Example 205
Opening of HAGCOPCOM *in traditional notation.*

with beginnings). Obviously it can and has worked quite often in a great many musics, yet it seemed to this observer to be *out of style*. Analytical study of other of the author's works provided valuable insight: these works often proved too predictably sectional. A lesson learned, the elongated surprises of this sequence were left in as transition. The output as translated in example 205 is indeed loaded with Ds, as was earlier predicted, and the remaining notes scattered in an indiscriminate manner. While the computer can create possibilities, the composer can only surmise or envision at best; the computer does have a complete separation from artistic standards. The compositional process from this point on was a more or less keeping of what tended to work and a changing or dropping of what didn't. The effect of the opening chord, for example, as shown in example 205, is loaded with unison Ds. While these were left in, however, the nonovertone series construction of the chord was not, as the lower notes proved only to weight the chord into a bass mass of sounds with pitches barely recognizable (something the composer did not wish). These lower notes were simply range-altered (or even left out if duplicated higher in the chord) to give more space to the lower chord area. With the more or less constant soundmass (though very much spread), constant timbre and articulation (nonprogrammed elements) become vital and choice of instrument and effect (violin: pizzicato, etc.) could be composer-controlled to fit the design of the work or even possibly assigned to a given column already extant in the program for a random approach.

The computer in this work serves as a speed processor, surprise maker, and a prolific provider of raw materials within composer-prescribed limitations. While HAGCOPCOM is not an exact stochastic treatment (far too few "ping-pong balls" [32] to give predictable results), it did prove to be a highly successful self-teaching device (both in regard to what should and should not be composer-controlled, and a device for reevaluating one's composition *habits*). It did secure very random clouds of sound at times, thus proving valuable in at least some potential of stochasticism. It constantly challenged composer ideals in its completely inartistic and unprejudiced outputs. While transcribing HAGCOPCOM and similar compositions takes great amounts of time (possibly equal to the experimenting of computer-generated sound), the results for at least one full effort seem quite distinctly positive. The end result is to be performed live and not on tape (as computer-generated sound), with the resulting imperfections of a performance situation, but as well the visual complement of something other than playback equipment.

Detailing HAGCOPCOM was not a choice born of prejudice in types of computer composition, but purely of available resources to readers as well as space for discussion. Appendix II gives a select list of books excellently designed for further study into computer-generated sound and other types of computer composition, all of which the author hopes the reader will aggressively devour. Computers are incredibly versatile beasts of burden. They are more than competent at doing what they are told to do (quickly and accurately). Computer technology has just begun, and the future holds a great variety of uses for this instrument, many of which will become standard technologies for performance of *human* (composer) directions, organization, balance, etc. Its variants and futures extend as far as imagination will allow.

ASSIGNMENTS

1. Locate any computer printout sheet from any source. Carefully examine it for any suggestions which might lend themselves to particular parameter interpretation. Place the chosen parameters and at least begin the work for piano. Complete enough that it can be performed.

2. Transcribe the first ten numbers of sequence 2 of HAGCOPCOM as shown in example 206. Divorce it from the composition described in the chapter and treat the translation as an element in itself. Make clear choices as to what works and what does not. Define clearly the reasons for those elements which do not work.

Example 206

```
SEQUENCE NUMBER  2           START TIME     5.00 SECONDS FROM START OF PIECE

          START                    STARTING  CRESC. OR   SUNG BY   IN SECTION
     N    TIME   PITCH   DURATION   DYNAMIC   DIMIN. TO   NUMBER    NUMBER
     1    5.00    42     10.00        1          2          2         3
     2    9.32    43      4.77        1          2          3         2.
     3   10.30    43      2.24        2          2          2         2'
     4   11.90    40     10.00        2          3          1         3
     5   12.46    42      8.37        2          3          1         2'
     6   14.16    42      9.20        2          3          2         2'
     7   15.99    43     10.00        2          4          3         2
     8   16.34    45     10.00        3          3          1         1
     9   16.80    43      3.44        3          3          4         2
    10   17.99    45      5.11        3          3          2         1
```

3. Analyze the chord shown in example 205 according to the principles discussed at the beginning of this book. Construct a new chord but based on this one which is stronger and more overtone-oriented. Use the new chord to create a short work for three available instruments (the notes obviously becoming melodic more than harmonic; the vocabulary is the important element to keep intact).

4. Using the computer printout of sequence 1, switch the meanings in either a random or intellectual way so that they no longer represent the column previously designated. Translate the new sequence into traditional musical symbols for two-piano performance.

5. Using example 205, choose a set of instruments which you feel would effectively render the chord. Use piano, etc. in order to get all the notes performed. Do not change any note or duration or make any octave displacement.

6. Create a simple computer program with any student, teacher, or available person. Create a short piece by using an overview process and complete the work for any available instruments in traditional notation.

7. Utilize any existing computer program as given in any music computer book and run the program on an available computer. Use the program to create a work as in the last assignment.

8. If possible, visit a computer center with a D/A interface and computer-generated sound potential. Do as much composition as time, money, and antagonized personnel will allow.

WORKS FOR ANALYSIS

Consult the most recent Schwann Catalog for current in-print recordings of these works. Publishers are usually found through libraries, music stores, or distributors of music. This list is not meant to be comprehensive, only suggestive of further study.

Cage, John, and Lejaren Hiller: *HPSCHD* (uses computer printout sheets for random knob control of playback on the home record player; each "performance" then becomes unique unto itself).

Dodge, Charles: *Changes* (computer-generated sound with a wide range of dense clouds of sound).

————: *Earth's Magnetic Field* (based on the concept that any bit of information can be used for input to composer-controlled computer parameters).

Hiller, Lejaren: *Computer Music* (for tape of computer sounds and percussion ensemble).

ILLIAC: *Suite for String Quartet* (a work composed by the computer with a set of stylistic parameters imposed).

Randall, J. K.: *Mudgett: Monologues by a Mass Murderer* (computer-generated sound for tape and soprano).

Vercoe, Barry: *Synthesism* (computer-generated sound with many of the results sounding synthesizer-oriented).

Xenakis, Iannis: *ST/48-1,240162* (a work for large orchestra which uses computer aid with stochastic means by the composer, who invented the application of probability theories to music frameworks).

————: *Atrées* (for ten soloists using similar techniques as described in this chapter for computer aid).

20

Texture

Texture is the combination of pitch, timbre, and rhythm measured in terms of density. Texture can be as thin as one sound or as thick as a large aggregate of sounds. For the centuries preceding the twentieth, textures generally were conceived in terms of from one to eight simultaneous pitches moving in a fairly regular rhythmic pattern and with generally static or set timbres (from string trios to large orchestral works). Exceptions are few and include only rare multivoiced Renaissance double and triple canons and the like. For the most part, texture control was limited to the solo versus tutti applications of changing densities in orchestral literature with elements such as rhythm limited to metric and notational traditions.

New-music compositional concepts have founded a vastly expanded texture vocabulary inclusive of single-note concentrations (already discussed as *klangfarbenmelodien*) to immensely thick densities of sound. Before focusing on the latter of these (for reasons that the former has already been discussed and the middle ground covered for centuries), it is important to develop some concrete methods for analysis and compositional techniques.

Since density is the basic yardstick for texture, one can draw the conclusion that the most number of *notes* with different *timbres* occurring *as fast as possible* could represent the "thickest" texture. With this as the expansive extreme and *klangfarbenmelodien* as the thinnest, potential for concepts of texture progression are possible. Just as one does not compose works for *just* major triads or *just* quarter notes (although, it should be noted, some have), one is not

223

likely to compose a work for *just* one texture. Using graphing methods, example 207 shows a short work in terms of its overall texture measured in terms of its flexible densities. It demonstrates a straightforward directional approach and begins in such a manner that one or more of its texture components (pitch, timbre, rhythm) is very thin.

Example 207
Simple overview of work in terms of texture.

The texture grows evenly to a relatively thick density and returns to its beginning point (though not necessarily the same note, timbre, or duration, but merely the same in combination: pitch could be the same, for example, but duration longer with timbre less complex). This example tends to follow the basic traditional format for phrase, movement, and even work construction throughout much of the common-practice period.

Example 208 is almost the exact opposite of example 207 in terms of texture and approach. Large blocks of sound are dramatically stacked one against another with no overlap (silence here is the intervening texture). These could easily represent stochastic sections discussed in the previous chapter; huge conglomerates of thick densities in which pitch and rhythm become so complex as to be literally meaningless taken as individual events. Only timbre (from ping-pong balls to golf balls to balloons, to carry the analogy from the last chapter a bit further) and effects can separate such massive entities.

Example 208
Contrasting texture overview.

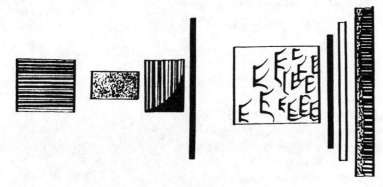

Example 209 shows a fusion between the fluidity of example 207 and the angular "blocking" of example 208 by piling density materials for developing texture thickness and soundmass and subtracting other density materials to thin the massive texture. Note here that the simplicity of direction of example 207 is not followed but rather a set of texture transitions applied to example 208 with additions of introduction and coda.

Example 209
Fusion of concepts in examples 207 and 208.

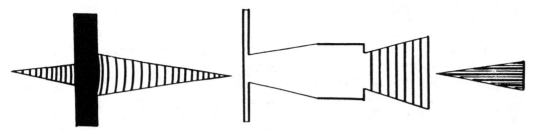

None of the three examples (207–209) is "right," as only context can secure such success. However, the concept of graphing texture in terms of wide- and thin-distanced lines of density for analysis and reanalysis for composition is vitally important. Many compositions seem not to work simply because texture was not a considered factor. Generally, works which avoid a multiplicity of textures become exhausting no matter what notes, what rhythms, or what timbres are included. While some composers attempt such exhaustion, it is important to note not what is *right,* but what is *what* (i.e., an understanding of the role texture plays in a given work). Texture can correspond to any other given parameter(s) of a piece, or remain entirely separate. Either can work as long as the composer is aware of the context in which his texture is intrinsically involved. Example 210 shows two small excerpts for piano, with one having conscious composer-control of texture as a compositional technique. The first excerpt shows the texture in total disarray (no two textures in the entire excerpt are the same), yet the music retains vital consistency in that the registrations used (pointillistic), dynamics chosen, and other elements are in complete agreement with this density extreme. The second excerpt shows the exact same texture arrangement with the material, however, being entirely tonal and within the span of two octaves. Dynamics, root progressions, and the other musical elements all function to help produce a directed phrase of music, yet the texture (though obviously adding interesting vocabulary to the somewhat overly consistent context) is at a completely opposite pole

Example 210
Two excerpts of texture usage.

in terms of composer control. If the latter example did exist in a work whose framework demanded this approach at a certain time then, as always, context could provide the situation for this combination of events to occur. If, however, one supposes that the excerpt continues in like manner with little regard to texture, the usefulness of texture contribution would be highly suspect. Though these are highly simplified examples, they do express the need for constant composer analysis of texture during composition.

Turning to the thick-density study promised earlier, one finds a large number of ways other than cluster techniques to achieve textures. Example 211 shows a density called *mikropolyphonie.* The thick texture is created by a multitude of different lines (twelve), different rhythms (especially rhythms which avoid duple classification: triplets, quintuplets, and the like), and many different timbres so that the effect is of an ever-moving mass of contrapuntal lines, none of which is important except as it contributes to the *whole.* *Mikropolyphonie* is in a sense a cluster-chord technique, but one in which the sophisticated texture is achieved by totally different means. The subtleties inherent in *mikropolyphonie* textures are indeed a far cry from the palm and forearm keyboard clusters mentioned in Chapter 7.

While the *mikropolyphonie* effect is most easily obtained in large ensembles, the density concept can be created on a single instrument such as the piano, but in a quite different manner. Note the incredible diversity of rhythms and pitch combinations in example 211. It would be nearly impossible to construct a single composite rhythm or root line for this mass. Example 212, on the other hand, is a thick density constructed from repeated and very simple rhythmic entities with a nearly drone root. The thickness of textures is obtained by the slow separations of the polyrhythms and the multitude of repeated notes.

Example 211
Mikropolyphonie.

Example 212
Mikropolyphonie *by rhythmic means.*

Nothing is really changing here but the texture (from thick to thin). The notes remain the same throughout, the rhythm in each hand changes only slowly (as ostinati), the timbre is piano only, yet the density is very thick due to the single aspect of complex composite rhythms. Nothing ever really quite sounds the same (though the materials *are* the same), and it is this attribute, combined with the tempo and speed of notes, that creates the thick densities.

Before progressing to other means for dense textures, some techniques for composing and analyzing *mikropolyphonie* (especially since root movement is so quick and relatively inaudible, and melodic direction is lost amid the multitude of lines) should be expressed. First, like clusters, the outer lines make for the general outline of the mass and serve as general curves for study as well as more often than not being the most important notes present. If inner notes are present only to contribute to the mass, they should be of like dynamic (especially consider the register of the instrument in question, as a *forte* high trombone is not the same as a *forte* low flute) and rhythms should be as diverse in vertical and horizontal relationships as possible. Inner note contribution also helps if one is very careful to note constantly the vertical structures. A sudden appearance of a major triad, for example, out of a texture of relatively constant panchromatic dissonances would prove quite surprising (possibly usefully, but not contributory to a consistent mass). Similar motives used in all the instruments, with variations due primarily to rhythmic structures, can add consistency to mass densities of *mikropolyphonie* when the motives are of relatively small intervals (a suddenly leaping piccolo, for example, could penetrate the consistency and bring attention to one note or line quite quickly). All of these techniques presuppose the desire for consistency in *mikropolyphonie* masses. Inconsistent textures could be created by reversing one, some, or all of the ideas presented above. Improvisation can be used for achieving variably dense textures. Example 213 shows a climax for six instruments in which probability would suggest the thickest of densities possible: ". . . do everything you can do with the loudest, fastest, and most aggressive techniques possible. . . ."

Example 213
Simple thick and diverse density.

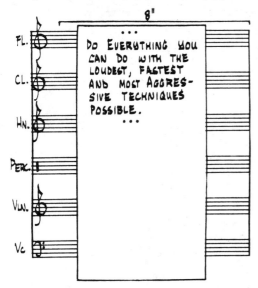

Example 214 is a bit more subtle and is controllable with small improvisation boxes providing raw material from which the performers are to create fast and even (F.E.) and fast and uneven (F.N.) textures. The order of the pitches shown is not to be kept intact. The probability of notating either of these in traditional notation (especially the latter) is slight indeed, and one wonders if the effect of such notations would not be a studied and stifled lack of texture definition.

Thick textures can be achieved by a lack of fast and intricate rhythms but, as is shown in example 215, can be accomplished by layering. Each note in this (again, 12-line) passage enters and dies out at different times, staggered in such a way as to achieve a moving texture with thick density. Techniques for analysis of this type of texture are similar to those of *mikropolyphonie.* Consistency can only be maintained if constant consideration of vertical sonorities is

Example 214
Improvisation mikropolyphonie.

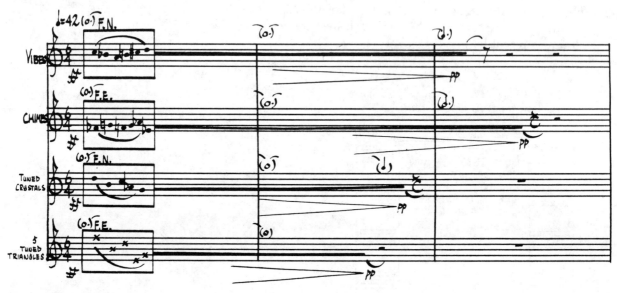

maintained (e.g., a chord of twelve notes which remains the same except register alterations and change of timbre).

Obviously orchestration (timbre concepts) plays a very important role in texture creation. Each of the previous examples would vary greatly if different timbres were chosen. Note that the substitution of a set of twelve sets of chimes for the instruments shown in example 211 would greatly vary the concept of texture. The monochromatic example of example 212 (piano) would be completely altered if the excerpt were for a small chamber orchestra or choir. The point is made here not to achieve a defined timbral standard (as each of the aforementioned excerpts could work in a multitude of orchestrations and circumstances), but to point out that, with the aid of timbral variation, whether it is slowly modulated (see following chapter) or sudden, can make textures (thick as they may be or stagnant as they may become with extended duration) evolve and grow. They may achieve variation within themselves while contributing to a consistent density for the context of the work.

Combinations of the above techniques can achieve a continuous thick density with flow and direction quite apart from orchestration changes. Example 216 is an overview from a textural viewpoint of a continuous broad density.

Example 215
Thick texture by 'layering.'

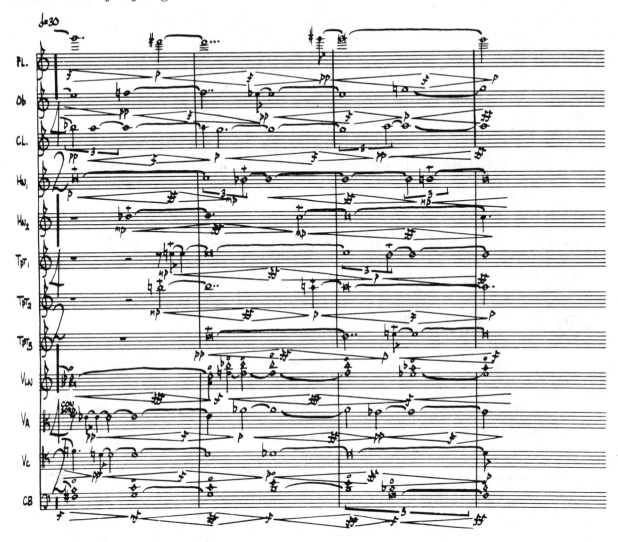

Example 216
Overview of continuous thick density yet with variety.

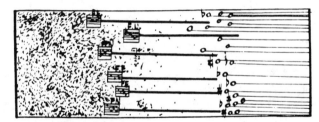

Within the large graphic rectangle, however, are the varying elements of change as previously discussed. Note the beginning of *mikropolyphonie* slowly dissolve into an improvisational framework of composite F.E. and F.N. This is followed by a modulation to a layered texture by the slow infusion of first a single staggered continuous note and then another, etc. The layering finally becomes complete. The composer has begun with a most incredible mix of complex pitch, rhythm, and timbres and developed to an undulating chord of single sustaining pitches. Example 217 shows a reverse possibility as the layering slowly gives way to ostinati (polyrhythmic to provide the complexity of ever-changing composite rhythms). The notes slowly evolve distinctly new rhythms, and *mikropolyphonie* has been created. In both these examples (216 and 217), the texture in terms of density has remained much the same, with only the technique being changed. With the potential addition of orchestration changes and modulations, the number of possible variants of thick densities becomes nearly endless.

Example 217
Thick density modulating from 'layering' to polyrhythms.

Effects can contribute to texture definition, and example 218 shows how *mikropolyphonie* can modulate smoothly to improvisations with the constant use of glissando, maintaining a consistency throughout.

Example 218
Texture in mikropolyphonie *from glissandi to improvisation.*

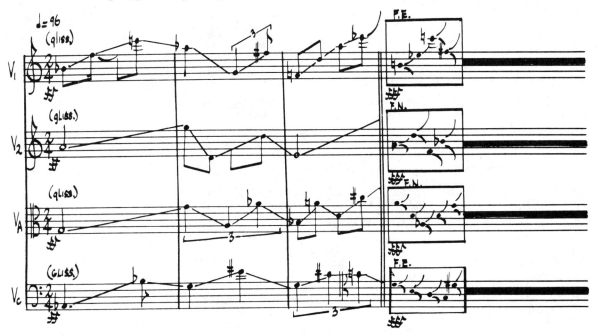

General "mean pitch" (see Chapter 19) can also play an important role and, while an improvised section or use of layering may remain at the same technique and density, *direction* can be achieved by clustering the fast moving notes (in one case) or the sustaining pitches (in the second case) around a moving central area. Example 219 shows a small excerpt of improvisation boxes moving upward (in this case by lines indicating that the pitch areas shown should slowly move) in mean pitch until a full climax is reached with the blast of a cluster chord.

Example 219
Directional texture usage in improvisation.

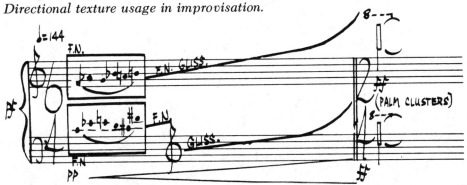

Example 220
Example 207 in more detail (beginning and climax).

Note the contribution of dynamics to the direction. One can see quickly how texture can be used, even in a constant state of thickness of density, for variety and direction. As this is accumulated, along with the variety of ways in which dense textures are created, it is possible to revert to the first three examples of this chapter to envision the sophisticated ways in which compositional processes can interplay with texture analysis. Example 220 shows the first example of this chapter (example 207) in more detail. Note how the fragment descriptions modulate and layer texture such that it becomes as viable a compositional process as, for instance, melody and harmony. It is interesting here to view the slow flexibility of the note as an end in itself. The beginning of this overview presents a slow melodic solo in which the nuance of every note is extremely important to the continuum of the work. As the density increases, the notes become less and less important until at climax they indeed (in *mikropolyphonie*) do not retain any validity in themselves at all. Surely a missed note at this point in the composition would not be observed at all. The value structure of pitch to timbre to rhythm to density all change under the guise and structuring of texture concepts. Without the knowledge of the contributions in variety, direction, climax, modulation, and other musical elements which texture can provide, the composer is significantly lacking in foundations. Whether he wishes to use this knowledge to create static textures of drones or dramatic compositions is completely beside the point. Texture, like pitch or timbre, is inherent in compositional processes and, if not composed, will surely be as random as *indeterminacy*, regardless of whether the composer's style is rich in *determinate* concepts or not.

ASSIGNMENTS

1. Analyze any previous assignment in terms of texture. Make any changes in the work you may now feel necessary due to the consideration of the analysis.

2. Using as many available instruments as possible (including piano and voices), realize example 208 in terms of *mikropolyphonie* with written out (in detail) lines.

3. Analyze example 211 in terms of traditional techniques used in the first chapters of this book. Analyze again according to the texture and density approaches described in this chapter. Compose a layered mass of sustained pitches which conforms to this analysis-structure as closely as possible.

4. Using as many available instruments and voices as possible, realize example 209 in any texture manner described herein or one you may conceive yourself. Adhere to the texture outline as closely as possible.

5. Compose a work for piano in which a continuous dense texture achieves motion by varying pitch mean. Use rhythmic means to attain the constant thick density. Do not employ cluster techniques of a previous chapter.

6. Analyze example 215 both in terms of traditional roots, consistent densities, and especially for the notes present vertically at every event entry or departure. Continue the example and slowly, almost unnoticeably, modulate to a mikropolyphonic texture of like density.

7. Orchestrate example 212 for available instruments, attempting to maintain the thick texture present. Do not use piano at all.

8. Realize example 213 following the textural (verbal) advice as closely as possible. Compose the work for six or less instruments not inclusive of piano. Note the ability of texture to be viable even in smaller chamber situations as well as thick textures to be achieved.

9. Construct a texture overview of your own choosing. Create a short work for any kind of ensemble following the overview carefully. Compose a second work made up of exactly the same notes, rhythms, etc., but do not follow the overview (move sections, or make vertical notes horizontal to vary the texture, or use any other device to avoid the previous texture).

WORKS FOR ANALYSIS

Consult the most recent Schwann Catalog for current in-print recordings of these works. Publishers are usually found through libraries, music stores, or distributors of music. This list is not meant to be comprehensive, only suggestive of further study.

Berio, Luciano: *Sinfonia* (contrasts of bursts of texture changes in the first movement; layering of texture for thick densities in the fourth).
———: *Circles* (use of improvisation boxes for obtaining occasional thick textures for small ensemble).
Cope, David: *Re-Birth* (constant use of texture development through the use of most of the techniques described herein in one form or another).
Crumb, George: *Black Angels* (begins with extreme textural density with only a string quartet as sound provider; uses a large number of the textural techniques described in this chapter).

Husa, Karel: *Apotheosis of This Earth* (uses layering especially to create extremely thick textures at times; very careful texture composition).

Ligeti, György: *Lontano* (very "directed" piece created from an almost continuous layering of textures very dense in nature, obtaining motion by orchestration and pitch movement as well as modulations discussed in the next chapter).

———: *Requiem* (great masses of *mikropolyphonie* by the composer who first began to use the term).

Lutoslawski, Witold: *Concerto for Orchestra* (creates thick densities for overall texture variation by using almost all of the techniques herein).

Penderecki, Krzysztof: *Capriccio for Violin and Orchestra* (as with most of this composer's output, thick textures are created from wide bands of minor seconds packed upon each other).

Stravinsky, Igor: *Firebird Suite* (extraordinary variety of texture control through a multitude of orchestral devices and techniques. The texture in this and many of Stravinsky's works is very closely tied to formal and dramatic overviews).

Xenakis, Iannis: *Pithoprakta* (like many of this composer's works, it is texture-oriented to a great degree, with blocks of textures often more like example 213; with little transition).

21
Modulations

Modulation will herein be defined as a smooth transition from one state of being to another. In tonal languages, it refers to the act of moving from one key center to another key center, usually by the use of a chord common in one way or another to both keys. Twentieth-century modulation has been expanded to include a vast new vocabulary of possible uses. This chapter will discuss a few of the current potentials of modulation and hint at some of their usages.

Spatial modulation requires first a discussion of space as a definitive parameter of composition. Spatial works have appeared here and there throughout most of music history, but for the most part the stage/audience relationship has remained immaculate with the "antiphonal" intruders considered as "effects" for a single work. Introduction of acoustical ideas, however, presents a quite opposite view. All works are spatial in a sense, since by reflection of sound from the top, sides, etc. of any hall, sound comes from a multitude of directions. This being the case, composers can draw upon this by controlling what sounds come from where rather than leaving it to the indeterminate acoustics of the hall. (This is much like media concepts: if visual and tactile sensations are present in a perform-ance situation anyway, why not control them?) With this concept, works can involve performers being placed in balconies, scattered throughout the audience, surrounding the audience, with a multi-tude of controllable spatial effects. Example 221 shows three setups

(A, B, and C) which will be used for examples as discussion of spatial modulation progresses.

Example 221
Three hall setups for potential spatial modulation.

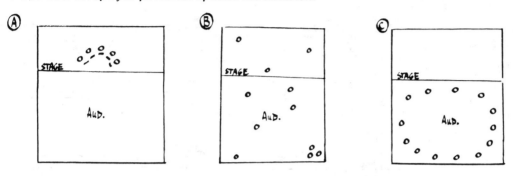

Note that A is a somewhat standard stage setup, B has performers scattered throughout the hall, and C, the performers surrounding the audience. Each of these will have a particular effect both in terms of instruments used and the relationships present (e.g., antiphonal, modulatory). Such effects are primarily justified by the individual work, and the variations of these are so numerous that detailed study cannot be made here. Spatial *separation* does, however, suggest spatial *modulation*.

Example 222 shows a conceivable use of spatial modulation in a type-A situation (see example 221). Note first the stage setup and then compare with the musical excerpt to its right. Violin 1 and violin 6 have exactly the same pitch staggered and overlapped so that one is ending as the other is beginning. Now observe that these two violins are at opposite ends of the stage, unlike standard stage setup. The sound will tend to slowly modulate from one side of the stage to the other (*pan,* in electronic jargon) and, depending on the material coexisting (very minimal here), spatial modulation will take place. More observable modulation can take place in a type-B arrangement (see example 221) in which a sound can literally pass around the hall. In example 223, a pitch (D) originates from the stage and is slowly taken up by performers in an angular manner throughout the hall, each performer leaving off as approximately the third succeeding begins. Note that the second trumpet (the excerpt is for complete trumpet ensemble) is in the balcony so that a three-dimensional modulation begins the excerpt. The idea ends back with the first trumpet, thus coming full circle. Though in itself

Example 222
Spatial modulation on a stage (or example 221-A setup).

an effect, the idea is viable and, with imitative events happening in other performers, a solid work could be conceived.

Example 224 shows a type-C arrangement with modulation traveling from player to player in a counterclockwise motion around the audience. Speeding up and slowing down, the entropy could result in a sort of physical panning effect (used with a multiple of speakers in electronic music with a joystick or a 360-degree pot for churning the sound around the hall). Again, in and of itself this is an effect without much depth. Placed, however, in the context of a work where musical direction and the like are enhanced by the spatial modulation, the effect becomes a viable parameter of the language of composer style. Example 225 shows a situation-B example which employs quick glissandi. Some of these glissandi are

Example 223
Spatial modulation in example 221-B setup.

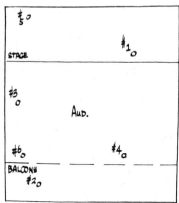

Example 224
Spatial modulation in example 221-C setup.

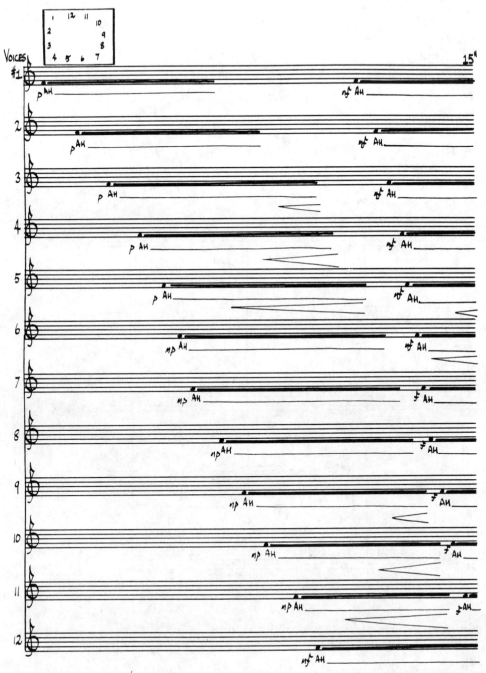

Example 225
Setup and excerpt for variety of spatial modulation and separation.

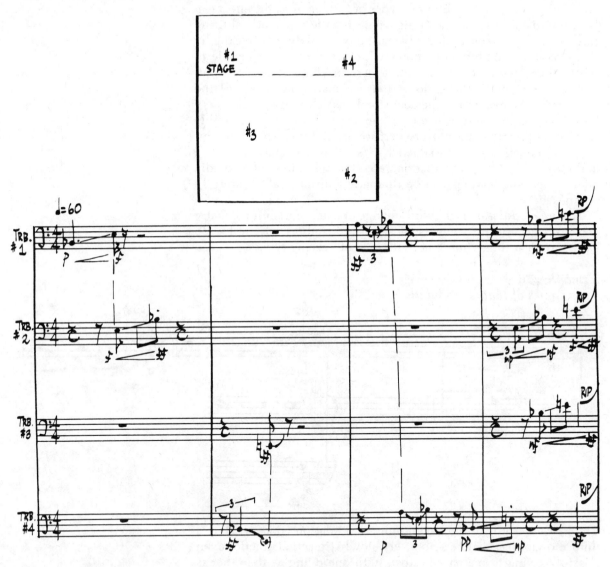

connected and continued, while others are separated with still others overlapped for a variety of modulations, echoes, and interplay. These ideas, placed in conjunction with the others presented, give spatial concepts—and modulation in particular—a more than credible listing in useful composer parameters.

Other potentials include the actual moving of performers during the course of the work. This gives an extra sense of motion, especially when the moving performer is playing. As well, if the ensemble is made up of different types of instruments, the effect can be quite dislocating for the audience in that the constantly shifting timbres leave no security for expectation of aural direction. Equally valid are those performance notes which request the ensemble to locate themselves in the hall for a certain effect to be achieved. Noteworthy here is the concept that no matter how careful the composer is in evaluating the acoustical spatiality of a work, every hall is different, and control in the exact sense is impossible (excepting his presence at every performance). Often spatial modulation is effective in a darkened hall so that expectations of the audience are completely disoriented. Though more of a media effect, such applications can be dramatic and musical if carefully composed.

Timbre modulation is the slow change of color of a sound, usually accomplished by instruments of semi-like timbres. Example 226 shows a set of three timbre modulations of varying types.

Example 226
Three types of timbre modulation.

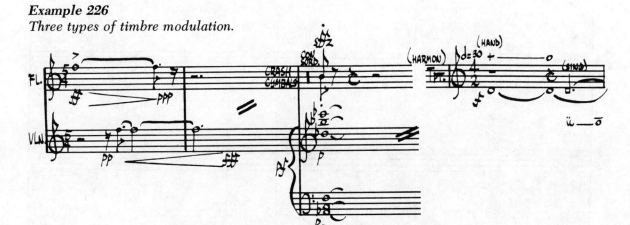

The first excerpt is of the basic timbre modulation concept. Here a flute and violin exchange a note very slowly (in actual practice even possibly trying to match vibratos), with one dying as the other is growing. A certain effect is observed at the pivot point where the timbres are dynamically balanced in such a way that a new instrumental sound is created for a brief instant: not a violin and not a flute, but a "flutin" or "violute." Other combinations such as "obet" (trumpet and oboe), "viorn" (viola and horn), "basset" (bassoon and trumpet) can be very effective if the right register and dynamics are selected. Matching is very important and "flubas" (flute and tuba) seem remote and unlikely indeed.

The second excerpt of example 226 is quite different in that the modulation is created by ringoff. The muted crash cymbals here completely overshadow the piano chord struck simultaneously. But, once the cymbals have been dampened, the piano (with damper pedal down) rings, creating a unique sound. "Cymbianos" and the like can be most effective in proper context. The third type shown in example 226 is timbre modulation with one instrument through a variety of elements. The trumpet begins with a harmon mute, the plunger in and hand over opening. As the hand is removed, the timbre modulates to a brighter sound. With the embouchure change created by the vocal addition, a third timbre is slowly evolved. Thus, in one instrument timbre modulation is not only possible but eminently usable.

Example 227 shows a quartet of voices modulating by vowel sounds with a percussion instrument used. All three of the previously mentioned timbre modulations are used here, primarily by vowel sound exchange and bass drum mashing (at the outset).

Example 227
Three types of timbre modulation used in a continuous excerpt.

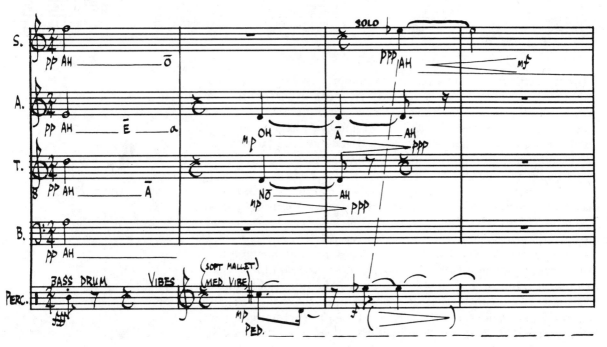

Timbre modulation, like spatial modulation (or, for that matter, any parameter of sound), if used for its own sake, becomes monotonous. If used in musical context with reason, the result is an added extension of musical dimensions.

Rhythmic modulation implies the change from one rhythmic idea to another as smoothly as possible. For the sake of clarity, both the ensuing examples will use ostinato ideas for the modulations (they need not be so, but are used here because it generally takes some time to set a rhythmic figure so its modulation is recognizable; such time, as symbols on paper, is not available in a book of this size). Example 228 is for piano and is one rhythmic idea repeated four times. By the fifth time the rhythm has developed a small variation (very slight displacement).

Example 228
Rhythmic modulation.

This slight boost of direction slowly modulates the rhythm, variation upon variation, until a related but quite different rhythm is achieved. Example 229 shows a larger ensemble of three instruments repeating *rhythmic* motives over and over. One of the voices, however, begins to change slightly and generates a like movement in the others. By the end of the excerpt, the total composite rhythm has new breath and a very different composite rhythm and direction.

Articulation modulation is quite possible in one instrument and can be very effective if it occurs subtly during a musical passage. Example 230 shows a fairly long flute line which begins with harsh "tongued" material and ends in a lyric style remote from the beginning. The articulation modulation is not flagrant due to the interesting material itself. Moreover, the modulation is not as straightforward as obvious step-by-step production would make it, but rather, hidden by constant "backstepping" so that one is never sure of the direction. This is only one type of articulation modulation, and the list of potential compositional processes is very large.

Example 229
Rhythmic modulation using motivic ideas.

Example 230
Articulation modulation.

Dynamic modulation (besides the obvious *crescendo* and *diminu-endo* usages in any traditional phrase of music) is usually spatially or timbrally oriented. Note how the dynamic modulations (or staggering and overlaying of dynamic increase with decrease) give the potential drive of modulation to most of the preceding examples of this chapter.

These five modulation types just begin the possibilities, as any new parameter can exist in a modulatory way (e.g., pitch modulation, such as motion Doppler effects). With just these five, however, one can form a framework for the concept of *combinative modulation*.

Example 231 shows first an auditorium setup and the instruments in each location and, secondly, a short musical excerpt which employs spatial modulation, timbre modulation, and articulation modulation in combination.

Example 231
Excerpt showing spatial, timbre and articulation modulation along with hall setup.

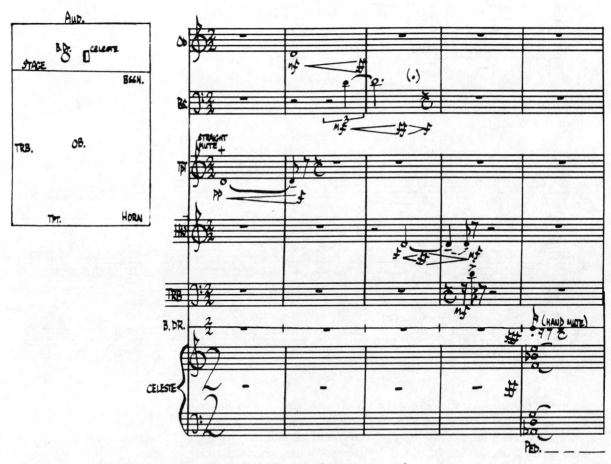

The idea begins in the back of the hall with the very legato tones of a straight-muted trumpet. The last note of the solo slowly modulates spatially to the center of the hall and also modulates in terms of timbre, as the new instrument is an oboe on the same pitch. This "obet" moves spatially to an "oboon," to a "bassorn," with subtle subtraction from the duration of each sound until the penultimate trombone is very staccato followed by a bass drum *fff* hand-muted with celeste ringoff (on the stage). While this remains more of an example to point out the combinations, such ideas can be made more musical by concurrent developments, important enough to detract from the "pure effect" of modulation but not strong enough to destroy it.

With the concept of *combinative modulations* comes the potential of *texture modulation:* many instruments adding to and subtracting from the unfolding modulations. Example 232 is a texture modulation for five voices surrounding the audience. Note the slow texture modulation from the single voice at center stage moving outward to include the entire ensemble in a thick density of rhythmic and spatial modulations.

Example 232
Texture modulation.

Example 233 is an additive- and subtractive-type texture, with the very short staccato notes splattered in the instruments (surrounding, within, and above the audience in the balcony). Note the exact placement of each instrument on the chart and then carefully examine the score excerpt.

Example 233
Combinative modulation.

The points of sound "cluster" in certain parts of the hall and then suddenly burst out in a defined direction, only to return to clusters but in different locations. As the sounds burst out of a space, they become more legato, as if slowing down and wearying, but return to staccato when clustered. As well, note that the bursts often shoot upward into the balcony, crisscrossing the audience in three-dimensional spatiality.

Example 234 includes the entirety of example 233 but with it is a choir of voices at four centerwall locations. The circular spatial modulation and obvious vowel control for timbre modulation continue the concept of the piece. Yet, more than this, they move in the directed fashion of continuous sound with notes ever moving upward in pitch modulation (bending).

Example 235 shows graphically some of the spatial crisscrossing of ideas through the use of arrows in an imagined hall. The careful construction of this last example (example 234 with reference to 235) demonstrates the need for substantial processes in other than modulation itself. While the concept of modulations has just begun to create a credible dramatic impact on even a "suspecting" audience, modulations alone are void of anything but circus manipulations when used as the sole source of musical direction. Consideration of *all* musical parameters is particularly important here, as combinative modulations—possibly even more than electronic music and media forms—possess an incredible fascination often born not of their musical relevancy but of their novelty.

ASSIGNMENTS

1. Compose a short work for three instruments (not piano) in which each of them is placed on the stage (or performing area) so that the most benefit of spatial modulation can be employed. Use spatial modulation, but as only one concept of the work, not as the sole feature.

2. Conceive of a performer placement different from those offered at the beginning of the chapter. Diagram it out in detail. Compose a brief example for such, exploiting the spatial potentials to the fullest yet maintaining musical direction.

3. Using as many performers as are available, write a work for an ensemble surrounding the audience. Spatially modulate evenly in circles with the rate of modulation increasing to a spiral effect.

4. Use staccato notes and other short durations to create a type-B (see example 221) setup and modulations. The work should contain

Example 234
Example 233 with spiraling vocal spatial modulation upwards.

Example 235
Graphic hall possibilities of modulation.

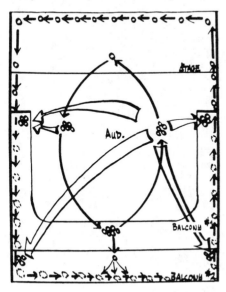

antiphonal as well as modulatory spatial effects. Use as many available instruments as possible.

5. Using three instruments of semi-like timbre, create a work employing timbre modulation as a continuous drone of undulating sound (same pitch). With a fourth (solo) instrument of quite unique timbre, create counterpoint of concepts.

6. In a work for voice and piano, create timbre modulation by having the voice slowly come out of harshly struck notes on the keyboard. Have this be intertwined with the pianist singing and exchanging vowel sounds with the vocalist.

7. Without using ostinati, create a work involving rhythmic modulation born of frequently repeated variants of a rhythmic motive. The work should be for at least three instruments other than the piano.

8. Conceive of another type (other than mentioned in this chapter) of modulation and use it to create a work using any number of instruments and techniques.

9. Create a work for at least five available instruments in which articulation modulation is used. Use "backstepping" to make the modulation smooth, and involve spatial modulation in some way of

your choice. Start legato, grow to staccato, and return again to legato.

10. Complete example 234.

11. Compose a work which involves as many types of crisscrossing modulations as is possible while using twelve-tone processes. Use pitch modulation; as the sounds move spatially, bend the pitch.

WORKS FOR ANALYSIS

Consult the most recent Schwann Catalog for current in-print recordings of these works. Publishers are usually found through libraries, music stores, or distributors of music. This list is not meant to be comprehensive, only suggestive of further study.

Berlioz, Hector: *Requiem* (included here as a very early example of spatial considerations, notably the *Dies Irae,* which includes four bands at the four corners of the orchestra).

Brant, Henry: *Voyage Four* (the most notable composer of music involved with modulations, especially spatial. This work is for percussion and some brass on stage, violins on one side of the balcony, violas and cellos on the other, brass performers on the floor level at the rear of the hall, and woodwinds and strings on two rear balconies).

Crumb, George: *Songs, Drones and Refrains of Death* (includes a number of effective timbre modulations).

Debussy, Claude: *Prélude à l'Apres-midi d'une Faune* (contains a number of remarkable timbre modulations, especially between flute and oboe).

Erb, Donald: *Fanfare* (includes brass players on stage and in the balcony for both sustained and articulative modulations and antiphonal effects).

Ives, Charles: *Fourth Symphony* (while not demanding it, Ives suggests the possible separation of performers for spatial movement and contrasts).

Ligeti, György: *Lontano* (includes a large array of spatial, timbre, and dynamic modulations throughout the work).

Riley, Terry: *In C* (through ostinati and combinations of motives, the work is literally structured around rhythmic modulation).

Schwartz, Elliott: *Elevator Music* (the audience rides up and down in an elevator with the floors the performance areas; the work achieves most interesting moving spatial and timbral modulations).

Stockhausen, Karlheinz: *Gruppen* (for three orchestras surrounding the audience; interesting effects with some texture modulation).

————: *Gesang der Jünglinge* (an electronic work which in live performance has many loudspeakers surrounding the audience for spatial modulations).

Stravinsky, Igor: *Le Sacre du Printemps* (constant uses of all of the types of modulation herein with the exception of wide offstage spatial modulation).

Varèse, Edgard: *Poème Electronique* (originally for many loudspeakers surrounding a closed area through which the audience walked).

22

Notation

In general, notation falls into four main categories:

1. metered (usually standardized around the grand-staff concept and the G and F clefs);
2. improvisational (often based on traditional concepts of note-heads, etc., but only as raw material from which the performer may interpret as indicated);
3. proportional (meterless notation in which a given time-block of indicated duration exists with notes in locations very close to where the composer intends; avoids strict metric ideas; visual is proportionate to aural activity in terms of time);
4. indeterminate (includes a wide range of graph musics and combinations of other types mentioned above in nonspecific situations).

For the most part, each of the above categories has been utilized by composers in such diversity that symbols often are contradictory to other composers' uses of the same symbol, even occasionally contradictory to their own. While at least semistandardization is imminent (as testified to by the author's own book on the subject), most composers and performers should be geared to face a variety of situations without pessimism. In examining concepts and symbols in this chapter, the author will avoid any attempt at standardizing one symbol over another, but rather attempt to demonstrate symbols and their usages as most commonly composed today.

255

Before facing the symbols themselves, the major categories of notation will be examined through more explanation and examples. This should give a groundwork for the more exact and specific notations.

Determinate metrical notations, though often considered so "common practice" that study seems only for the beginner, are often extremely complex and difficult to understand. Example 236 shows a few of the more difficult manifestations of metrical notation. Note the use of metric modulation (bar two to three), inner beat complexity (bar one: triplet inside quintuplet), complex meter (3+2+3 over 4), and confused linear clarity (though this excerpt is for piano, there are actually seven lines present in the structure; it would take four staves—rather impractical—for the rests, stem direction, etc. of each voice, for the counterpoint to be made clear). None of these are mentioned to detract from the significance and usefulness of metered notations, but rather to give some insight into the need for the creation of the somewhat newer categories.

Example 236
Complex metric notation.

Example 237 shows an improvisational example. Note that the bar lines are here but that they have little meaning except to help the performers keep some sense of where they are in the work.

Example 237
Improvisational notation.

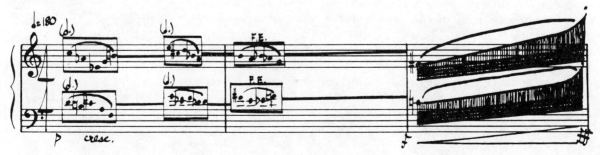

This example is again a bastard one in that it is purposely inconsistent in order to show three different notations for improvised structures (moreover, there are many other possibilities). The first bar shows improvisation boxes followed by a solid line to show duration (note the small parenthetical stemmed durations so no confusion can exist as to how long the improvisation will last). The notes should be freely improvised here with the problem being that performers generally rely on "comfortable" realizations, falling back into historical traps that the composer may not wish. The second bar includes the F.E. (fast as possible and even) mentioned earlier in the text. The third measure shows no noteheads at all, but rather an approximate number of stems in pitch areas to allow the performer to rip up the line (following the general pattern of the stems) without having to apply endless practice to individual notes (which in the end result, due to the speed of the example, would not be that important anyway). Each of these can be used for successful results, limiting the performer in one set of parameters (i.e., first: notes; second: rhythm and notes; third: rhythm) and freeing him in others (first: rhythm; second: order of notes; third: notes). The bar lines could be removed or utilized without set meter for purposes of organization.

Example 238 is a proportional section of 25-second duration showing three different, often-used types of notations. The opening

Example 238
Proportional notation with new symbols.

notehead, followed by a duration line, is very common, freeing the composer from strict metric concepts, yet allowing some control in terms of attack and duration timings. The second entrance is a series of effects (symbols described later in the chapter) which, like improvisation, are freely ordered in terms of which action, which order, and when (rhythm). Note that some of these symbols are defined in such a way that metric application would be rather ridiculous (e.g., how does one apply a stem to the marking?). The third entrance is of cluster type (note the indication of notes below the thick line) which in its glissando motion begins to seem more graphic than expressive. While meter and some of its implications are gone from this example, so are the chances for *controlled* intricate rhythms. For this reason, many composers have adopted a composite metrical-proportional (metriportial; see Chapter 10) composite.

Example 239 is one of indeterminate nature (type 1: graphic; see Chapter 11). A first glance at the picture seems to present little that would be useful for musical performance. But, as has been mentioned previously (see Chapter 11), there are many possible applications of musical rhetoric for the performer (whether composer-intended or not). Note how, on careful observation, the score folds slowly inward from graphic to proportional to improvised to a single highly structured measure.

Example 239
Graphic notation.

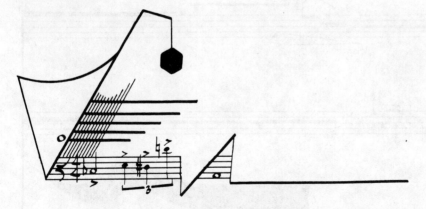

Whether involved program and performance notes go with these types of notations or not, they will remain outside the general frame of this chapter in that to clarify them would be to destroy their inherent intention. However, it should be observed that many of the new symbols are graphic in themselves though determinate in nature.

Coverage of the symbols themselves will progress in the chapter order of the text (i.e., as the need for new notations occur; Chapters 1 through 6, for example, need little notation explanation). It should also be stated that many notations explain themselves (verbal, for example) or are explained elsewhere in the book (especially in chapters beyond this one), and thus do not need redundant explanation here.

Cluster notations are numerous, with just a few shown in example 240. The first shows all notes present and all the attendant accidentals (for a full chromatic cluster).

Example 240
Different cluster notations.

This octave-span cluster notation is effective if one or more notes are missing, but is cluttered and difficult to read. The same cluster exactly is notated in much more legible fashion to its right. Here only the outer notes are shown with connecting lines giving the cluster identification. White-key clusters are notated by a natural sign, black-key clusters (key referring here, of course, to the piano keyboard) with a sharp sign, and both natural and sharp signs used for completely chromatic clusters. Some composers use the symbols white equal to white keys, black for black, and a half (or divided) black, half white symbol for the same set of clusters. This, however, leads to great confusion as to duration of notes, due to the half-note/quarter-note connotation of black and white, and should therefore probably be avoided except in proportional notations. The third symbols shown in the example illustrate only the general cluster outline (with the same potential for preceding large sharp, natural, etc., indications as before) which allows for some indeterminacy in terms of exact cluster (variance of palm size, etc.), but is very helpful for notation of quick cluster slaps as shown in example 241 where exact notation would only bring nearly impossible performance limitations.

Example 241
Readable clusters at the keyboard.

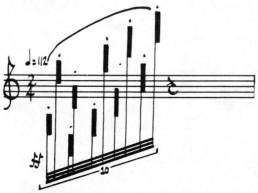

All three of the types shown in example 240 could be used in metered or proportional categories with the presence or removal of the stems. It is important to realize that these cluster notations are keyboard-oriented and that in ensemble writing, one should revert to example 238 (third entrance) or use traditional notation. This study is a mere beginning of that of notation of clusters. The space and time allotted to the discussion of clusters is only an indication of the vast amount of discussion that could go on with any of the subsequent symbols mentioned in this chapter. Clear study and understanding of which symbol to be used depends on performance situation, at least some personal codification, and a study of scores and reference materials listed at the end of this chapter and in Appendix II.

Example 242 shows two types of quarter-tone notation of the "arrow" type. The first has the arrow attached to the end of one "stem" of the accidental, while the other is separate. Both mean that the pitch is to be altered by a quarter tone in the direction indicated. While the first would seem the least cumbersome, one finds the latter in most "used" orchestral parts for tonal quarter-tone indications.

Example 242
Two quarter tone notations.

Example 243 shows the plethora of other symbols often used, with even this listing being merely a sampling. The number of cents (see

Chapter 8) seems most adequate for other microtone notations (with 100 cents per semitone), though complexity here (such as 27 cents) becomes a bit farfetched except in terms of electronic or computer realization. The list of other microtonal notations is incredible indeed, with most requiring vast practice for any convincing performance. Example 244 shows just one such type, a variant of traditional sharps and flats which has been used.

Example 243
Other notable quarter tone notations.

Example 244
Difficult microtone notation.

In general, however, the best solution seems to be to use a traditional or nontraditional instrument already tuned to the microtone scale desired, with the use of traditional notation for performance.

Percussion notation has developed visual symbols for instrument and mallet. Example 245 shows a few of these while not attempting to be complete.

Example 245
Visual percussion notations (samples).

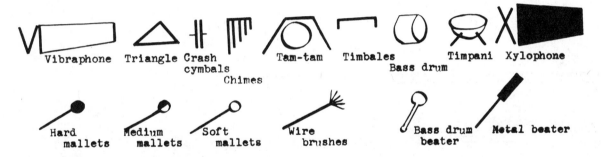

While not at all standardized, the concept of visual usage is growing in popularity. Example 246 shows the use of the symbols in an actual passage for percussion quartet.

Example 246
Example 245 in use.

Verbal indications work well but depend on common language between composer and performer for understanding. At the same time, the visual symbols require some new acclimatizing in terms of visual vocabulary. Regardless of choice, it is imperative that the composer bent on determinate results notate exact instrument, mallet, and mallet placement, as all produce different sounds. It is no longer possible to rely on traditional prototypes of just noting "timpani," as (while indeed there are set ways for performing such passages) in newer scores the performer is left to rather indiscriminately choose a mallet and its placement.

Percussion effects are often aided by the visual symbols. Example 247 shows a timpani struck with snare sticks on the metal sides. While the indication ". . . strike the side of the timpani with snare sticks . . ." could be used, the reading time and space occupation on the page seem self-defeating.

Example 247
Visual action symbols.

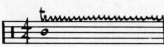

Example 248 shows a sample chart for piano preparations:

Example 248
Samples of notation for piano preparations.

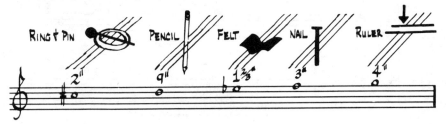

Note that the exact placement in inches from the damper is notated as well for an exact-as-possible sound. Each composer tends toward his own technique of notation in preparation; these should be placed at the beginning of the composition and not as they occur. Piano crossbars differ from make to make and model to model so that often composers prescribe this as well (frustrating to try and apply a preparation at an exact location only to find that a crossbar is at this place on this type of piano). If preparations are to be taken off or must be added during a composition, ample time should be allotted for this as well as clear notation. (See Appendix II for sources of notations in this area.) If performance of nonprepared notes is required (or even if the entire keyboard is not to be prepared), it is advisable to mark the minority areas (prepared or nonprepared, as the case may be) with masking tape.

Inside-piano techniques, if determinate, can be facilitated by marking a small piece of tape with the note name and attaching it to the back of the damper inside the piano. Verbal notations seem best for most inside-piano effects excepting a few such as harmonics. Example 249 is a short excerpt of a work mostly for the innards of a piano, with attendant suggestions for notation (though others have been used quite successfully). The example seems clear enough, with the possible exception of the + sign for muting (placing the right hand forefinger between the endpin closest to the performer and damper and playing the note thus dampened on the keyboard).

Media form notations are as complicated as the gear required for performance. Often performance and setup instructions are longer than the work itself. Since almost all such works depend on brand of visual device used, etc., it is impossible to even hint at the notations to be used. Combination of verbal and visual symbols are suggested and any real codification and/or suggestions are completely out of the realm of possibility (excepting works which leave large gaps of indeterminate performance possibilities).

Example 249
Excerpt involving piano 'insides' and notation.

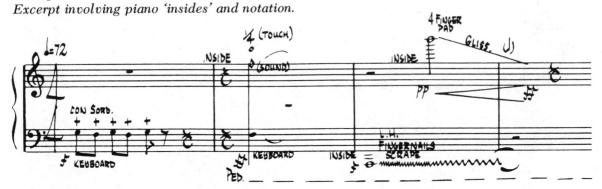

Electronic notations are usually more the composer's business than for the realizations of performers (the basic guidelines are overview and the concept "whatever works"). In any of the types of performance requiring live and tape coordination, some form of visual signal or cue is required in notation. Example 250 is for oboe, tape, and projections. Note the use of graphic (not always in the realm of indeterminate concepts) notation which gives both the projectionist and the oboist entrance cues.

Example 250
Graphic media and electronic notations.

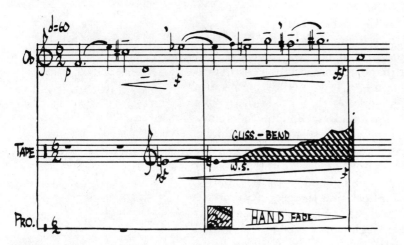

Other notations for either performer construction of tape part or for re-creation of tape are so varied and personal that viable suggestions or even examples are irrelevant here. The composer should use whatever notations are appropriate to his needs.

Synthesizer composition for the live performer (or even the studio tape composer) usually takes a duple form. First there are patch sheets (printed mock-ups of the particular synthesizer facing) which are filled in (usually by colored pencils for easy readability, making certain not to mark unused modules). Secondly, there is an overview in some form of the entire composition with reference marks for the exact patch to be used (usually cross-referenced numbers).

Example 251 is a brief look at some of the more general symbols in the music of today. Note the use of finger charts for multiphonics, carefully notated mute markings, and the like. Speed alterations of vibrato, flutter, etc. are common and no composition of recent times with variable wave or triangular lines for either of these should be taken as a printer's or copyist's error. Many of the effects (such as highest and lowest notes, square notes for singing while playing, and so on) apply to most instruments equally. Other notations (such as playing across the bridge and pedal tones) apply to one type of instrument group alone.

Example 251
Other often used new notations.

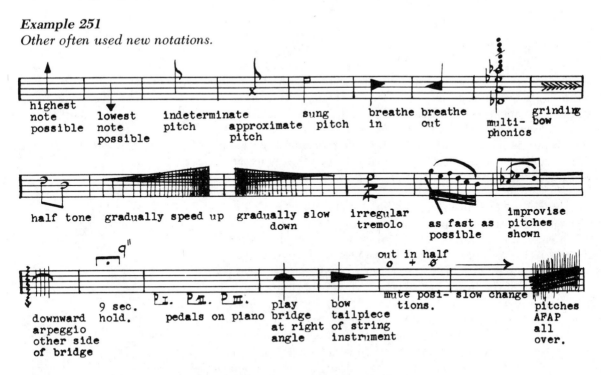

Rhythmic notations, such as the "gradually speed up" symbol, take a variety of similar forms as shown in this case. Each, however, is basically readable as a variant of the other. These symbols represent a fairly recognizable group of concepts and graphic representations that, while not standardized, are as common in new music today as "un-Webstered" slang is in literature. Scores of the most conservative composers use many of these, and it is rare to find a serious composition without at least one of the notations of example 251 present.

Some of the symbols represent a certain technique in and of themselves, and one should be careful not to have the notation box his personal style. The highest-note symbol generally reflects an indeterminate result (as players differ in potential). When a large number of highest-note notations are used for a large number of performers, there can be, however, a determinate stochastic result. Certain symbols (especially highly graphic ones such as "play across the bridge") can force a composer to use proportional notation when possibly he does not wish it. Intelligent creativity can usually be applied to avoid such boxing (in this case, the symbol placed above a metered set of headless stemmed rhythms). The number of stems in the rhythmic "speeding up slowly" notation is usually (though not always) suggestive only. Care should be maintained to express this in the performance notes. Usage of these varies from solo passages to a multitude of offset strata, producing a type of *mikropolyphonie* (if enough voices are present). Note particularly that these rhythmic repetitions do not have duplications of the repeated noteheads (indicated by headless stems which are not indeterminate, but repetitions of the same note).

Many other effects are best represented in verbal notations in English (slowly becoming the international language of music). A brief reminder is again in order regarding the placement of as many symbols and/or written effects in performance directions at the beginning of the score (or at least in the part, if one believes large sets of performance notes tend to scare conductors). This is far better than having to wait until the effect is to be performed, leaving the player with little or no preparation. Example 252 shows a work in which each of the symbols has been previously explained (both herein and in the assumed performance notes for the excerpt).

Two important new contributions are present in this example. First is the lack of staves for "resting" instruments (which gives the work a very unusual look to those "prepped" only in pre-twentieth-century scores), making the score to most much more easily readable. Secondly, along with the metriportional concept explained earlier, an overlap of determinate and indeterminate concepts is present. Note that the traditional hymn quote is metric notation overlapping the end of a proportional section. Moreover, there is a plentiful use of symbols recognized from example 251. At midpoint, there is a breakdown in two of the parts (horn and piano) into

Example 252
New notations in music excerpt.

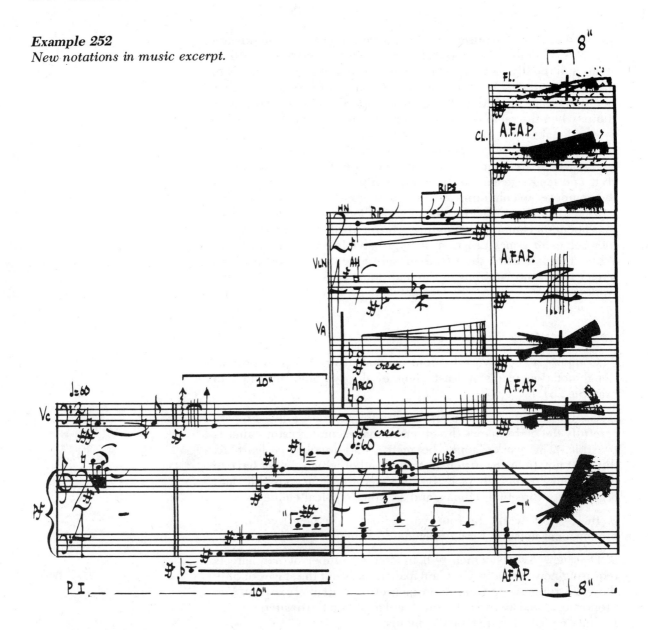

improvisational bursts of chords and rips followed quickly by a
completely graphic climax with only the signs of *fff* and *AFAP* (as
fast as possible) to indicate style of play (though the clutter of
specks and lines does suggest a high intensity of notes and thick
texture). While this is an excerpt of an incomplete piece, it suggests
a composite potential for all types of notations to be used as needed

and as best serve the purpose. It would indeed be absurd to notate a four-part chorale in completely proportional notation (without stems and the like) and expect the same result as metered notation of the same material. It would be equally absurd to try and shape a freely complex structure of extremely fast rhythms within metric limits when the same results could be so much more successful in proportional notations.

Notation is best which serves best. The more notations a composer has which are valid for his uses, the more creative his musical style and language can be. Notation of any kind must be the *tool* of the composer to communicate musical ideas (determined or nondetermined) through a performer to an audience. Notations (at least those bent on communication through sound) should *not* be ends in themselves or a masturbation of impressive-looking *augenmusiks*. While the latter are discussed in subsequent chapters, they no longer represent notations in the traditional sense, but become the work itself.

ASSIGNMENTS

1. Compose a short work for four or more instruments in proportional notation using at least eight of the symbols indicated in example 251.

2. Compose a work for piano using the insides only. Prepare carefully the performance directions so that accurate performance is possible. The work should be metric and involve at least six different notations for various activities, all of which do not have to be present in this chapter. Be as determinate as possible and organize for direction, climax, and all other musical elements.

3. In a short work for four voices, use *only* new symbols in proportional notation for a directed and structured work.

4. Overview a work which will involve a number of new effects requiring new symbols. On blank paper, mark out the staves of only those instruments performing (a quartet of available players). Use proportional and metric notation at will to obtain the desired results. Include no less than five new symbols.

5. Compose a traditional (tonal) four-part chorale with all attendant rules. Transcribe this chorale into as exacting a proportional notation as is possible, and perform.

6. Devise ten new symbols not shown in this chapter or known to you. Define them explicitly in the performance directions of a work for any number of players desired. Write the work, have it performed, and note the problems or lack of problems with the new notations.

7. Complete example 252 (both beginning and ending) in like notational style.

8. Write a traditional metrical version of the graphic section of example 252. Take care in being as complex and "climactic" as possible.

9. Use improvisational notations and compose a short work for as many available performers as possible. Attempt to be as specific as possible, but do not avoid the improvisation aspects. Perform the work twice, recording the first, and compare. Use at least five new notation symbols of this chapter.

10. Compose a work for available instrument and piano. The piano should be notated in strict metrical style while the instrument should be proportional and use only new symbols for performance.

WORKS FOR ANALYSIS

Consult the most recent Schwann Catalog for current in-print recordings of these works. Publishers are usually found through libraries, music stores, or distributors of music. This list is not meant to be comprehensive, only suggestive of further study.

Crumb, George: *Ancient Voices of Children* (uses empty space for instruments "resting" and novel uses of notation in circles, etc., for improvisation structures).

Haubenstock-Ramati, Roman: *Mobile for Shakespeare* (a variety of boxes, each with a different kind of sub-type of notation present; an exercise in notation understanding).

Kagel, Mauricio: *Sonant* (utilizes a large number of new symbols and ideas for their visual relationship with the act of performance).

Lentz, Daniel: *Sermon* (uses color as representing various performing activities, as well as circular and other collages of standard notations).

Ligeti, György: *Aventures* (extremely good source of notations of both metric and proportional bent; also uses a host of symbols for the vocalists).

Moran, Robert: *Bombardments No. 5* (very graphic appearance until one looks at the performance directions for some clarification; very instructive as to how one might achieve new notations from graphic ideas).

Oliveros, Pauline: *Sound Patterns* (excellent use of new symbols for vocal effects).

Penderecki, Krzysztof: *Threnody for the Victims of Hiroshima* (uses the somewhat standard Polish symbols, many of which were included herein).

Reynolds, Roger: *The Emperor of Ice Cream* (uses extensive verbal and graphic notations as well as a very clear set of performance notes).

Stockhausen, Karlheinz: *Zyklus* (use of percussion symbols presented herein).

Yuasa, Joji: *Icon* (electronic notation for white-noise variations).

23
Minimalization

Minimalization is a concept borrowed from minimal art. As applied to music, this concept is primarily a minimal amount of material and applied structural elements in a work. Duration, as will be seen, is quite often *not* minimal, and can be extensively prolonged. Minimalization, though possibly not at first seeming to be a broad subject for compositional process, does involve a variety of significant techniques. Each of these (listed below), regardless of its immediate impression in terms of usefulness, can become a more than valuable technique to master for use in other personal styles of composition. Each of the ideas below will be discussed in listed order:

1. silence
2. concept music
3. brevity
4. continuities
5. repetitions

A study of the potentials of *silence* would soon bring even the most scientific of researchers to a rather startling result: silence does not exist (at least in terms of human contact). Even in the most rigidly controlled of circumstances where no external sound is allowed to reach an individual, there is a turning inward in which the mind begins to reckon with sounds of the body (such as the heartbeat) and imagined sounds (from either past experience or from

271

creative imagination). A simple reader experience could be obtained by merely finding a quiet spot and plugging one's ears with the forefingers of the hands. An interesting roar of sounds usually prevails with the "composer-performer-audience" being submerged with sounds born of muscle tension, air pressure, blood pressure, and other physical activity. As will be seen later, this simple experiment could be in fact a complete work in itself, working with sound—attempting silence—as much as those who compose for ensembles of highly skilled and trained musicians.

While traditional composers hold silence in esteem, saving it for hiatus before climaxes, breath pauses between phrases and movements, and other such moments, the contemporary composer has used the most minimal of ideas as a tool for creating music from "silounds" (sounds created from silence, or a manifestation of an attempt to create silence itself) not usually considered potential for even the most indeterminate of compositions (some minimal forms *are* extremely determinate). Example 253 is but a brief verbal description of a situation in which the composer has controlled some parameters, leaving others open for variation of circumstance. Note that the "silounds" here present audience and performer as being "as silent as possible," allowing the performance situation to produce the music.

Example 253
A 'silound' work.

BE AS SILENT AS POSSIBLE!
OPEN UP YOUR EARS UNTIL
EVERY POSSIBLE SOUND IS
HEARD! START
NOW!

This particular work (and it is complete) is performable in almost any quiet locale where one can ". . . open up your ears until every possible sound is heard. . . ." All considered, the audience may have gained an insight into the concept of *sound* and be more aware of its subliminal relationship to their lives (whether this is composer-intended or not). More often than not, music attempting silence is really directing audience attention away from the concert situation towards listening to those sounds which occur naturally (or unnaturally) in the environment, portending a type of *biomusic* (to be discussed in Chapter 25). Even our traditional hiatus before climaxes is often marred by such extraneous noises as a car horn, a birdcall, or a neighborhood rock band. Though often programmed to resist acceptance of such sounds as part of the work, the audience more often than not greets such external sounds with *more* attention than they would seemingly deserve (e.g., a laugh, a turn of the head, or disgust). Attempts at silence, as unsuccessful as they may be, can be fruitful in terms of a more genuine understanding of "silounds" and especially musical *dynamics.* Clearly the most intense performance problem of any music—a true "soft as possible" passage—may be significantly improved by any ensemble attempting silence. These concepts of silence, as unrelated to actual silence as they may be, are useful and pregnant raw material for any composer, whether conservative or avant-garde, if they help him to *listen.*

Concept music can relate to the silence approach as shown in example 254. Here the control reference to ". . . as quiet as possible . . ." suggests the undesirability of sound.

Example 254
"Concept music."

In general, concept musics are those ideas borne of the mind and not of actual performance in traditional terms. Concept musics can vary from one- or two-word statements which bring Rorschach images to mind, to extensive programs in which the performer (now audience as well) creates an intricate mental environment for himself. Many concept musics are notated events for which performance is impossible. Example 255 shows a traditionally notated motive for flute, most of which is at least two octaves below its performance range.

Example 255
A 'concept' excerpt.

The mind of most observers tends to hear the line anyway, without the aid of the instrument or sound waves of any kind. The concept of the flute timbre at that low level is communicated in a most minimal manner indeed.

Many concept musics make no reference to sound at all, and only suggest situations, assuming all physical faculties will be in play. Example 256 briefly describes a conceptual situation in which one sets the stage for conceptual realization. Note that no reference to sound or visual activity is made in the slightest. This music is "thinkable" and even extraneous sounds are not a part (if possible) of the situation.

Example 256
Conceptual situation.

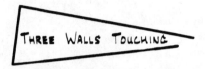

Example 257 is but two words: "Touch-Hear." Exploration of this could be as erotic or automated as the personality encountering the "score." While no laws prohibit one from actual performance in extended concert ritual, one presupposes a constant "touching-hearing" existence, and the words here reflect only a conceptual poetic reexamination of such.

Example 257
Total 'concept' score.

With these minimal notations, the composer has set such vague parameters that the performer/audience is as well a composer, his personality the true score. With the media concepts encountered in Chapters 12 and 24, even the word *composer* loses its meaning to a degree: the individual *is* the vessel into which the work is poured through a combination of experience and situation. These first two minimal musics (silence and concept) are well removed from the concert hall and, while valid in and of themselves, are as well fuel for those more determinate composers wishing to better understand themselves, this music, and the composer/performer/audience relationship.

Brevity situations bring back the concept of concert ritual. Example 258 is a work (complete) for solo bassoon.

Example 258
'Brevity' work.

It contains a bit of the previous two ideas in its lengthy internal "silound" (though it is notated in such a way that it could be less than a fraction of a second). Two single notes enclose this "rest" and give the work the brevity connotation. Example 259 carries the idea a bit more in the direction of composer-controlled brevity in that the bassoon here is but a single notated note with an "as fast as possible" slash through the five-note (indeterminate stems) rip.

Example 259
'Brevity' concept score of more control.

Works of this brevity (examples 258 and 259 are complete with double bar lines) are less interesting on repeated hearings as the shock value wears thin. It is interesting to note here, however, that one is hard put to admit boredom.

Continuities carry the concept of a single idea to a less than brief minimalization, at least in terms of length. Example 260 shows a work titled *A* in which the note A is performed by as many instruments as possible (transferred slowly from one to another) for the indicated duration.

Example 260
'Continuity' work.

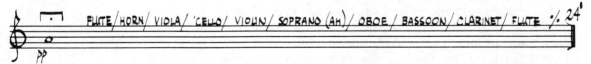

With this extensive length, the audience reacts in a variety of ways.

To the less calm or resilient listener, the only observation would be to leave the hall with a few well-selected four-letter words. To the ones that last the duration, however, an enormous variety of manifestations can begin to take place (some actually present, some imagined). Moods can come and go: boredom, monotony, laughter, contemplation, conversation; observance of overtone makeup and movement of sound in terms of space and modulation just begin the possibilities. The critics (who more often than not have left early in the performance) are more maddened at the "pretended" composer than at the work itself. If, as with indeterminacy, the control source is not considered important, one can bring more patience to the sound(s). More important, one must ask why, with the constant diversity of aural phenomena randomly packing our everyday soundscapes, a single note should bring such a paradox of reactions?

While certainly containing some audience-performed subtle variations, continuities can contain composer-programmed developments which can increase awareness of how carefully one listens. Example 261 shows an overview of a work of long duration for synthesizer in which the complex sound is continual but subject to a number of slowly applied processes of filtering. This type of entropy leads to a final passing away of a timbre which is very unlike the beginning.

Example 261
Graphic overview of work for synthesizer (continuity).

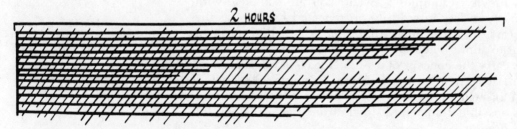

Continuities take a great many forms involving slow change of one or more parameters controlled by the composer, the audience or, in most cases, a combination of both. Indigenous to the form is the concept of a change of perspective away from what sound should be to what sound *is.* Sticking with continuity-type works can be a valid experience and an important contribution to personal style.

Minimal musics in the form of *repetitions* are very useful and often are of the more subtle continuity type. Example 262 gives but a single motive with a repeat sign *ad libitum.* As one can see in this example, the concept of continuity here is expanded only by the

Example 262
Minimal music via repetitions.

inclusion of a rhythm and pitch structure at a very simplified level. Example 263 is much more indicative of the types of minimal constructs based on ostinato repetitions. It shows five motives with a line between each. Note that the motives are very similar but not exactly the same. The score is indeed minimal but with the attendant performance notes (". . . repetitions should go for as long as the performer feels capable . . .") the work is quite substantial in length. This example is for right hand on piano alone, which would indeed limit the performance duration. As well, it would give the indeterminate length a built-in physical parameter for the perfor-

Example 263
Minimal ostinato music with modulation.

mer. Example 264 shows a work for piano (two hands) in which the sync of the repeated motives is varied. At times the two ideas will overlap exactly, while more often they will present an array of rhythmic and note *mikropolyphonie.*

Example 264
Material minimalization with mikropolyphonie *results.*

Such works usually need more than one performer for accurate performances, so intricate are the inner relationships of pitch and rhythm. The minimal aspects of the music have come to the opposite extreme of that of "silence" techniques. Here (example 264) the cells are in such constant variation with one another that, while the listener is almost immediately aware of what is going on, the interest in the fluctuating relationships is always changing (consider this as a distant cousin of the ideas expressed in examples 256, 257, and 259).

Each of the examples in this chapter shares a single common idea of minimal concept and technique: regardless of the potential resultant complexity, the composer has supplied but a situation, note(s), or idea(s) which are totally minimal in nature.

The variants of each of these concepts are as numerous as works themselves. Exact definition of many such hybrids is often impossible (and really unnecessary). It is often more the idea of the work than the work itself which inspires the composer. Moreover, points are often proved, ideals expressed, or situations explored rather than strict compositional process. Protagonists and antagonists alike can and will undoubtedly struggle over these forms, but one again finds a single assertion overwhelmingly significant to the truly creative individual: regardless of the viability of these works, to be exemplified as either "great" or "non-art" is both useless and a waste of time. What is really at hand here is to deal with the process, learn from it regardless of how far it may seem from any mainstream of familiar styles, and *discover* its potentials in any working personal style. Insight into *any* approach to compositional process or technique is the only potential for musical growth and development.

ASSIGNMENTS

1. Compose a score for audience in which silence is the only structural element. Fix a duration unknown to the "performers" (audience) and record the work. Analyze the tape carefully in terms of direction, idea, content, order of events, and other musical considerations. *Compose* a work for performers doing exactly the same actions in the same context and observe the communications.

2. Compose a passage for any available instrument with the attendant instructions; perform exactly as written but without any sound from the instrument (except breathing at appropriate points). Name the work *Listen* and perform before an unsuspecting audience.

3. Realize in traditional notation example 257 for as many available instruments using as many new techniques or ideas as you wish. Try to accomplish as similar a result in your realization as that engendered by the words.

4. Analyze example 263 (the motives, not repetitions) in terms of Chapter 3. Compose a work using cluster techniques (see Chapter 7) which achieves the same direction, continuity, and balance (for piano).

5. Compose a work for as many instruments as possible or desired (piano and voice included) which contains only three quick chords. By using any technique, process, and/or notation discussed up to this point, make these chords work as a piece of music.

6. Choose an environmental sound complex which will have a very long duration (no less than one hour). The work can be for any instruments of the composer's choice. Small, unobservable changes should be prescribed so that the work will develop to some degree. Vertically analyze for strong progression as per Chapter 1.

7. Realize example 261 for any combination of instruments.

8. Compose a work of three-measure duration for solo piano. The materials should be polytonal in nature. Add a repeat sign with no less than one hundred repetitions notated. Perform the work at the composer-indicated tempo. Shift performers (spell them) if necessary. Do not consciously vary any aspect of the written material.

9. Compose a work for any number of performers which in some way combines elements of all the techniques described in this chapter simultaneously.

10. Devise a new minimal concept other than those stated in the chapter and compose a work with attendant techniques.

WORKS FOR ANALYSIS

Consult the most recent Schwann Catalog for current in-print recordings of these works. Publishers are usually found through libraries, music stores, or distributors of music. This list is not meant to be comprehensive, only suggestive of further study.

Cage, John: *4'33·* (three-section work in which performer times his acts of silence; the audience makes the sounds for the work; prototype of this genre).

Corner, Philip: *One Note Once* (brevity in action, with the work being exactly as its title indicates).

Fulkerson, James: *Triad* (continuous performance of a C-major triad of from twelve to twenty hours in duration).

Glass, Philip: *Music in Fifths* (continuous work with a minimum of materials).

Oliveros, Pauline: *Sonic Meditations* (a group of works in verbal notations, many of which are concept minimal musics).

Reich, Steve: *Violin Phase* (phasing of minimal ideas).

Rzewski, Frederic: *Coming Together* (motivic work in which overlays of minimal materials slowly come together).

Riley, Terry: *In C* (work made up of a number of small motives which the performers repeat as often as they wish, slowly moving from one to the next, creating a tonal environment of minimal materials and maximum duration).

Satie, Eric: *Vexations* (32-bar waltz to be performed 840 times; a prototype of this idea of minimal repetitive form).

Young, La Monte: *Compositions of 1960* (a group of works of mostly conceptual nature, often with little reference to sound or music).

24
Mixed- and Inter-media

Multimedia has been defined (see Chapter 12) as a combination of art forms which is predominantly indeterminate in nature. Expression of such is primarily in terms of theatre pieces and light shows. Mixed- and inter-media, on the other hand, are combinations of art forms in which the contributing element (music, projections, etc.) draws more and more dependence on its participation in the total form, with less and less ability to stand viably on its own. In mixed-media, the art forms are dependent on each other for the success of the work, yet one or more could stand alone and remain potentially significant. Opera could be considered a predecessor of mixed-media in that, with a full-scale production, each element contributes to the totality of the work (music, staging, acting, dance), yet a performance of the music on records or over a tape playback system would not necessarily be a grave loss to the work's substance and quite often retains successful artistic survival.

Inter-media represents the complete opposite of multimedia and a further extension of mixed-media. The art forms are so closely interconnected that a separation of any entity subtracts meaning from every facet of the whole work and as well produces a greatly altered and nearly useless single form. It is important to note that inter-media is loosed from the theatrical proscenium space and exists (usually in the form of environments) as a complete entity in itself. One no longer considers individual elements as weak or

281

strong, contributing or non-contributing, but rather as one single correlated whole. The progress of this chapter will follow a course from the simplest mixed-media to the most complex of inter-media.

Projected scores offer a clear break from multimedia light shows in that correlation between the aural and visual forms is complete (at least for those able to comprehend the notation). While indeed the music should be playable without the projected score with equal success, more often than not a strong motive has inspired the composer to this form of communication. Example 265 shows two potential inspirations for the belief that the composer has conceived of the work as a dual entity. Note that the projected score (incomplete; one of ten slides) is of mobile structure and, for the eight instrumentalists, a much more readable one than a microscopic stand version. The conductor can indicate the number of the performed module with the performers relating to the single visual score image. Aside from this more practical aspect, the score itself is graphically artistic so that audience perception will not only present visual stimuli to follow the performer through the maze, but a defined knowledge of what the composer has "composed" and its visual artistry.

During the performance of such projected-score mixed-media works, there are a variety of crisscrossing elements: the aural, the visual, the combinatory, and most certainly the "game" (of the audience) of keeping up with the activities (performer and score) so that a recorded version on tape could not capture *all* of the psychological drama present in live performance (each of the elements indeed contributes to the whole). In the same sense, a film production of the score itself would prove of little use except for possible study or, at best, an interesting exercise for those bent on hearing such works completely in their head. The success of the projection, therefore, is only in a fully realized version.

The aspect of "game" can be very much a part of mixed-media concepts and performances. Example 266 is a collage of sound, projections, and spoken and acted costume drama. While the example is not the entire score (only the layout in terms of objects and general activities), it does give a graphic outline of the mixed-media concept. Note here that the performer triggers a variety of media events which in turn randomly trigger further events. Each projection or recorded sound which results from the random triggering in turn forces the performer (by full-score definition [not shown]) to turn to a set of actions (dramatic and musical), ending in a free choice of activity again. The "game" continues in theatre style as a string of events forming a media continuity. Further instructions (not shown) give exact content of the projections, music, drama, lines, action, and costumes. This is mixed-media in that the ele-

Example 265
Projected 'mobile' score.

ments are all contingent on cause-and-effect relationships in the work, *some* of which are random and some, performer- or composer-controlled. Many of the art forms could possibly stand on their own in this example, though it is difficult from this outline to abstract which ones.

Example 266
Schematic for collage of sound, projection, speaker and acted costume drama.

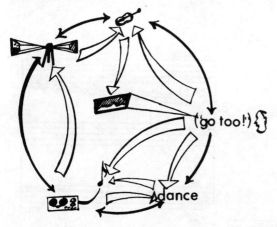

As one closes towards inter-media, the forms increasingly overlap. While one may mistakenly assume that such "media games" are really happenings (thus multimedia), a careful consideration of the total action-reaction process involved here (and communicated eventually to the audience as events are repeated) demonstrates far greater command of the art forms present and much more correlation.

Example 267 shows a stage setup for seventeen slide projectors (many of which have overlapping projections or even projections within projections), three dancer/actors, four musicians, and five audience participants. The performance directions (not shown) express details such as "slow hand fades" of projections, cloth coverings of projectors to prevent sound and light leakage into the darkened hall, and exact placement of projectors in the hall. This expresses one of the problems often encountered by the media composer: how to keep the performance from becoming either too provincial (home slide-show) or too self-indulgent (more interest in the technical complexities than the resultant form of art). Moreover,

Example 267
*Stage setup for 17 slide projectors, 3 dancers, 4 musicians and 5
audience participants.*

the media composer is very much in the position of the composer at
the synthesizer: how does one keep up with the proliferation of new
and better designs of equipment? The only difference between the
composer at the synthesizer and the media composer is that, in the
latter case, this problem is often multiplied many times over.

Example 268 is the first page of the score to the work shown in
example 267. Note the lack of real musical interest (direction) in the
extended "minimal" ostinati. Its significance lies in its contribution
to the complete body of the work and not in itself. Nothing about the
work suggests the gamesmanship of the previous example, but
rather a concentrated mixed-media form with possibly the dramatic
action and text being separable from the whole. They would be
damaged by the lack of projections, etc. but could retain the
integrity of the initial concept and a directed useful art form. The
"total theatre" of this example is observed in the parts of the
audience participants. With the opening blast of light and sound
come the tossing of marshmallows (soft) into the unsuspecting (and
no longer "safe" from the performance) audience, slowly modulating into a soft spray of perfume.

Example 268
First page of score to example 267.

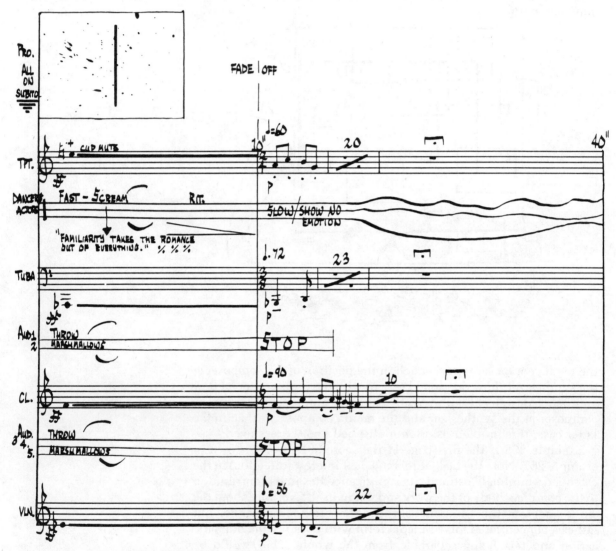

Eliminating the proscenium space (stage-to-audience relationship) from this total-theatre concept gives rise to the idea of controlled environments. Environments have no significant historical prototypes. They stem partly from "nature designs" and, while many exhibit a quite less than "natural" habitat, they do possess a correlation with environmental "scapes." This inter-media form (environments) is separate from mixed-media in that the "beginning, middle, and end" concept is virtually eliminated, creating a time-space continuum (no real form in one sense, or participant/audience-created form). As well, audiences are often considered a part of the work and generally walk in, around, or through the "structures," many times becoming part performer, composer, or both.

Example 269 demonstrates the immediate intense correlation of yet another art form not too often considered a performing art: architecture. Indeed, the structure shown is just the beginning of a work designed in this case by a determinate composer "determined" to be in control of every possible parameter of the work at hand (environment). With this architecture in mind, note the extensive sculpturing of one room in the context of the environment (example 270).

Example 269
External design of 'environment.'

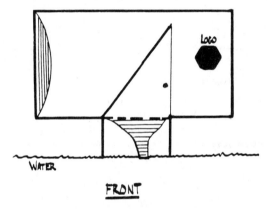

Example 270
One room of example 269.

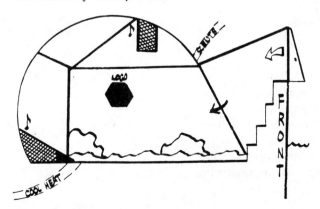

Here the design exactly locates the open and closed spaces, speaker locations for controlling spatial modulation and the like, cooling and heating ducts (inclusive of changing and controlling scents), color, floor covering (everything here is pure white), and other environmental elements. With such environments the audience becomes a part of the work, moving at will through (usually) all rooms first, then finding rooms, areas, and positions which are personally suitable. When one tires of any or all of the "works," freedom is available for exiting at will. In a sort of paradox, the composer (now an architect, designer, sculptor, etc., though these may be subcontracted or shared responsibilities) has controlled every element but form, that being left to the whim or semicontrol of the audience (i.e., the better psychologist could inform the composer of probable outcomes of an entering audience, but could never guarantee any true duration, direction, or form).

With this in mind, the composer can construct environments in which the audience can control *more* elements of the formal aspects of the environment. Example 271 shows one possible laser device which could have been placed in the environment of example 270. The harmless beam is projected across a walking area which, when broken, changes the sonic environment drastically (loud to soft, fast to slow, for instance). A retripping of the beam could produce a return to the former sound sculpture with the audience now able to control exactly which of two different musics he prefers.

Example 271
Laser device for audience control in environments such as example 270.

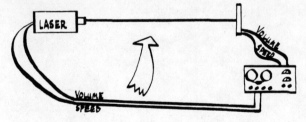

With a great many of these and like devices placed within an environment, one can easily envision a nearly completely audience-controlled atmosphere, an atmosphere in which one can choose not just the better of situations but possibly the best (at least for the moment).

A total reversal of this principle is possible with random selection of change programmed into most of the aspects of an environment, creating a self-contained *living* art object. For example, the output of a number of sample-holds (sampling white sound) could control each other and the environmental forms. Another possibility could require that the composer (or an observant and artistic controller) be at the controls to carefully program the elements as they interrelate to the audience. A sensitive programmer could observe various audience reactions to various stimuli and find those which produce a desired result.

All of these inter-media environments assume a vast knowledge of a wide variety of art forms or a cumulative effort of many artists for completion. While they can become experimental laboratories for understanding human behavior or massive collages of unrelated art forms (the potential for simplistic multimedia is ever-present), the mere expense in terms of time and monies invested suggests an artistic effort in all elements present (sensitivity to like ideals in all areas). While observer perception and spatial identities will always shift from one art form to another, the best of environments keep this crisscrossing of idioms at as equal a level as possible.

Example 272 is a type of "score" for the room shown in example 270 with composer control. The sound source is electronic but the graphic score is relatively clear in intent: smooth modulating timbres as a result of filtering white sound.

Example 272
Possible 'score' for room in example 270.

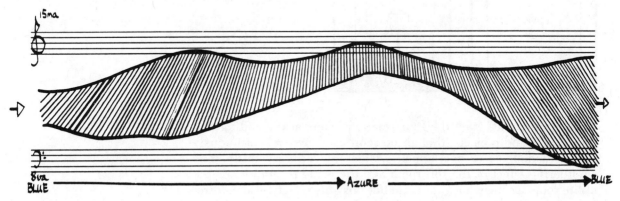

Being without beginning, middle, or end, it suggests little value in itself other than its intended environmental contribution, except in possibly the most permissive of minimal concepts (minimalization is usually a very important contributor to environmental structures, though not necessarily so). The light is a slowly changing hue from within the walls (note the lack of windows in example 270, making lighting a controllable element of the environment). The score is necessarily limited, as so much of the work is architecturally and spatially conceived. While this scoring and room design is fastidiously calm and restful in nature, it underscores a limitless set of correlative media environments from a simply conceived "tunnel of horror" to elastic rooms, stringed passageways, "ballooned" bedrooms, etc.

For the composer bent on experimenting and learning from these media concepts without devoting years to conception and completion, there are a number of less sophisticated possibilities. The use of pre-existing rooms available for modifications is one viable alternative. Example 273 shows an area (of any size) of usual rectangular construction to the left, with a fairly simple environment to the right. The voluminous supply of foam rubber bits and pieces upon a soft and thick foam rug, combined with the centrally located shade lamp (circa 1940) for lighting, convert the room into an entirely different environment.

Example 273
Empty room (left); potential environment (right).

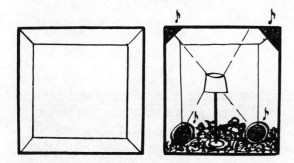

The music comes from the four small speakers at the ceiling and floor levels and projects (though no score is shown) a continuously repeated montage of overlapped waltzes played very softly. The smothering effect of the soft room and the paradox lamp lends the entire room a somewhat simplistic but possibly effective semicorrelation of inter-media art forms. Certainly the lamp alone in a bare room would bear little significance, as would the music in like circumstances. The composite provides a supply of tactile, auditory, visual, and psychological perceptions provocative enough to prove at least the potentials of "inexpensive" inter-media. Other solutions include institutional media centers now complete and being built, as well as home "conversion" to inter-media environments (as opposed to their more often multimedia existence).

The problems of mixed- and inter-media are immense and quite numerous. One, however, is so overpowering that it suggests potential disaster at every attempt: if one man attempts to master the *gesamtkunstwerk,* can he be truly master of all the arts involved (and their resultant trades, techniques, and processes) for the creation of even one large inter-media structure? If a group of individuals attempt the work, can they supplant their inherent egocentricity so as not to overpower other art forms with their own? This single problem has proven the most contributive to the lack of numerous successful environments.

The critics of these media forms usually cradle the above problem. The music critic, the architecture critic, the art critic all view the final product from their own ego-centered viewpoints. With the whole concept of environments being the relinquishing of individual significance to the concept as an entity in itself, one must await an "environment" critic (if one can exist) for credible value judgments. Those who view such media potentials as the future of musics and art in general predict more than what at present seems possible except in the most general and simplistic of terms. If such 'entities' do come to pass, with their incredible degrees of sophistication (hinted at in some of the examples), one can only imagine the potentials of modulations (light to sound, touch to visual aspects, etc.), live and electronic techniques (see Chapters 13, 14, 15, and 17), dramatic new instrumental sources (indeed, the environment itself could become the instrument), and other considerations available to the imaginative creator. The limits would be only self- and/or work-imposed.

ASSIGNMENTS

1. Compose a short work for available instruments in which the entire work is on one page only. Consider the fact that the score will eventually be projected in some fashion (overhead or slide, for example), and compose this media concept into a useful work in which the combination of visual and aural activities are meaningful.

2. Compose a work for one available performer. The work should consist of a number of fragments each related to some form of audience behavior (e.g., a short passage played for a cough, another for a giggle). A second performer should turn off the lights if an audience cue is not received after ten seconds of silence.

3. Complete the score of example 268 (or at least continue it).

4. Compose a work which is to be folded in a variety of ways and suspended from the ceiling into a circle of performers. Use only techniques from Chapters 1 through 7 for composition. The performers are to play whatever is before them, changing immediately as the mobile moves around. Only the score should be lit in an entirely darkened hall, with the audience as close to the performers as possible for the reading of the score. As well, the score should be notated in different colors, each with a meaning given in separate performance directions and known only to the performers.

5. Create a work using as many sources of projections, musics, aromas, etc. as possible. Relate all of these as closely as possible to create as coherent and closely knit a work as you are able. It should be notated as fully as is needed.

6. Taking an available empty room, create an environment based on the fact that the room will be packed with balloons (from floor to ceiling, wall to wall). Compose the music, lighting, and other elements all to fit exactly with the overall effect hinted at by the nature of the environment.

7. In a totally empty white room, place some kind of available triggering devices (thin thread, for example) which, when tripped, turn on or off some element of sound or lights. Use as many devices as possible and correlate the probable order of triggering to a concise set of organized sounds and sights.

8. Realize the score of example 272 as closely as possible. Perform in a room which is as close to that of example 270 as possible.

9. Build a large box, big enough for a man to stand upright within. Design potential control of every environmental aspect of the occupant of the box (inclusive of sound, lights, smells, tastes, touch). Create a highly unified work for the box in which all elements interrelate constantly and one does not dominate except for possibly short periods of time. The work should exist for as long as the box is turned on, so that during a performance period numerous people could enter and leave the performance.

WORKS FOR ANALYSIS

Since the often highly interwoven media concepts explored in this chapter very necessarily imply complete performance for full study, records (unless correlated with live production of other art forms) are usually not applicable. Scores are quite useful and can be obtained through libraries, music stores, or distributors of music.

This list is not meant to be comprehensive, only suggestive of further study.

Ashley, Robert: *Public Opinion Descends upon the Demonstrators* (a work in which the electro-performance is dictated by the actions of the audience as per a set score).

Cope, David: *The Deadliest Angel Revision* (projectors, actor, musicians in an inter-media situation, all elements contributing to the whole without any being viable independently).

Erb, Donald: *Souvenir* (a full media event in which a vast number of objects are thrown through black-light projections with performers surrounding the audience; very effective inter-media).

Ellis, Merrill: *Mutations* (a work which turns the entire hall into an environmental situation).

Kasemets, Udo: *It: Tribute to Buckminster Fuller, Marshall McLuhan and John Cage* (computer control of an auditorium environment of visual, aural, and audience participation).

Lentz, Daniel: *Sermon* (work for string quartet with the score projected at the back of the stage, using color and other graphic concepts for visual interest and correlation).

McLean, Barton: *Identity* (a complete environmental work which involves audience interaction in buildings for which the works were composed).

Stockhausen, Karlheinz: *Musik für Ein Haus* (a work especially designed for performance in the various rooms of a house).

Subotnick, Morton: *A Ritual Game Room* (a work which employs media game techniques for complete performance).

Tudor, David: *Reunion* (a media work produced with David Behrman, John Cage, Lowell Cross, Marcel Duchamp, Teeny Duchamp, and Gordon Mumma).

Young, La Monte: *Dream House* (like many of this composer's works, an environment in which every aspect, no matter how simple or minimal the realization, is controlled).

25
Biomusic

Extrapolated forms of biomusic range from simple "situation pieces" to extremely complex brain-wave compositions. Biomusic (music created as a result of any life—bio—or natural phenomenon, usually without traditional implementations of any kind excepting electronics when necessary), along with antimusic, poses probably the most radical concepts and ideas to music and art in general. It is not a matter of bearing with these ideas, but of examining them carefully for possible personal stylistic digestion that is important. As far removed from tradition as the examples herein are, the intelligent composer will not reject or laugh off their implications. If they seem to pose a threat to any definition of music or seem unworthy of study in a book on composition, it may be time for one to re-examine his own parameters of intelligent creativity. The possible use of twelve-tone techniques would have most probably been equally as foreign to its ancestors as biomusic is to contemporary tradition. Change is vital to any viable art form. Though many changes, when viewed in their raw and extreme states, seem extraordinarily uncomfortable, they can develop into unique and even comfortable additions to a personal arsenal of techniques and processes (when understood and practiced).

Listed below is a basic outline of biomusics from the more simple in structure to the more complex (note that no value judgment is intended: simplicity is as viable an element to art as is complexity). The chapter will follow this basic listing:

1. situation pieces
2. circumstance music
3. soundscapes
4. animal composition
5. plant composition
6. brain-wave musics

   Situation pieces are more often than not verbal in notation. Example 274 is a work which briefly describes a situation in which sounds are heard. What sounds, or what other media events which might take place, are beside the point in this composition. The composer has merely placed the audience (preferably one or two persons only) in a position in which auditory phenomena will occur. While this work, as well as the many which exist in "situation literature," may seem more a back-to-nature refresher course in what sounds indeed surround us (or can surround us if "situated right"), they can offer the composer a revitalization of his own concept of personal style (the sounds heard are equally "personal" to the "composers" present in the situation), repetition and form (indeed the natural sources abound in simple and complex forms), and originality (the best of composers with timbre control and usage *might* learn a great deal from a performance of a situation piece).

Example 274
'Situation piece.'

"... Stand amid tall trees in deep spring forest at sunset... "

   Circumstance music is very similar to situation pieces but more minimal and often concise in nature. Again, the notation is usually verbal and a circumstance in which sound events will occur is described. Example 275 is but one brief work: *Storm.* The composer has not given the slightest clue as to whether one should "walk through," "watch," "listen to," or even possibly "avoid" the "Storm." The work is part conceptual, certainly minimal, and definitely biomusic (note that in this piece the stress is on the natural phenomenon rather than the biological aspects of biomusic).

Example 275
'Circumstance music.'

STORM

Example 276 is a *soundscape* graph (for three seconds) of a room with open windows in New York City near Park Avenue on a summer afternoon at 3 P.M.

Example 276
Soundscape of room in New York City with 4 graphs: loudness, timbre, rhythmic diversity and pitch fluctuation for three seconds.

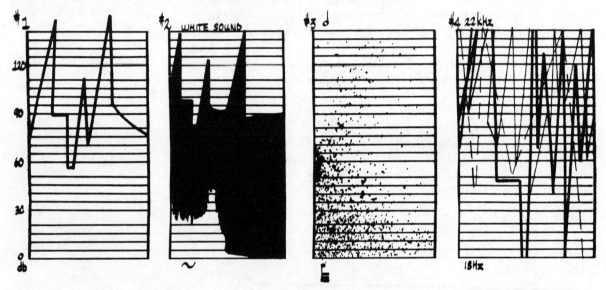

Note the high decibel levels reached (graph 1: 120–140 db is the pain threshold; beyond 140 db, damage to the ear can set in), the near white-sound complex with "blasts" of new timbres (graph 2: timbre), the rhythmic diversity (graph 3: basic rhythmic density measured as close as possible), and the wide pitch fluctuation and range (graph 4: 18 to 22,000 Hz is generally the human limit, inclusive of even extraordinary hearing potential). Each graph was made from an electronic apparatus (e.g., loudness: decibel meter) and affords a good deal of accuracy. This set of graphs is shown only to give basic groundwork to soundscape composition. The basic concept is to rework what would appear to be haphazard and an often cruel set of relatively random levels on members of the environmental audience so that potential parameters of sound can be observed and utilized in a framework for composition. Muzak is often used to hide the random soundscape vocabulary, but, like the using of the sides of a building for the canvas of a painting, or "sculpting" a city, the future potentials of soundscape composition are fascinating alternatives indeed. Example 277 is but a start to this and shows a two-block area of any city downtown section at two different times of day.

Example 277
Possible graph for soundscape work.

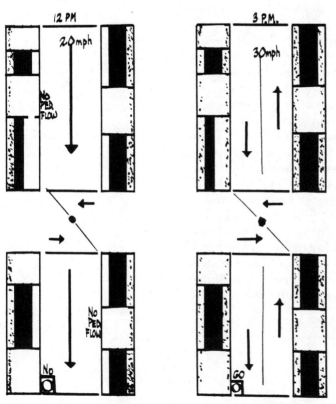

Note the change of traffic patterns and speed limits for automobiles as well as the pedestrian flow alterations. Sound-pollution controls for work signals, construction sites, etc., are also shown. With such things being possible indeed, one could compose works with the basic raw sonorities of a city as the only sound source. While such soundscapes are not an integral part of composition at this writing, such "sculptures" are imminent. Unlike situation pieces and circumstance music, the composer here can use his sources as determinately as he wishes for as finite and predictable a work as predesigned.

Animal composition is simply listening to animals create music.

Often this manifests a sort of natural theater not unlike the verbal implications of circumstance and situation musics. As used here, however, it is the particular listening to *one* type of animal in detail for performance. Birds have been studied for years for their song literature. More recently, the sounds of certain types of whales and other underwater creatures have brought attention to this immense sound source. Essentially one does not "compose" animal music (the animal takes care of that) but tries to record, amplify, or use other techniques to hear the unique "compositions" of particular animals. This form of biomusic does not require a score except when special electronic modification is to take place. It is here that two basic categories of animal music are created: (1) works which are truly animal-composed and untouched by human controls; and (2) works which involve human alteration in some small way (a large way would result in *musique concrète*). With little to be said about category 1 except in the form of an assignment at chapter's end, it is with category 2 that some interesting manifestations can occur. *Harmlessly* prodding animals to certain "performances," amplifying or using echo processes for greater audibility and/or effects, filtering electronically (especially to pinpoint one sound or another, singling it out from usually a diversified sonic background), and like devices all add human scoring to the work at hand. Example 278 shows an amplification and random filtering system placed into a gopher hole with attendant microphone pickup at one end and speakers at the other (placed just outside the hole).

Example 278
Bio (gopher) amplification.

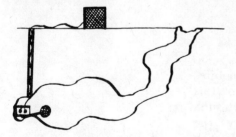

Besides being animal music *per se*, the leaving of such electronics unattended in a semisocial (human) environment would bring most interesting resulting candid audience reaction (a definite "natural theater" event).

Other forms of animal composition which have been used include "animal notation" (motion of animals through areas designated for predetermined realization by traditional ensembles) and "animal instruments" (*live* instruments such as human-trained animals which "sing" or perform in certain ways). Both of these seem rather unique to a single work (in the first case) and more valuable to the circus (in the second). One should, however, note that the musical saw is now considered a mainstream instrument, while until recently it was a bizarre folk instrument (to some, more a joke than a musical instrument). Certainly a *Concerto for Amplified Dog and Chamber Orchestra* seems a bit remote, but audience potential, if only for curiosity or a laugh (not such an evil thing in music), would be high.

Example 279 shows a potential schematic for *plant music.* This has been successful with the small bits of electric current in plants acting as voltage-control inputs to a synthesizer.

Example 279
Possible setup for plant voltage control of synthesizer.

Such plant compositions are more a result of a human set of controls (choice of which modules are to be controlled or used). Experiments do show potential for "prodding" plant outputs by various forms of motion around the plant (including vocal stimulations). This too, however, is human-controlled with the plant only "reacting." Such biomusics do exist, though, and have perhaps more than scientific value.

Possibly the most important biomusic yet to be discussed is *brain-wave composition.* In brain-wave biomusic, electrodes are connected (as with plant music) to a part of the subject or composer (in this case, the brain—which emits a small but definitely controllable electric current). These currents supplied by the electrode pickups are in turn amplified and used as control voltage sources for a synthesizer. The potentials of this type of electronic biomusic have just begun to be touched upon at this writing, but portend an enormous future. With a composer well versed in electronics and having set up his own sound sources and sets of control voltages (through some form of patching according to the synthesizer used), the connection of electrodes to the skin of the head of the composer/performer brings immediate sound. While this can be a dull and lifeless droning of alpha waves, no matter what the modules used, it can become a controlled and very lively sound production. Practiced composers have the potential of altering the electric brain wave outputs quite distinctly and with predictable results. Indeed, the concept of a composer "thinking" a work with its amplified and electronic determinate results emanating from the speaker in a concert hall may be a most significant new concept in music. It is the "practicing" which will give the potential, and the creativity of the composer himself which will secure a possible place for brain-wave composition in future musics.

ASSIGNMENTS

1. Incorporate any one of the six biomusics discussed in this chapter into a work for traditional instruments (any number available). Techniques which may be employed include minimal music and indeterminacy in particular.

2. Perform example 274 as exactly as described. Return and compose a short work in any style which suggests itself.

3. Compose a work for traditional instruments (as many as are available) with example 276 as a basic score outlay. Realize this example using procedures of Chapters 1 through 10 only.

4. Discover a potential soundscape environment (e.g., practice rooms) and, by using signs and the like, control the raw materials until a work of as determinate nature as possible is achieved.

5. Choose a sound-producing animal and record as much continuous sound as time allows. Study the tape for elements of form, repetition, direction, balance, and other applicable musical parameters. Compose a short work for piano which follows at least five basic concepts learned or observed in the animal music. Do not imitate the animal. In fact, avoid any potential for audience knowledge of inspiration. Only the basic suggestions of abstract observations should be compositionally employed.

6. Write twenty-five single-word circumstance musics. Choose three for performance (or observation) by as many people as possible. Follow performance with aesthetic discussion with all involved (recorded if possible without the knowledge of the participants). Review the tape made. Carefully re-evaluate every pro and con you have about what such music's value might be.

7. Using any amplification instrument available (and echo if possible), compose a work with diagrammatic notation for placement of electronics near a natural sound source. Record the entire operation from a distance with inclusion of all other sounds present as well as the distorted original single entity. Perform the work on tape as a whole without any further alteration before as large an audience as possible.

8. Compose ten situation pieces. Perform them all. Note which tend to work and which do not. In an otherwise nonbiomusic composition, use verbal instructions (e.g., at the climax) in the form of a situation piece. Return to the original nonbiomusic material before the work's conclusion.

9. If synthesizer potential is available as well as proper safe electrode inclusion as a voltage control source, create a composition by thinking "events." Practice as time is available for better control and more determinate outcome.

10. Analyze in graph terms and verbal identity every sound that you are hearing as you read this. Be as complete as possible, making sure that none have been missed. Try to discover direction, balance, or climax in any or as many as possible of the sound complexes heard. Note if any correlation occurs between the different sources. Note carefully how many you were not conscious of at the time of reading. Attempt conscious intellectual control over which sounds you wish to hear and which not. Experiment by shifting "blocked sounds" and sounds heard one to another.

WORKS FOR ANALYSIS

Consult the most recent Schwann Catalog for current in-print recordings of these works. Publishers are usually found through libraries, music stores, or distributors of music. This list is not meant to be comprehensive, only suggestive of further study.

Barnett, Ed, Norman Lederman, and Gary Burke: *Stereofemic Orchidstra* (plant music generated by electrodes through a synthesizer as voltage control).

Chiari, Giuseppe: *Fuori* (a situation piece and soundscape in one; the performer is instructed to sit in a chair and tell the audience what he is hearing).

Hassell, Jon: *Landmusic Series* (wide range of musics inclusive of situation pieces of simple verbal notation to extensive drawings of amplifications of natural phenomena).

MacKenzie, I. A.: *Notes in Discontinuum* (a book of circumstance and situation musics in graphic prose notations, with realization by David Cope, relating many of MacKenzie's ideas and thoughts published posthumously).

Oliveros, Pauline: *Sonic Meditations* (many diverse works involved with situation, circumstance, and soundscape contexts, along with concepts often born of extrasensory perception).

Rosenboom, David: *Ecology of the Skin* (one of many works by this composer very much involved with brain wave musics).

Rzewski, Frederic: *Love Songs* (a set of mostly situation pieces in verbal notation).

Schaffer, R. Murray: *World Soundscape Project* (soundscape studies on record with emphasis so far on the city of Vancouver).

Songs of the Humpback Whale (recorded on Columbia ST-620; shows some of the extraordinary potential of animals to create music).

Yannay, Yehuda: *Bugpiece* (a work for "living notation" in which bugs provide the moving notation across a checkerboard with parameters set up for a quartet of traditional performers on traditional instruments).

Young, La Monte: *Piano Piece for David Tudor No. 3* (this is a seven-word circumstance music, as are many of this composer's minimal-type musics).

26
Antimusic

The definition of *antimusic,* like that of antiart, often embraces a variety of forms (many of which have already been discussed: biomusic, minimalization, concept musics, and the like). As examined herein, antimusic will connote basically those forms which definitively attempt destruction of sound, the concept of audience or composer, and any combinations of these. Again, while these concepts are extremely foreign to any rational approach to music, they should be carefully examined in order to evaluate any potential they may have beyond the raw states in which the examples in the chapter protray them. Avoidance of study of antimusics is only "head in the sand" philosophy; they *exist.* Each of the ideas expressed herein, coupled with other more traditional forms, can prove useful (especially when utilized in a less extreme or at least less total state). Many of these potentials will be examined in more detail at the chapter's end.

Like most art forms, music has remained somewhat immaculate and docile through most of history, contributing primarily benign emotional impacts on audiences. *Danger* concepts of sound have arisen partly out of the electronic creation of sounds louder than the human ear can tolerate (beyond 140 db) and the temporal lack of knowledge of "when" such effects might take place. As well, the media breakdown of proscenium concepts brings the potential of "where" the sound will come from, another danger ingredient.

"Danger musics" actively exploit the audience's breakdown of security. Example 280 shows a work in which an ephemeral environment surrounds the audience, only to be punctured time and time again by random crashing chords, ear-splitting and frightening by context. The theatre of the work, only graphed in overview here, is not in what will happen, but when. Contributing to the antimusic definition, the work lasts two days, with each unpredictable bone-crushing sound of different loudness with each punctuation (note the db levels in the overview). An electronic performance would lead the most stalwart soul rushing from the hall long before the work ends. It is this element (that the audience or human listeners are no longer important) as well as the concept that performances are no longer safe that is implicit in antimusic.

Example 280
Overview of two-day danger music in terms of loudness (db).

Danger-music "mobiles" are, and have been, effective antimusic. Example 281 is a sound museum which has twenty-four buttons and connected speakers. Each of the tape decks (hidden behind the front plates) has a sound of some kind on a self-contained loop. Some of these sounds are soft modulations of rich sounds, environments of aural luxury. Others contain single blasts of sound rendering even the most prepared listener—temporarily at least—partially deaf. The Russian roulette performance by a single participant is exciting, masochistic, and, to be sure, quite insane. Yet, ear-cleansing works such as these first two, as well as others with continuous sounds of db danger levels reached and passed, exist commonly in certain popular musics and abound as well in the avant-garde. In serious musics, danger music (like most concept and minimal music) provides a podium of some communication of political or social comment. In its purest form, danger music poses some of the most critical aesthetic questions one can encounter. Following the continual expansion of not only art combinations but art concepts throughout this text, one must inquire: where to from here? More apropos to the avant-garde situation is the question: how does one invent something more extreme than or at least totally different from any other artist? In the escalating processes and change of the twentieth century, is it no wonder that artists have examined and re-examined every conceivable potential for exploration of sound and idea? While many composers are content to avoid the aesthetic questions or believe that they really do not need answering, the composer of danger music deals with such as a constant in his art form.

Example 281
'Sound museum' with audience choice of various benign and dangerous sounds.

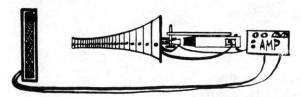

An offshoot of danger music and a definitive member of the antimusic group is that of destroying extant music. While composers have done this to their own musics for centuries, the anti-composer does it to works of others. The nearly incomprehensible act has indeed manifested itself clearly in the avant-garde. Some have even specialized techniques in which a destruction ritual is displayed. Example 282 is that of a one-page work slowly destroyed through five stages. In some sort of integrity of means, the score is first determined to be the only copy and only rendition of the work. If the composer is living, permission is often asked for the destruction (depending on the "decomposer's" state of being). In stage one, the work is written over in black ink in great time-consuming detail so that virtually nothing is legible. Stages two and three are exact cutting by (a) parallel horizontal lines, and (b) parallel vertical lines. Stage four is the crushing of the mutilated score into a ball with the aid of flammable glue, and finally, stage five completes the process by burning the work to the finest ashes possible. Many such works are saved in clear plastic containers with a label exclaiming both the original creator and the eventual destroyer. A number of museums have such containers in their collections. The act, as meticulously insane as it may appear, is clearly again born more from an idea and an aesthetic: what matter if the work dies now or a million years from now? Is art defined partially by potential immortality? If a work, a composer's name, all will die in the millennia ahead, what matter if things begin a bit early? If potential audiences are the answer, then one must question seriously what exactly one's music *is* to an audience: entertainment? drama? communication? If antimusic does nothing more creative, it brings to the open the aesthetic questions that every composer must at some time face.

Example 282
'Destruction ritual' of a musical score.

Example 283 is of a self-destructing work which its composer completes with full knowledge of its impending end. In fact, as the page shows, the composer must work with incredible speed to beat the consequences of the completely disappearing ink (nonretraceable).

Example 283
Self destructing work through use of disappearing ink.

Some composers deal with instruments or works which have no audience, not even the composer's presence. Example 284 shows a popular type of wind-sound sculpture discussed earlier under new instruments (see Chapter 16). Its destiny will be to remain in total isolation from any human audience as much as that is possible. Quite harmless compared to danger and destruction works, this at least suggests more creative potentials of antimusic. The aesthetic questions are, however, no less real.

Example 284
Wind sound sculpture.

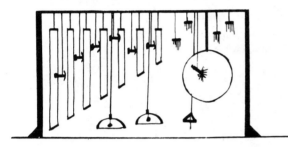

All of these examples in one way or another typify the antimusic concept: add *anti* as a prefix to every possible parameter of music tradition, e.g., antidirection, antimovement, anticreation. Only "anticlimax" is the possible exception, as certainly most antimusics are not that. The question enduring through most of this maze of confusing acts is: Why? Or possibly of more direct import, why should a composer, especially a student of the art, become involved in such acts? One might respond by suggesting that, like any "evil," it should be exposed and understood as thoroughly as possible. To follow such reasoning one must definitely possess the knowledge that indeed such acts are "evil." In antimusic one has exposed the composer to the end towards which many of his previous experiments point (if indeed he is going to expand his artistic consciousness).

Possibly the most important content of danger musics is their potential creative uses. The theatre potential for high db levels is extremely useful. Note in example 285 the overview of a relatively short piece in which the bursts of example 280 are less violently utilized but create the danger threat to the audience. Such bursts are especially useful as climactic techniques. In this example, each burst of sound gets louder, portending an eventual danger to the audience, yet it is never reached. Within the brevity of the work and the clear-cut form, the probability is that the audience will remain for the entirety of the work, though probably feeling no more safe than they were in example 280.

Example 285
Overview of short work with danger 'threat.'

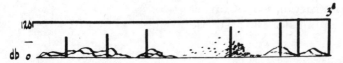

Example 286 shows a simplistic version of example 282, in which a composer's own score is completely destroyed by fire. The example is *shown* completed for constant demonstration, and not just described, to accentuate the fact that actual destruction, not just hiding away or "grounding" a composer-viewed bad score, can truly be a creative act defining a creator's personal aesthetics.

Example 286
Storage of destroyed work (ashes in labeled jar).

Antimusic extends the consciousness of the composer to the extreme. While it possibly seems insane, the art world holds many such similar activities with singular enthusiasm. Self-destructing sculptures, erased drawings, and similar artifacts, are extant in many major museums. While music has often paralleled art events, more often new ideas in art are evidenced years ahead of music and its ideals.

Previous chapters are categorizations of the manifold forms of endeavor which will undoubtedly continue to unfold for years to come. It is only hoped that, by defining the *complete* parameters of music, the composer will find his personal style and place with a combination of them, uniquely his. Antimusic completes the cycle from study of strong direction and strength in traditional music notation to the selfsame destruction of such with as many alternatives in between as possible. For the critics of these latter chapters (as useful substance for composition study), the author merely suggests said critic define any aesthetic or scientific concept without defining equally its opposite (e.g., good/bad; beautiful/ugly;

object/vacuum). For the protagonists of antimusics (especially in the extreme) and those who choose such as a sole compositional technique, one can only suggest that the dead-end features of this concept will surely spell successful completion of a "musical career" in short order. As has been stated many times up to this point in the text, responsibility to any *single* technique or process is usually self-defeating and uncreative. The diversity presented in this text is surely the evidence of crossed potentials and truly personal styles which is the topic of the next chapter.

ASSIGNMENTS

1. Select the weakest assignment produced for this book. Carefully use the procedures of example 282 to completely destroy the piece. Save the ashes in a plastic container if desired. Redo the assignment so that it is no longer the weakest. Repeat the process if necessary.

2. Construct an instrument which in some way plays itself (by wind, fire, rain, etc.). Place the instrument in the most remote area accessible to you and never return to its location.

3. Reread Chapter 1 of this book. Apply the prefix *anti* to every aspect of the concepts. Compose a work in traditional notation which is the weakest and clearest example of every conceivable negative aspect derived through "anti" technique.

4. By any electronic means available (radio, if necessary), create a sound which borders on the danger level of db response. In a work for as many instruments as possible performing softly, use this source as sound threat to the performers and/or audience.

5. In a verbal score of quite extended length (to be read to an audience), suggest potential actions in a believable way so that no member of the audience is capable of staying in the hall. Boredom should not be an available factor (the work should not last over twelve minutes).

6. Using techniques of Chapters 1 through 10 only, compose a short work for piano in which it is known that the performance will be total destruction of the score by the performer. Outline the destructive procedures at the beginning of the score in detailed performance directions.

7. In some way create a selection of sounds to be chosen at random by a "performer." Follow the same concept as described around example 281. Make sure that the "performer" is unaware of any of the sounds to be produced as well as the db-level contrasts. If speakers are the source, hide them so that direction of sound is as surprising as content.

WORKS FOR ANALYSIS

Consult the most recent Schwann Catalog for current in-print recordings of these works. Publishers are usually found through libraries, music stores, or distributors of music. This list is not meant to be comprehensive, only suggestive of further study.

Acconci, Vito Hannibal: *Works* (much of the work of this poet-artist-composer deals with self-destruction of not only the work but of audience and/or performers, though to date no one work has actually been so consummated).

Ashley, Robert: *Wolfman* (a work which—when on record—gives program notes to turn on as loud as possible; since the original performance was equally loud, damage to ears can be potentially quite extensive).

Ay-o: *Finger Boxes* (these are small sculptures, some of which contain sharp blades and other very soft silk, etc.; which box contains which is only discovered by performing the piece, i.e., placing one's finger into the small opening).

Cage, John: *HPSCHD* (composed with Lejaren Hiller; a work for large multimedia happening, but the recorded version contains printed computer readouts to perform the piece on the record-player dials; certain settings for the already loud performance can lead to most intense danger music connotations).

Higgins, Dick: *One Antipersonnel Type CBU Bomb Will Be Thrown into the Audience* (needs little discussion as to its antimusic concept).

Lentz, Daniel: *Anti Bass Music* (graphic score of weaponry for advanced warfare in which the performer is to produce the relevant violent and destructive sounds as best as possible).

MacKenzie, I. A.: *Wind Sound Sculptures* (works, as described in the chapter, which are even at this moment performing for no human audience).

Paik, Nam June: *Danger Music for Dick Higgins* (a work which in short verbal language suggests performance the completion of which would surely destroy the performer).

——: *Hommage à John Cage* (a work in which two pianos are destroyed, cutting of Cage's necktie occurs along with his complete soaking with soap and water without prior knowledge; other works by this composer involve destruction of a variety of musical instruments).

Tinguely, Jean: *Homage to New York City* (a large self-destructing sculpture which included a player piano. The work took nine months to build and less than two hours to self-destruct).

27
Decategorization

Most personal styles are not born of *one* concept, process, instrumentation, or technique. Up to this point in the book, the focus has been to give examples of a variety of ideas for the purpose of allowing the reader (actively composing his way through) to find those modes of his use. Once found, these models can be decategorized in a number of useful ways so that the composer can form a unique and imaginative musical frame of reference. By definition, decategorization is the molding of more than one concept so that perception of technique and process are no longer the end or point of composition but the *means* to an end. While many of the ideas expressed in this chapter do exemplify one or more techniques in an obvious way, the concept is still intact: the technique is being used by the composer, and not the reverse.

The combinations of just two of the techniques, processes, concepts, instrumentations, or notations discussed herein equals 26 factorial (or 26 × 25 × 24 × 23, etc.). That is to say that harmonic progression techniques could be used with twelve-tone processes, melodic direction, pointillism, polytonality, etc. and, with few exceptions (indeterminacy, for example), all ideas up to and including antimusic. Likewise, twelve-tone techniques could be effectively combined with melodic direction, pointillism, polytonality, etc. The total possible combinations are in the multibillions. This, combined with the factorial combinations of the use of three chapter

311

contents, four chapter contents, etc., give the composer more selectivity and possibilities than composers who have lived, are living, or will ever live (if only half of this prediction be true, it is a comforting thought for those bent on originality). While authoring a potentially secure spot for an individual style, the large number of combinations for decategorization does present problems of combining various processes and techniques together. This combining *process* (or decategorization) is the basic motivation for this chapter's content.

Assuming the composer has chosen a set of stylistic parameters within which to work, one can formulate some cognitive suggestions for their combinative use. It should be clearly noted that the author does not exclude other new ideas or additions of the multitude of traditional techniques available to the composer. Decategorization is a concept applicable to any set of ideas. Choice of materials of this book for "example use" in this chapter is merely a launching pad for further exploration. Likewise, it seems best to utilize ideas discussed within this book because of their easy accessibility.

The list below gives some of the potential decategorizing processes and will be the chapter order of discussion:

1. eclecticism
2. quoting
3. sectionalization
4. leakage
5. overlay
6. fusion

Each of these new techniques can be as important in decision-making as the processes described in many of the previous individual chapters. Indeed, it is most critical for a composer to musically evaluate why certain combinations of techniques sound as they do, so that he might choose the *right* decategorization procedure for the desired result. Many of the above-listed concepts dovetail and/or overlap significantly with others present on the list. It is the author's intention here not to be redundant but rather to express basic concepts from many possible angles.

Example 287 is a combination of twelve-tone concepts, new instrumental techniques, melodic direction, and *mikropolyphonie*. The excerpt is for woodwind quintet and demonstrates one form of an *eclectic* approach (as defined in terms of ideas retaining formal technique or process identity). Note that the combination is most interesting in the noncollaborative ways the different processes contribute to the whole. While each of these ideas could be fused,

Example 287
*Combination of twelve-tone concepts, new instrumental techniques,
melodic direction, and* mikropolyphonie.

they are left principally in the raw, not intending to blend or correlate but rather to dramatize their uniqueness. At times (in the flute part) a strong melodic line is accompanied by a flowing *mikropolyphonie.* Later in the short excerpt twelve-tone techniques are lost completely in the use of new instrumental resources (multiphonics, mouthpiece alone, for instance). It is the purpose of such eclecticism to utilize the *differences* between source techniques rather than their similarities. These then provide the composer with the contrast and materials for compositional direction.

Eclectic techniques often defy decategorization concepts rather than implement them; however, by sheer composite use of more than one process the decategorization has begun. Eclecticism (in its simplest meaning) is most effective when used with an unstable continuity of concepts. If, for example, an entire work of extended duration were to explore eclecticism exclusively, it would more likely than not need carefully timed intrusions of the processes. Example 288 shows an overview of a composition of fifteen minutes. Note that only the processes—in this case, *klangfarbenmelod-*

ien (K), interval exploration (I.E.), indeterminacy (I), melodic direction (M), and cluster techniques (C)—are described in the boxes outlining the work. Each of the techniques remains intact and is separated (in the orchestral framework for which it was conceived) by instrumentation, pitch range, and tempo, as well as the overlap and often use of only one technique at a time. After a certain amount of the work has passed, the effect of eclectic technique is somewhat diluted. While one assumes that the ideas are good enough in themselves to hold the attention of the listener, the eclectic concept can continue to be viable not by *what* is occurring but *when*. Note in the example that there is an almost random quality at the outset between the various techniques. This is followed by a more organized development of each separate process and finally culminates in a stretto between the component ideas. Eclecticism on this basis can be a useful tool for composers to instill dramatic discontinuities in their works.

Example 288
Overview of work with a variety of techniques discussed as 'eclecticism.'

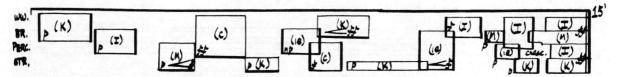

Quoting is in a sense a form of eclecticism, but with a bit more obvious contrast informing the compositional frame of reference. Example 289 shows part of a short work for piano and voice which includes cluster techniques, microtones, *mikropolyphonie,* and the added decategorization concept of quoting. Note here that until the piano begins the small portion of a Chopin sonata, the materials seem more cohesive than provided in eclecticism. While this is not necessary, it does provide a more effective base for the contrasting style and concept of the tonal intrusion. If the cohesion were not present, the quotation would be just one more contrast added to the already overfull pot of inconsistent elements. In example 289 the resultant theatre can be extraordinarily effective if the context is suitable and the timing right.

Example 290 shows "technique" quoting without style or composer attachment. Here the excerpt is for modulation techniques (timbre, and of one note) in the clarinet, violin, and trumpet parts, which is suddenly contrasted by the prepared piano.

Example 289
"Quoting" as well as cluster techiques, microtones and mikropolyphonie.

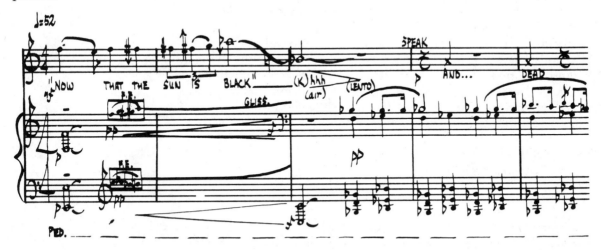

Example 290
'Technique' quoting.

This interruptive technique is a definitive potential of quoting, but not necessarily ideal (as the more obvious example 289 shows). Again, like eclecticism, quoting exploits the differences and not the similarities of the materials presented, suggesting anything but decategorization. Important to note here, however, is the increased effectiveness after quotation if the environment around it is fused.

Example 291 is a *sectionalized* decategorization process involving total organization, pointillism, *musique concrète,* new notations, and interval exploration. The excerpt is for tape and piano. Like eclecticism and quoting, the effect is diversification or decategorization by emphasizing the differences of the techniques involved.

Example 291
Sectionalized decategorization.

Up to this point, a more or less exact and thorough use of technique or process has been present. Since none of the chapters present rules *per se,* a simple procedure of blending the techniques together would be that of poetic license. Freedoms attained through the melting of one technique into another are quite possible and effective and, though they would weaken the effect of eclecticism and quoting, can make sectionalization ideas more rational and certainly less abrupt. Example 292 shows a work employing the exact same techniques as example 291, with the exception that the technique is not taken literally but *used* as musical intuition dictates. Note that even though the tape portion is partly graphic in notation, it clearly shows how the overlays and modulations of especially the total-organization technique secure a more fluid composition, though still separated. The total organization, rather than stopping, slowly expands its own parameters by subsetting subsets until the organization principle is lost and the interval of the second is explored.

Example 292
'Intuitive' decategorization.

Leakage becomes a more subtle decategorization process and involves a core concept of allowing a number of techniques to attract their *like* qualities rather than their differences. Example 293 is an excerpt for flute, projections, and synthesized tape (employing pointillism, mixed-media, electronic techniques, and resultant notations).

Example 293
Modulatory decategorization.

Note the modulations (here a core concept to the process of leakage) from flute to tape to projections, with the thread of a single concept growing throughout. The pointillism is an irregular but distinct feature of the excerpt, overlapping from the flute bursts to quick slide changes to abrupt slashes of electronic sounds. Each process is in its own way different but utilized in a similar manner, giving what might initially appear a noncohesive ensemble of processes a viable connective tissue allowing ideas to "leak" one into another.

Possibly a more dramatic form of leakage would be example 294, which shows minimalization, new notations, melodic direction, and indeterminacy in a work for voice and optional piano innards.

Example 294
Dramatic form of leakage.

Note that while the "repetition" form of minimalization is used for the single line of text, the melodic direction and drama of indeterminacy provides a useful leakage which adds variety and direction to the example.

Often "leakage" implies a use of very traditional or mainstream techniques spilling over into an avant-garde language. The resultant vocabulary is not "quoting" or difference exploitation, but rather the concept of using any technique or sound to compose a work without regard for historically imposed connotations. Example 295 is but a brief passage for piano in which completely tonal materials are interspersed with new-instrument resources and twelve-tone techniques (atonal). While the effect can often be humorous, the leakage concept can viably front any set of sounds if the musical context is right.

Example 296 shows *overlay* techniques in progress. This excerpt—for cugaphone (new instrument), soundscape (biomusic), and a separated group of instruments (*klangfarbenmelodien* and spatial modulation)—is to be performed in three separate buildings utilizing a composer-controlled natural environment.

Example 295
Traditional and contextual leakage.

Example 296
Overlay technique of decategorization: 3 buildings and controlled environment with new instruments, klangfarbenmelodien *and spatial modulation.*

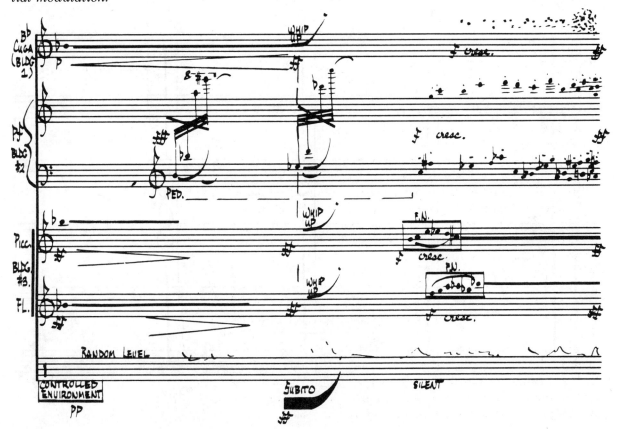

Imitation is the cue for overlay definition in that each of the processes exists simultaneously, one over the other, without straining the thread of consistency desired between them. Indeed, each of the techniques used benefits from the presence of the others, and the work perceived as a whole (though obviously hard to do, as an audience/performer–type situation does not really exist) is clearly a set of ideas folded in such a way that one is aware of the processes but not obsessed with them.

Fusion requires quite selective processes in techniques used, and the following three examples attempt to show what basis is needed for the selection. Example 297 shows pointillism, *klangfarbenmelodien,* total organization, twelve-tone processes and D/A (digital-to-analog) computer tape techniques in an excerpt for five instruments and tape.

Example 297
'Fusion' type of decategorization.

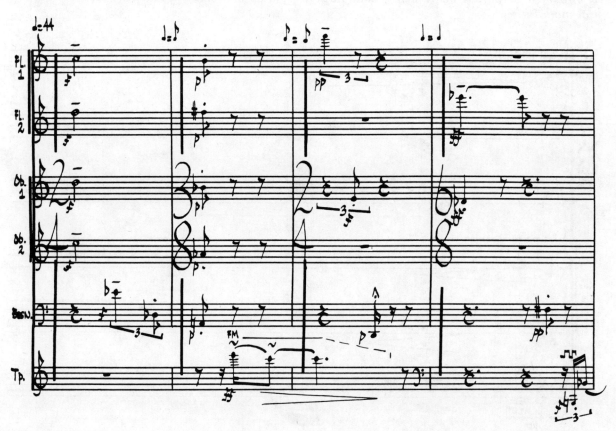

The choice of processes is based on the affinity of the techniques to be bound together without conflict. No eclecticism is apparent in the example, which typifies the "control" nature of all the concepts used. The tape part has been written out with close proximity of attacks of sounds, etc., so that the overall nature of the example can be observed.

Example 298 shows indeterminacy, notation ideas, and prepared-piano techniques to function in correlation in a graph piece. Note the ease with which these ideas work together. Here the concept of total organization would only bring back some form of eclecticism or technique quoting.

Example 299 is for piano solo and involves polytonality, interval exploration, metric and rhythmic concepts, and modulation (rhythmic) to function in a fused manner. Again, the "like" and "associative" concepts of each category fuse them into decategorized music in which process and technique serve the work and do not necessarily become aural to the perceiver; substantive or noticeable traces of any one technique's "seams" do not show.

Though the six processes of decategorization show substantial differences (from opposites exploited to technique digestion possibly imagined as simple-to-complex or vice versa), no single concept is better or worse than any other. The only precept is that a knowledgeable application of all these processes (or concepts) should be used so that a desired result is achieved. No two composers (or works, for that matter) are, or should be, alike. It is hoped that the diversity of ideas, concepts, processes, and techniques contribute not to confusion of priorities but to a more sensitive understanding of potentials. The various chapter contents, when understood as successfully as one hopes traditional musics have been, would, when forged into a style (a personalization of mechanics), become the successful realization of this book's intent. The composer can become alive with ideas born not of exercised self-plagiarism, but with a full, free choice of as many modes of expression as possible. This hopefully will not only bear rich new musics, but will be as well a seed of constant expansion for future icons.

ASSIGNMENTS

1. Compose a short work for unprepared piano which uses at least five techniques, processes, or concepts of five different chapters in the text. Use eclecticism as the basic decategorization and make the work as effective and musical as possible.

Example 298
Fusion in a graph work.

Example 299
Fusion of more traditional techniques.

2. In a work for voice and three available instruments quote a segment of your favorite piece of music (other than one of your own). Make sure the quotation is generally recognizable, at least in style, and set it with an appropriate text so that the quoting process is a viable and meaningful one in the context of the work as a whole.

3. Using sectionalization as a process for decategorization, compose a work using the techniques of spatial modulation, *musique concrète,* polytonality, and multimedia. Employ as many performers as are available with a composite of new and traditional notation.

4. Compose a work for solo voice with choir (as many voices as possible). The text should be syllables only, without recognizable meaning. Use tonality, microtones, special effects, and new notations (along with traditional ones) to create a "leakage" form of decategorization with as much fusion concept as possible; the ideas should feel as if they belong together, yet somehow retain their identity in terms of analysis.

5. In a work for inter-media, use spatial modulation, pointillism, cluster techniques, and one new instrument to create as fused a musical example as possible. Performers, notation, etc., are all up to the composer.

6. Analyze example 299 in terms of Chapters 1 and 3. Compose a work in tonal language only which achieves similar results.

7. Take any three previous assignments you wish and correlate them into two short works with as few changes of notes as possible. The first work should be actively eclectic and the second (using the same three assignments) should be fused.

8. Choose as many concepts (present in this book or not) as desired and compose a work (using any decategorizing process wished, present in this book or not) which exemplifies the most personal and

effective style and music you are capable of. The work may be for any instruments available and any length. It should *not* be a composite of all techniques learned but rather a selective and very personal creation of the best that you can produce.

9. Repeat assignment number eight in *concept,* but for at least different instrumentation. Note any techniques altered, changed, or present when absent before (and vice versa).

WORKS FOR ANALYSIS

Consult the most recent Schwann Catalog for current in-print recordings of these works. Publishers are usually found through libraries, music stores, or distributors of music. This list is not meant to be comprehensive, only suggestive of further study.

Babbitt, Milton: *Vision and Prayer* (for synthesized tape and voice; demonstrates highly fused techniques of synthesizer tape processes, pointillism, *klangfarbenmelodien,* total organization).

Berio, Luciano: *Sinfonia* (strong use of overlaid tonal quotes in the third movement, as well as every concept of decategorization presented herein at one time or another in the work).

Cage, John: *Variations IV* (fused work for soundscape [museum with bar], indeterminate and electronic sources inclusive of radios, etc.; fusion of techniques is so constant as to suggest mere "confusion" at times).

Crumb, George: *Ancient Voices of Children* (work using new instruments, very effective quoting techniques, new notations, new traditional-instrument resources; more fused but inclusive of every decategorization technique mentioned herein).

Davies, Peter Maxwell: *Eight Songs for a Mad King* (use of multimedia techniques, quoting, effective new traditional and nontraditional instrument techniques in an often fused but more sectionalized—by movement—decategorization).

Husa, Karel: *Apotheosis of This Earth* (homogeneous fusion of a wide variety of techniques which hold great affinities for each other: modulations, new traditional instrument resources, new notations, texture control).

Ives, Charles: *Piano Sonata No. 2 (Concord)* (like many of Ives' works, shows a complete variety of decategorization techniques; however, unlike most of his orchestral pieces, this masterwork explores fusion elements rather than his usual eclectic tendencies).

Ligeti, György: *Requiem* (fusion of *mikropolyphonie,* spatial and timbre modulations, interval exploration, cluster techniques).

———: *Aventures* (extraordinary fusion of notation, new traditional-instrument resources, pointillism, *klangfarbenmelodien,* and other techniques).

Stockhausen, Karlheinz: *Momente* (sectional type of decategorization using a wide variety of the materials discussed in the text).

APPENDIX I
The Composer's Table

The purpose of this appendix is to suggest possible approaches to composition, the tools of copying, and applications of works for performance which are often neglected in texts and teaching approaches. None of these suggestions need be followed, but rather are offered as possibilities which the reader may accept or for which he might find alternatives.

Approach

Overview has been stressed throughout much of this text. Such overviews may take a growing visual graphic idea or a conceptualized whole from which techniques and materials are derived. The overview approach helps avoid the problems often encountered in a continuous non-prestructured composition: aural suggestions of Monday's ideas, Tuesday's new ideas, etc. Overviews (while changeable to the very last note of the composition) provide frameworks in which the composition can take place. Titling (at least a temporary working title) is often a help. Composers often neglect the significance of a title to an audience. Indeed, the *concept* of *Symphonie Fantastique* by Hector Berlioz would change markedly with a new title, even if the change were minimal: e.g., *Symphony No. 1.* (Moreover, overviews do not force the composer to begin at the beginning, but provide any area of the work as a starting point for what might seem workable or inspired on a given day.)

It is suggested that composers work on a day-by-day basis. Just as a clarinetist needs to practice his art *and* craft, so must the composer. This practice may take the form of composing in the context of a work in progress, solving a given problem, reworking a passage, or even studying another work for its solutions. The hour(s) of the day (or night) spent at composing are variable, depending on the composer. Many find a set hour and/or duration is most effective, while others find inconsistency the most viable method.

While conducive surroundings are an asset to compositional approach, one is often misled as to what, exactly, the "conducive" surrounding is. It is most certainly different from composer to composer. Probability seems to suggest that the best-made plans go awry when programming comfort in an approach. The author has occasionally spent days attempting to discover the most comfortable surroundings (e.g., draftsman's table with swivel chair) only to discover that the most *uncomfortable* position of sitting on a chair with no back, composing at awkward angles, etc. produced the quickest results. The planned-ahead "composition in the woods" is most often disastrous (though this again is but a generalization of which the exceptions are numerous). In general, a steady workroom seems to provide the composer the security of knowing where each tool he uses is located, and avoids the complications of work-by-work change of surroundings.

In the day-to-day penciled first draft (final drafts will be considered under *tools*), one must be cautious not to let new ideas, completely foreign to the work at hand, be included just because they are good and work in themselves. The "composer notebook" idea is a very viable concept and is often used to great advantage. The point is to sketch the idea, concept, or whatever, in a separate pad, using it for later works, especially for when inspiration is at low ebb. It should be noted that pencils have two ends, and composition students are best forewarned to "write softly and carry a big eraser." Many a poor work was the result of a tired composer not wishing to erase a potential mistake. While this may seem an unusually practical suggestion, it has proven to be an important one. *Any* device to make a work better should be employed (including taping-on extra measures, throwing out entire movements, etc.). *Destruction,* as was shown in antimusic, can be a very *creative* act, and more than one composer of recognized great musics has admitted ending a day of composition with ten measures less than when he began.

Since music is a temporal art form, it is highly advised that timing a rough draft time and time again with a metronome produces a few changes that can prove the difference between mediocrity and successful creation. As well, such timings contribute to the composer's really *hearing* the work in his head. So often, works not heard or reworked bear witness to *augenmusiks* (works which may appear pretty on the page but do not work in performance). It is most important to evaluate compositions before final copy in terms of abstract versus performed time. A composer, wound up in his hearing of a passage for the fiftieth time, is successful only if he can retain the perspective of an audience hearing it for the first or second time. Repeated performances with increased amount of audience interest is one form of success, yet composers often get tied up in the extraordinarily personal act of creation and lose the second-person evaluation. One must ask constantly: Is the "judging" at this point (rough draft) one of a tired composer hearing a passage time and time again without context, or a fresh criticism born of truly becoming a dual personality capable of discerning the real from the abstract, the performance from the concept, the music from the mood? The potential here is in destroying a good passage only because it seems boring in a given minute (out of context and after repeated hearings) when a careful and objective reexamination might bring a different result.

An oftentimes successful approach technique that has proven itself with a number of composers is to make things purposely difficult in the compositional process. While it may indeed seem masochistic, the author has been known (for example) to take splicing tape from dispensers, purposely make tools of the trade difficult to find or place needed materials hard to reach to provide the extra grain of time to evaluate whether a certain sound or idea is worth the effort. While often dangerously maddening, such a system provides a framework for the composer demanding from himself only the very best he can produce.

Tools

There exists on the market at this time a wide variety of "final draft" tools for production. First of all, the *ozalid* method seems the most practical reproduction method to date for multiple copies of scores and/or parts (this is especially true considering that most publishers now distribute scores in autograph form). Other processes such as Xerox, while possibly successful in terms of one performance, prove practically useless: either the paper won't remain upright on the music stand or the result is unreadable. With the ozalid method, one is able to obtain an unlimited supply of strong and readable (as readable, that is, as the original) copies of the work or parts (including both sides of the paper or accordion-fold potentials). Most professional composers use this method.

The ozalid process is a light process in which a specially treated paper is imposed with the image of the original (called vellum master sheets). Anything on either side of the vellum is printed on the copy. One advantage of this is that producers of the paper can print the musical staves on the opposite side of that on which the composer copies, so that electric erasers will clean only the mistake and not the staff lines. The paper is opaque so that the composer can see the lines clearly for copying. The blackest ink (usually waterproof to protect from perspiration and spilling of liquids), such as india ink, provides the best results. Due to the fact that both sides of the vellum (often called onionskins) produce equal results, one can check the master sheet for reproduction levels by viewing both sides against a bright light. If the reverse side (from that of copying) is not readable, the final copy is bound to be the same.

The pen itself is an important tool for the "composing table." Since most dark india inks contain ammonia, regular fountain pens are not very useful (they usually contain rubber or plastic ink chambers which are slowly eaten away by the ink itself). As well, many of the newer pens which hold ink internally in some fashion have the problem of clogging (india ink dries fairly quickly and quite hard, not allowing the ink to flow and needing almost constant attention for usage). Thus, many composers use the "dunk" method for copying. While it is time-consuming, it does provide generally the most satisfactory results (one can use a dark pencil with the "copy" side of a carbon sheet underneath for double printing, but this smears easily and does not wear well in that it tends to leak from one vellum to another when kept for long periods of time). A point holder (speedball variety, usually found in art supply stores) is needed and, since they come in various sizes, should be carefully chosen for one's particular hand. Separate points are then purchased (usually very inexpensively, i.e., twenty-five to fifty cents), with the C-5 number a good starting point from which the composer can experiment to find his best and most suitable style.

A few practical hints might save the reader a great deal of copy time:

1. Empty the ink bottle in such a way that the right amount of ink is available at the bottom of the jar so that one does not overload the pen point (only to produce "lumps" of ink on the paper) or underload it (only to have to refill almost immediately).

2. Always follow the ink brand directions, but make sure to shake the bottle well before using. Be careful to use some sort of paper cloth or rag to clean the inside neck of the bottle before dunking, or

the sides of the holder (as well as your hands) will become messed with ink. This rag can then be used as a blotter, with the penpoint being tapped on it after each dunking to avoid ink overloads as well as offering the composer the time to notice any hairs or clumps of dried ink attached to the point.

3. The ink bottle can be kept at a fairly constant level by using the ink cap (which usually has a squirter attached) to add ink from another bottle. Always make sure to clean a penpoint carefully after use with plain water. If a point is new it often needs breaking in—easily accomplished by using a small amount of spit and leaving overnight. The acids in the spit eat small holes in the metal which make the ink cling to the point. This avoids the usual start of having all the ink run off the pen at once with a new point.

4. Make sure that the paper chosen is right for the piece you are composing (a good book for making such choices is available free of charge from Alpheus Music Corp., 1433 N. Cole Place, Hollywood, California 90028; other companies which do this copywork are in many cities around the world).

5. Use the pen gently, as the points tend to bend and become useless very easily.

6. A ruler should be used as often as possible for a neat copy. If the ruler you are using does not have a front "lift" to it (i.e., it does not separate from the paper by at least an eighth of an inch), you can tape pennies to either end to obtain such a lift. This avoids smearing the ink at the time of application. As well, the use of the coins at the very ends of a long ruler helps avoid smearing still-drying materials on the page as the ruler is moved around. Metal is the best choice for ruler material, as wood splinters and plastic tends to get nicks.

7. If time does not permit mailing a composition for reproduction, it can be taken to any blueprint shop for reproduction. Ozalid is essentially a "black line" blueprint process, and a blue (but legible) version can be obtained at most blueprint shops.

8. Erasing mistakes can be accomplished by electric erasers, some standard erasers, or by the razor-blade method. This latter and more traditional method involves the use of a single-edged razor blade and nonyellowing Scotch tape. The copied sheet with the mistake is placed directly on top of a similar "staved" blank sheet so that when the mistake is cut out an exact-shaped blank version accompanies it. This second (blank) portion of the sheet is then taped securely onto the original (tape on the reverse side) and the correct version is copied. While this last process takes time, it does avoid the problems often encountered with erasing: the eraser damages the vellum surface and the ink splinters out in tiny rivulets when reapplied.

The hints of copying and the copying process itself are very involved, entailing hours and hours of practice and patience. It is hoped that this time-consumption has been diminished by the suggestions given here. With the variety of covers, gold imprinting of the work's title, composer's name, etc., available, the composer who acquires a mastery of the craft of copying (there are many books in this area) can create a work which is publishable "as is" (an important ability to have in light of the next section).

Application

The "autograph" concept counts very strongly in the publication world of today. Indeed, most publishers do not "publish" serious works (in the printing sense of the word) but rather distribute their autographed ozalid copies. Do not get trapped into believing that the world has not changed drastically since the eighteenth and nineteenth centuries. Most composers no longer have the luxury of scribbling their musics and waiting for a calligrapher to study and recopy or print the results. Such methods are far too costly today. For the young or unknown composer in search of publication, a single word of advice is necessary: patience. Ten publishers can see a work and reject it, and the eleventh accept it with glowing compliments. Be sure to send a copy and not the original and, if possible, a tape or press recording of the work (many publishers cannot read music or hear it in their heads and in quick situations generally turn down an unknown "commodity").

Copyright of work can be done either by you or the publisher. If unpublished, it can be accomplished as an unpublished copyright. Complete information can be had on this subject by writing to the Copyright Office, Library of Congress, Washington, D.C. Serious musics rarely need unpublished copyright, and, when published, are usually copyrighted by the publisher. Since copyrighting costs six dollars and requires two copies of the work, as well as the time in filling out forms, it usually seems unnecessary, as most potential plagiarists in serious musics do the act in a much more subtle form (they don't steal the work, but just many of its ideas, etc., which are not really protected in the first place).

Commissions are usually very important to the composer even if they involve only a promised performance. A commission enables the composer to work within some sort of limits (hopefully not too unmusical) and as well work with a performer or group of performers from whom he can learn a great deal. Performing composers are also aided by the constant friction and inspiration of music and its craft of performance. A conductor-composer, for example, can learn a great deal about the instruments of his orchestra, orchestration, literature, and composition technique if by nothing but osmosis.

Great care must be taken in the act of composing a commission. If it is written for a performer of great gifts and/or specialized talents, one should be aware of the limited performance potential. If such a player is well known and performs a great deal, there is no problem. However, if the performer is a close friend who has little outlet for performance, creation of a work utilizing special effects which only he and a few other performers can do is a bit idealistic. On the other hand, one should not "water down" the work just to obtain performances. Indeed, techniques not known can be learned by creative performers. One guideline for success is to be able to perform the technique yourself; this enables the composer to confront the difficulties directly to ascertain if it is easy to learn, as well as help obtain performances by simply embarrassing performers into doing the work.

Grants and prizes are important if one wins, and certainly no sign of anything if one loses. Advice here is to evaluate whether you can take the loss in stride (loss is expected in many or most attempts unless luck is on your side or school or teacher "ins" make success possible; this is not to say that such grant or prizes are always rigged or a matter of chance, as great pieces have won deserved prizes and great composers have received deserved grants). If such loss is acceptable, further advice is to enter such "contests" and then forget them. If taken seriously (and awards and grants do play a role in job and tenure security), grants can usually be won if one stochastically approaches the problem. If the grant or prize is properly applied for and the chances are a hundred to one against success, there should be no need for worry until the one-hundredth loss.

Recordings are, for the unknown or young composer, mostly a matter of acceptance and paying. Even most of the major companies work on some grant type of project to obtain funds (or expect the composer or performer to do so). Unless one "waits success out," the best approach is similar to that of publication. Send tape after tape after tape without being discouraged. Once a work is accepted, you will learn of the monies required of either you or the company. One can then seek grants, pay off, or go begging (no disgrace for a composer worth his salt). Commissions can often help in this area as well, for many times performers and groups will commission a work, like it, and record it, taking the burden completely off the back of the composer. This is indeed the best approach in the long run.

This appendix has been a purely practical and simple structure which it is hoped will enable the reader to function more securely in a world which seems not to want him around in the first place. If one last bit of advice can be offered (by no means does this mean that all advice has been given; indeed, there is much more attainable through organizations, other composers, teachers, etc.): carefully examine the various performance-rights organizations (e.g., ASCAP, BMI, etc.). They play an extremely important role in most professional composers' lives by supplying monies earned from performances as well as keeping one posted as to what was performed and where.

The author hopes that this appendix will help the composer of new musics secure a more solid concept of himself and the world around him, and contribute more available scores and records of new music composition.

APPENDIX II
Further Reference Materials

Chapter 1

Backus, John. *The Acoustical Foundation of Music.* New York: W. W. Norton & Co., 1969.

Forte, Allen. *Contemporary Tone-Structures.* New York: Columbia University Press, 1955.

Marquis, G. Welton. *Twentieth Century Music Idioms.* New York: Prentice-Hall, 1964.

Persichetti, Vincent. *Twentieth Century Harmony.* New York: W. W. Norton & Co., 1961.

Yasser, Joseph. *A Theory of Evolving Tonality.* American Library of Musicology, 1932.

Chapter 2

Babbitt, Milton. "Set Structure as a Compositional Determinant." *Journal of Music Theory,* April 1961, pp. 72–94.

Babbitt, Milton. "Twelve-Tone Rhythmic Structure and the Electronic Medium." *Perspectives of New Music,* vol. 1, no. 1 (1962), pp. 49–79.

Basart, Ann Phillips. *Serial Music: A Classified Bibliography of Writings on Twelve Tone and Electronic Music.* Berkeley: University of California Press, 1961.

Perle, George. *Serial Composition and Atonality.* Berkeley: University of California Press, 1962.

Spinner, Leopold. *A Short Introduction to the Technique of Twelve-Tone Composition.* London: Boosey and Hawkes, 1960.

Tremblay, George. *The Definitive Cycle of the Twelve Tone Row.* New York: Criterion Music Corp., 1974.

Chapter 3

Dallin, Leon. *Techniques of Twentieth Century Composition.* 2nd edition. Dubuque, Iowa: William C. Brown Co. Publishers, 1974.

Lang, Paul Henry, ed. *Problems of Modern Music.* New York: W. W. Norton & Co., 1960.

Messiaen, Oliver. *The Technique of My Musical Language.* Paris: Alphonse Leduc & Cie., 1950.

Chapter 4

Berg, Alban. "Why is Schoenberg's Music So Hard to Understand?" *The Music Review,* May 1952, pp. 187–196.

Cage, John. *Silence.* Cambridge: The M.I.T. Press, 1961.

———. *M. Writings '67–'72.* Middletown, Conn: Wesleyan University Press, 1973.

Hansen, Peter. *An Introduction to Twentieth Century Music.* Boston: Allyn & Bacon, 1967.

Kolneder, Walter. *Anton Webern: An Introduction to His Works.* Berkeley: University of California Press, 1968.

Chapter 5

Boatwright, Howard, ed. *Essays before a Sonata, The Majority, and Other Writings by Charles Ives.* New York: W. W. Norton & Co., 1962.

Cowell, Henry. *New Musical Resources.* New York: Alfred A. Knopf, 1930.

Forte, Allen. *Contemporary Tone-Structures.* New York: Columbia University Press, 1955.

Persichetti, Vincent. *Twentieth Century Harmony.* New York: W. W. Norton & Co., 1961.

Chapter 6

Cowell, Henry. *New Musical Resources.* New York: Alfred A. Knopf, 1930.

Forte, Allen. *Contemporary Tone-Structures.* New York: Columbia University Press, 1955.

Johnston, Ben. "Proportionality and Expanded Pitch Relations." *Perspectives of New Music,* vol. 5, no. 1, pp. 112–120.

Messiaen, Oliver. *The Technique of My Musical Language.* Paris: Alphonse Leduc & Cie., 1950.

Xenakis, Iannis. *Formalized Music.* Bloomington: Indiana University Press, 1971.

Chapter 7

Boatwright, Howard, ed. *Essays before a Sonata, The Majority, and Other Writings by Charles Ives.* New York: W. W. Norton & Co., 1962.

Cowell, Henry. *New Musical Resources.* New York: Alfred A. Knopf, 1930.

Kagel, Mauricio. "Tone Clusters, Attacks, Transitions." *Die Reihe* 5 (1959), pp. 40–55.

Persichetti, Vincent. *Twentieth Century Harmony.* New York: W. W. Norton & Co., 1961.

Chapter 8

Boatwright, Howard. "Ives' Quarter-Tone Impressions." *Perspectives of New Music,* vol. 3, no. 2 (1965), pp. 22–31.

"Microtonal Music in America." *Proceedings* 2, American Society of University Composers.

Orga, Ates. "Alois Haba and Microtonality." *Musical Opinion,* July 1968.

Yasser, Joseph. *A Theory of Evolving Tonality.* American Library of Musicology, 1932.

Chapter 9

Brindle, Reginald Smith. *Contemporary Percussion.* London: Oxford University Press, 1970.

Bunger, Richard. *The Well-Prepared Piano.* Colorado Springs: The Colorado Music Press, 1973.

Reed, H. Owen, and Joel T. Leach. *Scoring for Percussion.* New York: Prentice-Hall, 1969.

Salzedo, Carlos. "Considerations on the Piano and the Harp." *Harp News,* vol. 3, no. 4 (Fall 1961).

Chapter 10

Carter, Elliott. "The Rhythmic Basis of American Music." *Score,* vol. 12, no. 27 (June 1955).

Erickson, Robert. "Time Relations." *Journal of Music Theory* 7 (Spring 1963), pp. 174–192.

Edwards, Allen. *Flawed Words and Stubborn Sounds.* New York: W. W. Norton & Co., 1971.

Kagel, Mauricio. "Tone Clusters, Attacks, Transitions." *Die Reihe* 5 (1959), pp. 40–55.

Messiaen, Oliver. *The Technique of My Musical Language.* Paris: Alphonse Leduc & Cie., 1950.

Chapter 11

Behrman, David. "What Indeterminate Notation Determines." *Perspectives of New Music,* vol. 3, no. 2 (Spring 1964).

Cage, John. *M. Writings '67–'72.* Middletown, Conn.: Wesleyan University Press, 1973.

———. *Silence.* Cambridge: The M.I.T. Press, 1961.

———. *A Year from Monday.* Middletown, Conn.: Wesleyan University Press, 1967.

Childs, Barney. "Indeterminacy and Theory: Some Notes." *Composer,* vol. 1, no. 1 (June 1969).

Xenakis, Iannis. *Formalized Music.* Bloomington: Indiana University Press, 1971.

Chapter 12

Becker, Jurgen, and Wolf Vostell, eds. *Happenings.* Hamburg: Rowohlt, 1965.

Cage, John. *Silence.* Cambridge: The M.I.T. Press, 1961.

———. *A Year from Monday.* Middletown, Conn.: Wesleyan University Press, 1967.

Cope, David. *New Directions in Music,* 2nd edition, Dubuque: Wm. C. Brown, 1976.

Gibb, Stanley. "Understanding Terminology and Concepts Related to Media Art Forms." *The American Music Teacher,* vol. 22, no. 5.

Hansen, Al. *A Primer of Happenings and Time-Space Art.* New York: Something Else Press, 1968.

Kaprow, Allan. *Assemblage, Environments and Happenings.* New York: Abrams, 1966.

Kirby, Michael. *Happenings.* New York: E. P. Dutton & Co., 1965.

Tomkins, Calvin. *The Bride and the Bachelors.* New York: Viking Press, 1965.

Chapter 13

Cage, John. *Silence.* Cambridge: The M.I.T. Press, 1961.

Cross, Lowell M., ed. *A Bibliography of Electronic Music.* Toronto: University of Toronto Press, 1967.

Davies, Hugh. "A Discography of Electronic Music and *Musique Concrète.*" *Recorded Sound,* vol. 14 (April 1964).

———, ed. *International Electronic Music Catalog.* Cambridge: The M.I.T. Press, 1968.

Luening, Otto. "Some Random Remarks about Electronic Music." *Journal of Music Theory,* vol. 8 (1964).

Schaeffer, Pierre. *A la Recherche d'une Musique Concrète.* Paris: Editions du Seuil, 1952.

Schwartz, Elliott. *Electronic Music: A Listener's Guide.* New York: Praeger Publishers, 1972.

Strange, Allen. *Electronic Music.* Dubuque, Iowa: William C. Brown Co. Publishers, 1972.

Chapter 14

Bartolozzi, Bruno. *New Sounds for Woodwind.* London: Oxford University Press, 1967.

Cummings, Barton. "A Brief Summary of New Techniques for Tuba." *Numus West,* vol. 5.

Howell, Thomas. *The Avant-Garde Flute.* Berkeley: The University of California Press, 1974.

Read, Gardner. *Thesaurus of Orchestral Devices.* London: Sir Isaac Pitman & Sons, 1953.

Yates, Peter. *Twentieth Century Music.* New York: Pantheon Books, 1967.

Chapter 15

Appleton, Jon, and Ronald Perera, eds. *The Development and Practice of Electronic Music.* Englewood Cliffs, N.J.: Prentice-Hall 1974.

Babbitt, Milton. "Twelve-Tone Rhythmic Structure and the Electronic Medium." *Perspectives of New Music,* vol. 1, no. 1 (1962), pp. 49–79.

Cross, Lowell M., ed. *A Bibliography of Electronic Music.* Toronto: University of Toronto Press, 1967.

Davies, Hugh., ed. *International Electronic Music Catalog.* Cambridge: The M.I.T. Press, 1968.

Luening, Otto. "Some Random Remarks about Electronic Music." *Journal of Music Theory,* vol. 8 (1964).

Schwartz, Elliott. *Electronic Music: A Listener's Guide.* New York: Praeger Publishers, 1972.

Strange, Allen. *Electronic Music.* Dubuque, Iowa: William C. Brown Co. Publishers, 1972.

Trythall, Gilbert. *Electronic Music.* New York: Grosset & Dunlap, 1973.

Chapter 16

Cope, David. "Chronicles of a Cause." *Composer,* vol. 1, no. 1 (June 1969).

Partch, Harry. *The Genesis of a Music.* New York: Da Capo Press, 1973.

Varèse, Edgard. "New Instruments and New Music." Edited by Elliott Schwartz and Barney Childs. *Contemporary Composers on Contemporary Music.* New York: Holt, Rinehart, and Winston, 1967, pp. 196–198.

Chapter 17

Appleton, Jon, and Ronald Perera, eds. *The Development and Practice of Electronic Music.* Englewood Cliffs, N.J.: Prentice-Hall, 1974.

Cross, Lowell M., ed. *A Bibliography of Electronic Music.* Toronto: The University of Toronto Press, 1967.

Davies, Hugh, ed. *International Electronic Music Catalog.* Cambridge: The M.I.T. Press, 1968.

Mumma, Gordon. "Creative Aspects of Live Electronic Music Technology." Audio Engineering Society Reprint no. 550.

Schwartz, Elliott. *Electronic Music: A Listener's Guide.* New York: Praeger Publishers, 1972.

Strange, Allen. *Electronic Music.* Dubuque, Iowa: William C. Brown Co. Publishers, 1972.

Chapter 18

Babbitt, Milton. "Set Structure as a Compositional Determinant." *Journal of Music Theory,* April 1961, pp. 72–94.

Boretz, Benjamin, and Edward T. Cone, eds. *Perspectives on Contemporary Music Theory.* New York: W. W. Norton & Co., 1972.

Boulez, Pierre. *Boulez on Music Today.* Cambridge: Harvard University Press, 1971.

Messiaen, Oliver. *The Technique of My Musical Language.* Paris: Alphonse Leduc & Cie., 1950.

Chapter 19

Appleton, Jon, and Ronald Perera, eds. *The Development and Practice of Electronic Music.* Englewood Cliffs, N.J.: Prentice-Hall, 1974.

Baker, Robert A. *Musicomp.* Champaign, Ill.: University of Illinois School of Music, 1963.

Chowning, John. "The Stanford Computer Music Project." *Numus West,* vol. 1.

Cohen, David. "Computer-Generated Music." *Southeastern Composers League Newsletter* 66.

von Foerster, Heinz, and James W. Beauchamp, eds. *Music by Computers.* New York: John Wiley & Sons, 1969.

Hiller, Lejaren, and Leonard Isaacson. *Experimental Music.* New York: McGraw-Hill, 1959.

Howe, Hubert S., Jr. *Electronic Music Synthesis.* New York: W. W. Norton & Co., 1975.

Mathews, M. V., and Joan E. Miller. *Music IV Programmer's Manual.* Murray Hill, N.J.: Bell Telephone Laboratories.

Mathews, Max. *The Technology of Computer Music.* Cambridge: The M.I.T. Press, 1969.

Vercoe, Barry. "The Music 360 Language for Sound Synthesis." *Computer Music Newsletter* 2 (June 1971).

Xenakis, Iannis. *Formalized Music.* Bloomington: The Indiana University Press, 1971.

Chapter 20

Backus, John. *The Acoustical Foundation of Music.* New York: W. W. Norton & Co., 1969.

Erickson, Robert. *Sound Structure in Music.* Berkeley: University of California Press, 1975.

Goldstein, Malcolm. "Texture." Edited by John Vinton. *Dictionary of Contemporary Music.* New York: E. P. Dutton & Co., 1974.

Chapter 21

von Bekesy, Georg. "Musical Dynamics by Variation of Apparent Size of Sound Source." *Journal of Music Theory,* vol. 14, no. 1 (1970).

Brant, Henry. "Space as an Essential Aspect of Musical Composition." Edited by Elliott Schwartz and Barney Childs. *Contemporary Composers on Contemporary Music.* New York: Holt, Rinehart, and Winston, 1967.

Xenakis, Iannis. *Formalized Music.* Bloomington: Indiana University Press, 1971.

Chapter 22

Behrman, David. "What Indeterminate Notation Determines." *Perspectives of New Music,* vol. 3, no. 2 (Spring 1964).

Cage, John. *Notations.* New York: Something Else Press, 1969.

Cole, Hugo. *Sounds and Signs.* London: Oxford University Press, 1974.

Cope, David. *New Music Notation.* Dubuque, Iowa: Kendall-Hunt Publishers, 1976.

Palm, Siegfried. "Notation for String Instruments." *Composer,* vol. 3, no. 2 (1972).

Pooler, Frank, and Brent Pierce. *New Choral Notation.* New York: Walton Music, 1973.

Chapter 23

Johnson, Tom. *Imaginary Music.* New York: Two-Eighteen Press, 1974.

Reich, Steve. "Music as a Gradual Process." New York: *Anti-Illusion Catalog of the Whitney Museum,* 1969.

Rzewski, Frederick. "Prose Music." Edited by John Vinton. *Dictionary of Contemporary Music.* New York: E. P. Dutton, 1974.

Young, La Monte and Marian Zazeela. *Selected Writings.* Munich: Heiner Friedrich, 1969.

Chapter 24

Chase, Gilbert. "Toward a Total Musical Theatre." *Arts in Society* (Spring 1969).

Cunningham, Merce. *Changes: Notes on Choreography.* Edited by Frances Starr. New York: Something Else Press, 1969.

Gibb, Stanley. "Understanding Terminology and Concepts Related to Media Art Forms." *The American Music Teacher,* vol. 22, no. 5.

Kirby, E. T. *Total Theatre.* New York: E. P. Dutton, & Co., 1969.

Subotnick, Morton. "Extending the Stuff Music is Made Of." *Music Educators Journal,* vol. 55, no. 3 (November 1968).

Tomkins, Calvin. *The Bride and the Bachelors.* New York: Viking Press, 1965.

Chapter 25

Henahan, Donal. "Music Draws Strains Direct from Brains." *New York Times,* November 25, 1970.

Moore, Carmen. "The Sound of Mind." *Village Voice,* December 24, 1970.

Young, La Monte, and Marian Zazeela. *Selected Writings.* Munich: Heiner Friedrich, 1969.

Chapter 26

Higgins, Dick. "Boredom and Danger." *Source,* vol. 3, no. 1 (January 1966).

Nougé, Paul. "Music is Dangerous." *Soundings* I (1973).

Young, La Monte, and Marian Zazeela. *Selected Writings.* Munich: Heiner Friedrich, 1969.

Chapter 27

Cage, John. "The Future of Music." *Numus West,* vol. 5.

Cope, David. "Footnotes." *Composer,* vol. 4, no. 2 (1973).

Johnston, Ben. "On Context." *Proceedings* 3, (1968), American Society of University Composers.

Ligeti, György. "Metamorphosis of Musical Form." *Die Reihe* 7 (1960).

APPENDIX III
Brief Glossary of Terms

amplifier: instrument used to increase the amplitude of a sound.

amplitude: the loudness of a sound, measured in hertz (Hz).

atonality: lack of tonality; also called pantonality.

band-reject filter: filter which eliminates a particular band of frequencies while allowing the remainder to pass.

band-pass filter: filter which allows a certain band to pass while rejecting the remaining frequencies.

chance music: indeterminate music.

classic electronic music: electronic music which is created primarily by splicing sounds rather than by using keyboards; involves as well techniques of *musique concrète.*

cluster: a complex chord in which the inner voices have little value in themselves but rather contribute to the complete mass.

decay: the last portion of a sound's envelope.

envelope: the amplitude characteristics of a sound: attack, initial decay, sustain, and final decay; envelope generators can control both the amount and duration of each of these factors.

feedback: sound fed back through a system many times to produce separate oscillation.

filter: instrument designed to allow a selection of frequencies.

hexachord: a six-note chord or set of different pitches.

improvisation: music involving performer freedom during performance within a certain set of limits.

indeterminate music: music composed and/or performed in which the outcome is not predictable.

klangfarbenmelodien: term meaning sound-color-melody; usually point-illistic, with separate pitches receiving separate timbres.

laser: beam of light connected to a receiving device such that, when the beam is broken, an oscillator is triggered.

linear: refers to "line."

microtone: measurement of intervals less than an equal tempered half step.

mikropolyphonie: thick densities of polyphony in which no voice dominates.

mixer: instrument used to combine signals.

modulation: process of change.

multimedia: two or more art forms in indeterminate combination.

musique concrète: music which employs nonsynthesized sounds with tape manipulation.

pantonality: atonality, or twelve-tone music.

parameter: the measurable limits of a given subject.

pointillism: sounds in points, separated by time and space.

program: computer language or software.

quarter-tone: one half of an equal-tempered semitone.

sample/hold: an electronic device which samples a given waveform generating a variable voltage and consequently a pitch, timbre or other voltage control parameter.

sequencer: 8–12 note electronic device which, using preset dials, can repeat and vary at any rhythm or tempo the resulting pattern (ostinato).

spatial modulation: apparent movement of sound through space.

timbre modulation: slow change of timbre.

white sound: all possible frequencies simultaneously.

INDEX

A

B